THE

BRITISH HO

OR, THE

COOK, HOUSEKEEPER's,

AND

GARDINER's COMPANION.

By

Mrs. MARTHA BRADLEY, late of BATH
(1756)

A FACSIMILE EDITION

VOLUME IV
June, July

PROSPECT BOOKS
1998

First published in Great Britain in 1998, by Prospect Books,
Allaleigh House, Blackawton, Totnes, Devon TQ9 7DL.

British Library Cataloguing in Publication Data
A catalogue record of this book is available from the British Library.

ISBN 0907325696
ISBN 0907325637 in respect of the whole set

Printed by Antony Rowe Ltd, Bumper's Farm, Chippenham,
Wiltshire SN14 6QA.

THE
BRITISH HOUSEWIFE

Mrs Martha Bradley's *British Housewife* was first published in weekly parts in 1756, then issued as a two-volume set that same year or the next. This facsimile edition is also divided, but into six, not two, volumes. As the original is itself divided into monthly chapters, this arrangement works satisfactorily.

CONTENTS

*Sections V–IX are numbered in error in the text as Sections VI–X.
† Section VI is numbered in error in the text as Section V.

SUBSCRIBERS TO THIS PRESENT EDITION

Priscilla Bain
Peter Brears
Alan Brown
Kit Chapman
Mrs K.M. Charlton
Covington & Burling
Mrs G.M. Cox
Caroline Davidson
Ove Fosså
Mr R.A. Grant
Dr E.S. Halberstadt
Geraldene Holt
Lynette Hunter
Mr S.H. Jollye
Katherine Knight
James Lamb
Fiona Lucraft
Reinhard Madlinger
Laura Mason
Mrs M.B. Maunsell
Pat & Jim McLavey
Stephen & Barbara Mennell
Michael & Joy Michaud
Joan Morgan

Pam Musa
Julia Neville
Elizabeth Orange
Helen Pollard
Dr Esteban Pombo-Villar
Dermod Quirke & Brian Holser
The Reform Club
Mrs U.A. Robertson
Liz Seeber
Roy Shipperbottom†
Mrs A.S.M. Smith
Mr D.R. Smith
Liz Calvert Smith
Professor R.J. Theodoratus
Malcom Thick
Gordon J. Van der Water
Bas van Oosterhout
Harlan Walker
Dr & Mrs R.J. Webber-Hill
Robin Weir
Barbara Ketcham-Wheaton
Dr Eileen White
Chris Young & Verni Tannam

The late Mr Roy Shipperbottom kindly communicated the text of this advertisement from the *York Courant* of 6 July, 1756.

The public in general, and the Merchants, Captains of Ships, or such as are concerned in the providing for the Sea Service in particular, Are desired to take Notice that
This Day is published
Sold by STABLER and BARSTOW, Booksellers in York
NUMBER XXIV. (Price only Three-Pence)

In which is contained compleat Directions relating to preparing for the Sea Service the following Articles: the several elegant Methods of preserving them for the use of the Cabin, and the particular Ways of eating and dressing them according to the Nature of their several Kinds; intended for the Service of all who are concerned in the Article of providing for Sea, viz. Veal in Butter, Geese in Fat, Greens in Brine, Tripe in Vinegar, Soles in Oil, Roots fryed and dry, Mushrooms dry, and the making Anchovy Sauce for the longest Voyage, and many other Articles of the like Kind.
The Whole to be compleated in Fifty Numbers, illustrated with many
curious Cuts,
of an entire new Work, intitled,
THE BRITISH HOUSEWIFE: Or, The COOK,
HOUSEKEEPER's, and GARDINER's COMPANION. Calculated for the Service both of London and the Country; directing what is necessary to be done in the Providing for, Conducting and Managing, a Family throughout the Year.
By Mrs. MARTHA BRADLEY, late of Bath.
Being the Result of upwards of Thirty Years Experience.
London, printed for S. Crowder and H. Woodgate, at the Golden-Ball in Paternoster-row.

Shortly will be published in this Work, an experienced, easy, and plain Receipt for making portable SOUP, communicated by a Lady, from her own Experience.

THE FACSIMILE

THE
BRITISH HOUSEWIFE:
OR, THE
COOK, HOUSEKEEPER's,
AND
GARDINER's COMPANION.

CALCULATED FOR THE

Service both of LONDON and the COUNTRY;

And directing what is necessary to be done in the *Providing for, Conducting*, and *Managing* a FAMILY throughout the Year.

CONTAINING

A general Account of fresh Provisions of all Kinds. Of the several *foreign Articles* for the Table, pickled, or otherwise preserved; and the different Kinds of *Spices, Salts, Sugars*, and other *Ingredients* used in *Pickling* and *Preserving* at Home: Shewing *what* each is, *whence* it is brought, and what are its *Qualities* and *Uses*.

Together with the *Nature* of all Kinds of *Foods*, and the Method of *suiting them to different* CONSTITUTIONS;

A BILL of FARE for each Month, the Art of *Marketing* and *chusing* fresh Provisions of all Kinds; and the making as well as chusing of *Hams, Tongues*, and other *Store Dishes*.

Also DIRECTIONS for plain *Roasting* and *Boiling*; and for the Dressing of all Sorts of *Made Dishes* in various Tastes; and the preparing the *Desert* in all its Articles.

Containing a greater Variety than was ever before publish'd, of the most Elegant, yet least Expensive RECEIPTS in

COOKERY,	‡	FRICASSEES,	‡	TARTS,	‡	DRY'D FRUITS,
PASTRY,	‡	RAGOUTS,	‡	CAKES,	‡	SWEETMEATS,
PUDDINGS,	‡	SOUPS,	‡	CREAMS,	‡	MADE WINES,
PRESERVES,	‡	SAUCES,	‡	CUSTARDS,	‡	CORDIALS, And
PICKLES,	‡	JELLIES,	‡	CANDIES,	‡	DISTILLERY.

To which are annexed,

The Art of CARVING; and the Terms used for cutting up various Things; and the polite and easy Manner of *doing the Honours of the Table*: The whole Practice of *Pickling* and *Preserving*: And of preparing *made Wines, Beer*, and *Cyder*. As also of *distilling* all the useful Kinds of *Cordial* and *Simple* Waters.

With the *Conduct of a Family* in Respect of *Health*; the *Disorders* to which they are every *Month* liable, and the most approved *Remedies* for each.

And a Variety of other valuable Particulars, necessary to be known in *All Families*; and nothing inserted but what has been *approved* by EXPERIENCE.

Also the Ordering of all Kinds of profitable *Beasts* and *Fowls*, with respect to their *Choice*, their *Breeding* and *Feeding*; the *Diseases* to which they are severally liable each Month, and *Receipts* for their *Cure*. Together with the Management of the *pleasant, profitable*, and *useful Garden*.

THE WHOLE

Embellished with a great Number of *curious* COPPER PLATES, shewing the Manner of *Trussing* all Kinds of GAME, wild and tame FOWLS, &c. as also the Order of setting out TABLES for *Dinners, Suppers*, and *Grand Entertainments*, in a Method never before attempted; and by which even *those who cannot read* will be able to instruct themselves.

By *Mrs.* MARTHA BRADLEY, *late of* BATH:
Being the Result of upwards of *Thirty Years Experience*.

The whole (which is deduc'd from Practice) compleating the careful Reader, from the highest to the lowest Degree, in every Article of *English* Housewifery.

LONDON:

Printed for *S. Crowder* and *H. Woodgate*, at the *Golden Ball* in *Paternoster Row*.

First Course

1. A Haunch of Venison with sweet sauce
2. Cods Head with Lemon garnish
3. A Chine of Veal in Bacon
4. Pigeon Pye
5. Almond Pudding
6. Pullets with Oysters
7. Scots Collops

Second Course

1 A Brace of Partridge
2 A Brace of Teal
3 Fry'd Smelts
4 Spitch cockd Eel
5 Butterd Apple Pyc
6 Cream Tarts.
7 Artichoaks.

THE

COOK, HOUSEKEEPER's,

AND

GARDINER's COMPANION.

J U N E.

SECT. I.

Of Provisions.

A Bill of Fare for the Month of June.

CHAP. I.

Of Butchers Meat.

LAMB and Veal are in Seafon at this Time, Beef and Mutton always, but in general lefs in Summer than Winter. Pork is not good, but Bacon never is more ufeful than in this and the fucceeding Month. Any Joint of Veal may very well come to Table roafted; the Breaft raggoo'd is alfo very proper, and any of the fmall Difhes that are made from it.

Lamb is very proper to fupply the Place of Mutton, and there is a fine Variety of Garden Stuff to fend up with it, as we fhall fhew under that Head.

A Raggoo of Lambs Stones and Sweetbreads is very proper, and all that Variety of leffer Difhes we have defcribed, as made under that Article of the various Parts of Lamb.

To

To the Butchers Meat we are to add Venifon; the Haunch roafted, or for Variety, where a great deal of Venifon comes into the Kitchen, it may be boiled with Cauliflowers. Some prefer this to the roafted Haunch, but I think that is a falfe Tafte; however it is very proper for a Change.

Fawns are alfo now in Seafon, and may be dreffed in larger or fmaller Quantities, according to the Family; and to this Kind we are to add Leverets, which are never finer than toward the Middle of *June*.

C H A P. II.

Of Poultry.

CHICKENS and Pigeons are now in high Seafon; and as we are fpeaking of what is to be had at the Poulterers, we are here to mention young Rabbits, though properly of the former Clafs: They are now in high Seafon: A Fricafee of them is a very good Difh in a firft Courfe, as is alfo a Fricafee of Chickens. Pigeons may be dreffed various Ways, but at this Seafon they come in very well boiled with Bacon and Greens.

Pheafants are now to be had in very good Order, and Turkey Poults: Thefe come in beft in a fecond Courfe. Quails are alfo in Seafon, and there are young Ducks for Variety, and thefe are now very fine.

C H A P. III.

Of Fifh.

CARP and Tench continue fine; and we have from the Salt Waters Turbot in very great Perfection; there are alfo large and very fine Soals and Mackarel.

Salmon

Salmon is in good Seafon, Pike are very fine, and this is the prime Time of the Year for the River Trout; they eat the May Fly during the laſt and in the Beginning of this Month, and it gives them a Colour and Flavour they have not at any other Seaſon; the very Spots on the Skin glow with an uncommon Brightneſs at this Time, and their Fleſh is of the fineſt red that can be conceived. All theſe Fiſh do very well in firſt Courſes, and the beſt Way of all is to have the Pike roaſted.

For the ſecond Courſe we have Eels, which may come in pitchcock'd or collar'd; and a Chine of Salmon broiled is a very good Diſh: There is alſo Sturgeon cold; and of the Shell Kind Lobſters, Crayfiſh, Prawns, and Crabs; which laſt come up beſt buttered

If to theſe we add the Store Diſhes, as Ham, and the like, and ſucking Pigs, which may come in occaſionally, and add the Aſſiſtance of the Paſtry, we ſhall find, before we enter on the abundant Products of the Garden, that there is this Month every happy Variety for the Houſekeeper's Choice and Management.

CHAP. IV.
Of Paſtry.

THE Articles of Paſtry moſt proper for a firſt Courſe this Month are, Veniſon Paſty, and Humble Pie, Marrow Puddings, and the like; and for a ſecond Courſe there may be ſent up a Potatoe Pudding, with all the Variety of Tarts, Cheeſecakes, and Cuſtards, for they are never in better Seaſon.

CHAP. V.
Of Garden Stuff.

NO Month of the Year makes the Garden more ſerviceable to an elegant Table than this, a very great Part of its Products are come in, and moſt of them delicate and fcarce; which, though it does not make them a Bit better, yet never fails to render them more pleafing at Table, as well as of a greater Price at Market.

A R T. I. *Roots and Herbs.*

Carrots are in great Perfection, they are juft grown to fuch a Size as to have their full fine Flavour, and Turnips are in the fame Condition. Thofe who are fond of the true Delicacy of thefe Roots fhould have them very frequent at their Table at this Time.

The large-rooted Parfley is alfo at this Seafon fine, tender, and full, and this deferves to be brought much more into Ufe, becaufe it is fo excellently wholfome as well as pleafant a Root.

After thefe we are to mention Celeri, which of all the Plants comes neareft a Root, being a Stalk buried in Earth. Some early Stalks of this will be now juft getting into Seafon, and never better or finer; they are fure at this Time to be very tender, juicy, and of a high Flavour.

Cabbages are come to be very fweet and fine, and thofe Cauliflowers which we advifed the Gardiner laft Month to cover in, by breaking upon them fome of the inner Leaves, will toward the End of *June* be in perfect fine Order; they will not be large, but hard, and as white as Milk.

Afparagus will continue in great Perfection, and there will be a Variety of very fine Lettuces.

2. *Fruits of the Kitchen Garden.*

Beans and Peafe come in now in Plenty, and in the well-managed Garden fucceed one another, a frefh Crop every ten Days, fo that they keep in the fame fine young State which fo highly recommends them at their firft Appearance.

This is not only the Cafe where there is a good Garden in the Country, but may be had in London in the very fame Manner, if a careful Houfekeeper
who

who underſtands theſe Products goes to Market. Our Gardiners who raiſe Things for Sale are as nice and careful as the beſt of thoſe retained in Gentlemens Families; they always have their Crops one under another, and it is only the Art of knowing how to chuſe them that is required to keep up the Elegance of the Table in this Article.

French Beans will now alſo be very fine : Indeed they are at no Time of the Year ſo fine as when they are juſt ripened for gathering in this Month; the ſucceeding Crops of theſe, altho' they ripen regularly one under another, yet have not the true Tenderneſs that theſe of the firſt Growth always have.

Artichokes are very fine this Month, and there will be Cucumbers and Melons in very great Perfection.

After theſe, which are properly Fruits, and are the laſt Products in Order in the Kitchen Garden, we are to obſerve, that there continues young Salleting in great Perfection, and the ſcarlet Radiſhes from a late ſowing will be very fine.

3. *Fruits for the Deſert.*

We have obſerved that in the End of the laſt Month Strawberries were juſt coming in; during the Courſe of this they will be every Day ripening in greater Plenty, and we ſhall have the ſeveral Kinds of them in their higheſt Perfection.

We ſhall have Cherries of ſeveral Kinds alſo ſucceeding one another; as the Kentiſh Cherry, the Duke Cherry, the Flanders Heart Cherry, and the white Heart.

The maſculine Apricot, that came in toward the End of the laſt Month, will in the Courſe of this be in perfect fine Seaſon.

Theſe are the Fruits which will ripen in their natural Growth; but as in large Gardens there are uſually forcing Frames, and ſome of thoſe who ſupply

the

the Markets have the fame, we are to mention their Products though before the natural Seafon.

Peaches will be had from thefe about the Middle of *June*, and toward the End of it fome Nectarines and Grapes.

Some Apples may yet be fent to Table, as the Golden, Ruffet and Stone Pippin, Pile's Ruffet, the Oaken Pippin, and the John Apple; and there may yet be preferved three Kinds of Pears; thefe are, the black Worcefter, the Cheynes Green, and the Englifh Warden.

The Number of thefe decreafes now greatly, becaufe all we can have muft have been preferved with great Care during the Winter and Spring, but it will in a few more Months multiply upon us beyond any other, for they will quickly begin to ripen in a vaft Variety and Abundance.

Among the Articles of Fruit we are not to forget the Pine Apple, raifed now in every good Garden by the artificial Heat of Stoves, and by many of thofe who fupply the Markets: Thefe, as the Heat that raifes them is artificial, may be had in a Manner throughout the Year, but the Time when they are moft plentiful, and indeed fineft, is when the natural Temperature of the Air is not very different from that made by Art in their Stoves, therefore this and the two fucceeding Months are the Seafon when Pine Apples are not only beft but moft plentiful in England.

They are kept alive by actual Fires during the Year, therefore the Expence of Coals and Attendance is very confiderable; yet they have now brought the Fruit to a moderate Price, Half a Guinea will purchafe the fineft in our Markets, and very good ones may be had for feven Shillings and fix Pence, others down to Half a Crown.

SECT.

S E C T. II.

Of COOKERY.

C H A P. I.

Of Roafting.

ART. I. *To roaft a Pig the Spanifh Way.*

TAKE out the Liver of the Pig, and fhred it into exceeding fine minced Meat. Set this by on a Plate: Then mince in the fame Manner two Anchovies, firft wafhed and boned, four Truffles, two Morels, half a Dozen fmall Mufhrooms, a Table Spoonful of Capers, a Slice of Bacon, half a Clove of Garlick, and fome Leaves of Thyme and Sweet Bafil, or in want of that Sweet Marjorum.

When thefe are all minced very fine, put the Liver to them, and mix them very well; tofs it all up together in a Saucepan.

Whilft this is doing, make the Pig ready for the Spit, ftick two fmall Onions full of Cloves, put the minced Meat and the Onions into the Belly of the Pig; put alfo into the Belly a Piece of Butter broke into feveral fmall Scraps, and placed in different Parts among the Meat and Onions.

When all this is in, few up the Belly, and lay the Pig down to the Fire.

Prepare for the Bafting a Quantity of the fineft Sallad Oil, and a large Goofe Feather: As the Pig roafts bafte it carefully all over with the Oil, dipping the fmall End of the Feather in it, and drawing it
from

from Time to Time well moiftened all along the Body of the Pig.

By this Means the Pig will be of a better Colour than all the Art and Dilligence of Cookery can make it any other Way, and the Crackling very crifp and very tender ; this Way of Dreffing alfo always prevents the Skin from bliftering.

When it is enough, take it up, open the Belly, and take out a little of the Stuffing ; put this into a Saucepan with a Piece of Butter and fome of the Pig's Gravy, and tofs it up for Sauce.

This may give the Reader a general Notion of the Spanifh Cookery. Here is a Difh very rich and yet not loaded with a Multitude of Ingredients, or with a Confufion of Taftes ; the Pig comes up in its own Form, only better than any Way eife, and the Sauce is made of its own Gravy.

The French have adopted this Piece of Cookery, and thofe of the beft Tafte among them, are very fond of it, preferring it to all the Manglings and Stewings of their own Receipts.

Thofe who chufe may leave out the coftly Ingredients of the Stuffing, and make the Difh come no dearer than a common roafted Pig, tho' it will be beyond all Comparifon better.

2.   *Pigeons ftuffed and roafted.*

Take out the Livers of the Pigeons and mince them very fmall ; then lay down the Pigeons to heat a little juft to blanch them. Mince very fmall a Handful of the young Leaves of Fennel, half a Handful of Parfley, and a few Chives : Mince feparately a Piece of Bacon cut very thin ; and when thefe are done, mix the minced Liver with them.

Stuff the Bodies of the Pigeons with this, then roaft them : Serve them up with a rich Gravy for Sauce.

The French ufually fend up a Raggoo of fome Kind with them ; but this is too much ; it runs into the

the common Fault of their Cookery, which is the Confusion of Tastes.

3. *To roast a Pike.*

Chuse a Couple of large fine Silver Eels, skin them, gut them, and cut the finest Part of their Flesh into long square Slices for Larding.

Chuse a large Pike, scale it, and clean it; scar it slightly with a very fine Knife, and with a careful Hand; lard it well with the Pieces of Eel.

Make a good Quantity of rich Seasoning thus: Strip some Sweet Herbs, and chop the Leaves fine, bruise four Cloves, mix them with a good Quantity of Salt and Pepper, grate in three Quarters of a Nutmeg, and mix these with the Herbs; roll the Pike well in this Seasoning, that it may get into the Scars, and then lay it down, tying it fast to the Spit the whole length.

Make a Sauce for basting it thus: Melt a little Butter, pour it into a Bowl, and put to it a Glass of white Wine; add two Table Spoonfuls of Vinegar, and squeeze in the Juice of a large Lemon.

Keep the Drippingpan extremely clean; baste the Pike as it roasts over and over again with this, and when the Fish is near done, make the Sauce thus:

Cut small a Couple of Anchovies, first washed and boned; put these into a Saucepan, pour to them all the Basting out of the Drippingpan, and toss it up over the Fire. Strain this thro' a Sieve, then put it into the Saucepan again; add to it a Dozen Oisters, and half a Score Grains of whole white Pepper, mix all, and laying the Pike carefully in a Dish, pour this to it.

4. *To roast a Pullet with Onions.*

Scrape some very fine fat Bacon, and mix it with the Leaves of savoury Herbs.

Chuse a fine young Pullet, raise the Skin of the Breast, and put in this Stuffing.

Then

Then pick it and lay it down to roaft.

Chufe a couple of Dozens of fmall fine round Onions; boil thefe in Water, take them up, fet them to cool, and take off the outer Skins; when they are clean and tender, fet them over the Fire in a Saucepan with fome Effence of Gammon of Bacon, and let them fcimmer together for fome Time.

When the Pullet is done, take it off the Spit, place it handfomely in the Difh, and lay thefe Onions round it; pour the Effence in which they were ftewed carefully round them, and ferve them up.

This is a very pretty Difh, and to be provided with little Expence or Trouble. The French improve upon it by parboiling the Fowl, firft tying up both Ends, and then covering it with Slices or Bards of Bacon, before they lay it down to the Fire. The Onions are to be dreffed as we before directed; and to thofe who chufe the Trouble, this is a great Addition.

5.   *To roaft a Calf's Tongue.*

Set on a Stewpan with fome Gravy, put in the Calf's Tongue, cover it up clofe, and fet it to ftew over a moderate Fire.

When it is three Parts enough, take it up, peel it carefully, and lard it with Bacon : Then lay it down to roaft. When it is of a fine Colour, thicken up fome of the Gravy for Sauce, and fend it up. 'Tis a fmall Difh but a very elegant one.

Several Tongues may be done thus together, running Skewers thro' them, and faftening them to the Spit; and this Way four make a very pretty Appearance.

6.   *To roaft a Shoulder of Venifon.*

Cut fome fine fat Bacon into Pieces for larding, and let them be pretty large.

Make a Seafoning of fome Pepper and Salt, mix it with grated Nutmeg, and about three Cloves bruifed; mix all thefe together, roll the Pieces of Bacon in it, and fet all by together on a Plate.

Then

Then put into a Soop Difh large enough to hold the Venifon, a Bottle of white Wine, and half a Pint of Verjuice ; throw in four bay Leaves a little bruifed in the Hand, and a Bundle of Savoury Herbs ; add fome Pepper and Salt, and ftir all well together.

This being ready, lard the Shoulder of Venifon well with the prepared Bacon, and ftrew the Remainder of the Seafoning upon it.

Lay the Shoulder thus prepared in the Soop Difh, in the Marinade prepared for it, and let it lay three Hours, turning it once in half an Hour.

Have a clear fteady Fire ready ; take the Venifon out of the Soop Difh and fpit it ; lay it down at a good Diftance from the Fire, and let it roaft leifurely.

Let the Drippingpan be made perfectly clean ; and pour into it all the Marinade out of the Soop Difh. Bafte the Venifon frequently with this, and when it is near enough, make the following Sauce :

Take out of the Drippingpan fome of the clean Liquor, fkim off the Fat, clear away any Foulnefs that may be on it, and pour it into a Saucepan. Chop a Couple of Spoonfuls of Capers and put them in ; add fome white Pepper, and fqueeze in a fine Lemon, when all is ready, lay the Venifon in a Difh, and pour this Sauce about it.

This is a very excellent Difh, and it the more re- quires the Notice of an Englifh Family, in that for want of knowing how to drefs a Shoulder of Venifon, we efteem it a very poor Joint. This Way it is equal to many a Haunch that one fees at a good Table ; it eats moift, mellow, and excellently well flavoured.

7. *To roaft a Haunch of Doe Venifon, or any other that is not very fat.*

Cut fome fine Bacon into fmall Pieces for larding, lard the Haunch very well with thefe without any Seafoning, and lay it down immediately to roaft, only covering it up very carefully with Paper.

N°. XVIII. 3 U When

When it is near enough, make the following Sauce.

Wash and bone four Anchovies, mince them small, and put them into a Saucepan with some Essence of Gammon of Bacon, and two Spoonfuls of chopped Capers, when they are hot; add half a Pint of hot Gravy of some rich Kind, or of some good Cullis if at Hand, and strew in some Pepper and Salt: Mix all well, then add half a Spoonful of Vinegar; and when the Venison is taken up, lay it handsomely in the Dish, and pour this Sauce round it.

We do not propose this Way to the Cook for a fine Haunch, but when she happens to have one of an inferior Kind, this is an excellent Method of disguising its Defect, and giving it an Air of Novelty.

As some may not like this French Sauce, who would be very well satisfied with the Dressing of the Venison, they may serve it up with the common Sweet Sauce, or with the following, which is the Sweet Sauce at French Tables.

Bruise half a Dozen Cloves, put them into a Silver Saucepan, or an earthen Pipkin, with a Glass of Vinegar; cut an unripe Lemon into Slices, throw that in, then add some Pepper and Salt, and a large Spoonful of the finest Sugar powdered. Break in a Stick of Cinnamon, and throw in a little Bay Salt; boil all together, and strain it thro' a Sieve for Use.

C H A P. II.

Of Boiling.

ART. I. *To boil Scate.*

CHUSE a large thick and very fine Piece of Scate, perfectly fresh and firm, for this is a Fish that soon spoils, and when it is but beginning to grow bad, no Art can make it do the Cook any Credit.

Set on a deep Stewpan with as much Water as will be sufficient to boil it; add to this a Pint of Vinegar,

or

or more if it he a very large Piece of Scate, and put in alfo a Bundle of Sweet Herbs, and fome Bay Salt and white Pepper, and half a Dozen whole Cloves. Put in the Scate and let it boil gently.

When the Fifh is near done, throw in the Liver, and let it boil two Minutes; take this out, and when the Fifh is enough, take off the Stewpan; and when it cools skin and perfectly clean it : Lay it on a Difh and the Liver by it, and then pour round it Parfley and Butter. The French make their Sauce of oiled Butter, Parfley, and fome Vinegar.

2. *To boil Sheeps Tongues.*

Firft put the Tongues into cold Water to clean them perfectly ; out of the cold Water throw them into hot Water, and when they have lain in it fome Time, take them out and peel them.

While they are peeling, fet on a fmall Pot for boiling them : Put into this a fufficient Quantity of Water, and half a Dozen Onions quartered. Add a large Bunch of Sweet Herbs, a Dozen Cloves, fome whole Pepper, and four Bay Leaves.

When this boils, and the Tongues are peeled, throw them in, and keep it boiling till they are enough.

When they are near ready, thicken up fome rich Gravy ; or if you have fome Cullis at Hand beat it ready ; drain the Tongues, lay them handfomely in a Difh, and pour this Gravy round them.

Thofe who have not feen this Difh, would not imagine what an elegant Thing is thus prepared from thefe cheap and trifling Ingredients. The Tongues by this Management are of a fine Colour, and they have a Flavour from the Ingredients boiled in the Water with them, which is light and pleafing, and extremely elegant, and the Sauce added they are very rich.

3 U 2   C H A P.

C H A P. III.

Of Broiling.

A R T. I. *To broil Salmon with white Sauce.*

CUT some fine Salmon into handsome Slices for broiling; lay these ready on a Dish.

Melt some Butter in a Saucepan, and add some Basket Salt.

Pour this Butter over the Slices of Salmon, roll them over and over in it, that every Part may be well covered; then put them on a Gridiron over a very clear but slack Fire, let them broil leisurely, carefully turning them as there may be Occasion.

While the Salmon is doing make the Sauce thus:

Wash and bone a couple of Anchovies, mince them small, and put them into a small Saucepan with some Butter, and a Pinch of Flour; season this with Pepper and Salt; add a Spoonful of Capers chopped, grate in some Nutmeg, and put in a whole Leek, a small one, and add a little Water and half a Spoonful of Vinegar.

Keep this scimmering over a gentle Fire while the Salmon is broiling, and when that is near ready prepare a Dish, warm it, and pour in the Sauce; take away the Leek, and lay in the Salmon, sending it up hot.

This is perhaps the best of all Ways of eating fresh Salmon.

2. *To broil a Shad.*

Chuse a fine and large Shad, scale it, clean it, and pour over it some melted Butter in a Soup Dish, roll it about in the Butter; cut some Scores in the Back and Sides with a very sharp Knife, strew some Basket Salt upon it, and turn it about in the Butter again.

When

When it is well covered with the Butter lay it on to broil; let the Fire be very clear, but not violently fierce.

While the Shad is doing make the Sauce thus:

Melt fome Butter, and put in a Spoonful of Juice of Sorrel, fome Nutmeg, Pepper, and Salt, and when it is all well mixed, add as much Cream as there is Butter: pour this Sauce into the Difh, and lay the Shad in it.

3. *To broil Lampreys.*

Clean them carefully, then cut them into Lengths, and fet them ready.

Cut fome fweet Herbs, a good deal of Parfley, and fome Chives very fine; add to them fome Pepper and Salt, mix them on a Saucer, and let them ftand ready.

Melt fome Butter in a large Saucepan, when it is melted throw in this Seafoning, and when that is well mixed put in the Pieces of Lampreys.

When they have been toffed together two or three Minutes, take them out, drudge them carefully and thick with very fine Crumbs of Bread, and lay them on a Gridiron over a brifk Fire.

While they are doing make the following Sauce:

Put a Piece of Butter into a Saucepan, add a Pinch of Flour, brown it; mince together an Anchovy wafhed and boned, a Couple of frefh Mufhrooms, fome Chives, and fome Parfley; add a little Nutmeg, fome Pepper and Salt, and a few Capers; mix up the whole, and pour it into a warm Difh; lay the Lamprey in it.

4. *To broil Trout.*

As this is the Seafon in which Trout are in their higheft Degree of Perfection, and many efteem this the beft Way of eating them, we can by no Means omit it in the prefent Chapter.

Let

Let the Trout be carefully cleaned, wafhed, and dried; tie them round and round with Packthread to keep them entire and in Shape; then melt fome Butter with a good deal of Bafket Salt, pour this over the Trout, and roll it in the Butter till perfectly covered, then lay it over a clear Fire at a good Diftance that it may do leifurely.

While the Trout is broiling make the Sauce thus:

Cut an Anchovy, firft wafhed and boned, very fmall, and chop fmall alfo a Table Spoonful of Capers; melt fome Butter with a Pinch of Flour, and add to it fome Pepper, Salt, Nutmeg, and thefe Ingredients; laft of all pour in half a Spoonful of Vinegar: When the Trout is done take it up, lay it on a warm Difh, pour this Sauce upon it, and fend it up hot.

C H A P. IV.

Of Frying.

A R T. I. *To fry Smelts.*

PUT into a deep Soup Difh a Quart of Vinegar, break in four Bay Leaves, put in a Nutmeg fhaved, not grated, four bruifed Cloves, fome Pepper and Salt, and a few Chives chopped, not very fmall.

This is a Marinade for the Smelts, and vaftly improves their Flavour.

Lay the Smelts cleaned in this Liquor, and turn them once in a Quarter of an Hour; let them lie in it an Hour and half, and then take them out; wipe them very dry with a Napkin, drudge them well with Flour, and fry them.

They will thus be of a fine brown, very delicate, and will have all their own rich and elegant Flavour vaftly improved by the Marinade.

Some fend up a Gravy Sauce for them, and others a Shrimp Sauce, but this is all wrong: If it be any

one's

one's particular Fancy to have fuch a Sauce, let it be
fent up feparate in a Sauce Boat, not in the Difh with
the Smelts

This Difh fhould be garnifhed with crifp Parfley,
and nothing fhould be eat with the Smelts but Salt.

2. *To fry Soals.*

Clean the Soals perfectly, then wafh them to complete it, and dry them with Napkins ; fet on a Stewpan with fome clarified Butter, drudge the Soals with
Flour, and fry them in the Butter till they are of a
perfectly fine brown Colour.

Drain them perfectly dry, lay a clean and fine Napkin over the Difh, and lay the Soals upon it; garnifh
with fried Parfley.

Send up with them in a China Sauce Boat, a Mixture of equal Quantities of Juice of Seville Orange
and Juice of Lemon, and fome Pepper and Salt.

This is the French Sauce, and none is fo proper.

Our People, when they fry Soals in this Manner,
commonly make a Butter Sauce, which they enrich
with Shrimps, or relifh with Anchovy, but this is
vaftly preferable.

3. *To fry Sweetbreads.*

Squeeze into a fmall Soup Difh four fine Lemons,
take out the Pips, and to the clear Juice put fome
grated Nutmeg, fome Pepper and Salt, four whole
Cloves, and fome Chives cut fmall; ftir all this together for a Marinade.

Blanch a Couple of Sweetbreads, and cut each of
them, if large, into three or four Pieces, if fmaller
only into two Pieces; put thefe into the Liquor, and
let them lie in it an Hour, frequently turning and
ftirring them about; then make a Batter for them
thus :

Beat up one Egg with a little Salt, mix it with
fome Flour and Water into a moderately thin Condition, then melt about an Ounce of Butter and add

to

to it; ftir all together, and if too thick or too thin bring it to be right by a little Flour or a little Water.

This being ready, take the Sweetbreads out of the Marinade and dry them in a Napkin; when thoroughly dry dip them in the Batter.

Set on a Stewpan with fome Hogs Lard, when it is hot take out the Sweetbreads from the Batter, and put them one by one into the Pan; let them be fried perfectly brown, then take them up, and drain them carefully from the Fat.

Heat a Difh, and lay over it a Napkin alfo heated; lay the Sweetbreads on this without any Sauce, garnifhed with fried Parfley.

4. *To fry Trout.*

For thofe who love the real Tafte of this excellent Fifh, there is no Way better of dreffing them than plain frying, it gives a Crifpnefs to the Flefh, and leaves its high Flavour entire; it is to be done thus:

Gut and clean the Trout, wafh them, and then dry them perfectly with Napkins; cut the Sides and Back flightly with a very fine Knife, ftrew a little Salt over them, and then drudge them over with Flour.

Set on a Pan with fome clarified Butter, and when it is hot lay in the Trout, fry them to a delicate brown, and fend them up in a Napkin, garnifhed with fried Parfley.

We fhall fhew the Method of making fome very elegant Difhes of Trout in the fucceeding Chapters, but this is the fine Way to eat them.

CHAP. V.

Of Baking.

ART. I. *To bake a Turbot.*

POUR into a Silver Difh juft big enough to hold the Turbot a Pint of Champaigne Wine, but firft rub the Difh all over with a Piece of Butter.

Shred

Shred fome Parfley and fome Chives very fine, fhave down a Nutmeg and put to them, add fome Pepper and Salt, and put all this to the Wine in the Difh.

When all is thus ready clean the Turbot perfectly, and cut off the Head and Tail, lay it in the Difh, and ftrew over it fome of the fame Seafoning as was put to the Wine.

Melt fome Butter, and pour a little of it at a Time upon the Turbot, rub it well all over the upper Side of the Fifh as it cools, and then drudge it thin with Crumbs of Bread made very fine ; fend it to the Oven, and when it comes home fend it up, with fome Anchovy Sauce in one Sauce Boat, and rich Gravy in another.

The French ferve up their rich Culliffes with this Fifh, and nothing deferves them better.

2. *To bake Tench.*

Clean a Brace of Tench perfectly well.

Then rub over the Bottom of a Silver Difh, big enough to hold them, with a Piece of Butter.

Sprinkle into the Difh upon the Butter the following Seafoning:

Cut fome Parfley very fine, cut alfo fome Chives, and mix with them fome Pepper, Salt, and grated Nutmeg ; pick fome fweet Herbs from the Stalks, and ftrew thefe and the other Seafoning over the Difh; laft of all fhred a large Onion very fine, and fcatter it over the Seafoning.

Lay the Tench evenly and regularly in the Difh, pour fome melted Butter over them, drudge them with very fine Crumbs of Bread, and fend them to the Oven.

While they are baking make a very rich Sauce with Gravy, Anchovies, and Truffles ; pour this round the baked Tench, and fend them up hot.

Tench ftewed in the Manner of Carp are a very fine Difh, and preferable in the Opinion of many to

N°. XVIII.   3 X   Carp,

Carp, but thofe who value Fifh for their true Flavour prefer the baked Tench to the ftewed.

The French make a very fine and rich Difh of baked Tench; they take out the Back Bone of the Fifh, and ftuff it with the Flefh of other Tench made into a Kind of Force-meat with Eggs and Bread, and then bake them, and ferve them up with their Cullis of Cray-fifh, the Way of making which we have defcribed before.

If any prefer this Method to the plain baking, there is fome Trouble but no great Difficulty in the doing of it, and it makes a great Figure.

C H A P. VI.

Of Made Difhes.

A R T. I. *A Bifque of Pullet.*

CHUSE a very fine Pullet, and let it be truffed in the neateft Manner, blanch it in hot Water, and then fet it ready for boiling.

Set on a large Saucepan with fome rich and very clear Broth or weak Gravy, put into this an Onion peeled and ftuck with Cloves, a Lemon cut into Slices, Peel and all, and four or five Slices of fat and lean Bacon.

Put the Pullet into this, and fet it over a moderate Fire; as it boils fcum it carefully, and when it is thus boiled very clean, and done enough, fet it over a Chaffing-difh of Coals that it may keep hot.

While the Fowl is boiling make a rich Raggoo of Sweetbreads, as we have before directed in its Place, let there be put into this fome Mufhrooms, Truffles, and Artichoke Bottoms, all cut fmall; let thefe be all toffed up together with fome melted Bacon, and then pour on it fome rich Veal Gravy.

Thicken this with Cullis of Veal and of Gammon of Bacon.

When

When all is thus ready foak fome Crufts of Bread in ftrong Broth, lay them round the Sides of a Difh, lay the Pullet in the Difh, and pour in the Raggoo round it, but not upon it.

This is a very elegant and very famous Difh.

A great deal of the Expence and Trouble may be faved by only making a rich Gravy, or a cheap and flight Raggoo, and pouring it round a Fowl thus carefully boiled: This would not be fo expenfive as the right and perfect Bifque of Pullet, but it would be an exceeding good Difh.

2. *Forced Cabbage.*

This is a cheap and a very elegant Difh, and the young Cabbages that are now juft coming into Seafon are the fitteft of all for it.

Pick out a Couple of very fine Cabbages, cut away the outer Leaves of one, and fave only the Infide or Heart for boiling; cut out the Infide or Heart of the other more carefully, that the outer Part may remain entire, throw this Outfide into boiling Water, and let it fcald till the Leaves are pliant and manageable, then take it out, and lay it in a Sieve to drain and to be ready.

Boil the two Hearts of the Cabbages very well.

Boil four Eggs hard, feparate the Yolks, and fet them ready, chop the Cabbages to Pieces and fet that alfo ready.

Cut very fine Half a Pound of Veal and a Quarter of a Pound of fine fat Bacon, mix with thefe the chopped Cabbage, and then cut to Pieces the Yolks of the Eggs, mix them with Pepper, Salt, fome grated Bread, and a very fmall Quantity of grated Cheefe; mix thefe with the others, and making the whole into a large round Lump put it into the fcalded Cabbage Leaves, tie it up, and fet it ready.

Set on a large Saucepan with a Gallon of very ftrong Broth, put in the forced Cabbage, and let it boil gently till it is thoroughly done, then ferve it up hot.

3 X 2   It

It is one of the Difhes which require no Sauce, for its own Sauce is within it, but fome ferve it up with Gravy, and fome with melted Butter; if any be ufed the Gravy is much the better.

3. *To drefs Chickens the Barbary Way.*

Cut off the Flefh of a Chicken, and make it into a Force-meat with fome Bacon, Yolks of Eggs, Bread, and a great deal of Spices; trufs another Chicken for boiling, beat it with a Rolling-pin to break the Bones, then fill the Body with this Force-meat.

Set on a large Saucepan with a Gallon of Milk, a Bundle of fweet Herbs, a Nutmeg fliced, and fome whole Pepper; when this boils put in the Chicken, and let it boil till it is near enough.

Then take it up, dry it, broil it to a fine brown, and ferve it up with a very rich Gravy, or with a cold Sauce made of Juice of Lemon, Pepper, Salt, and Capers: This is the true Way.

4. *To roaft Chickens with Gravy.*

Chufe fome very fmall and delicate Chickens, and cut for each of them a Piece of Bacon as long and as broad as the Body of the Chicken, and very thin; loofen the Skin of the Breaft all the Way down, and then feafon the Bacon with Pepper and Salt, fome Parfley, and fome Chives, all fhred fmall together.

When the Pieces of Bacon are well covered with this Seafoning lay one of them upon the Breaft and Body of each Chicken, juft of its Largenefs, and draw the Skin over it; then tie up the Chickens, that the Skins may not come off in any Part, and roaft them in Bards of Bacon, that is, wrapped up in thin and broad Slices of Bacon.

When they are near done make fome rich Veal Gravy hot for Sauce; lay the Chickens handfomely in a Difh, taking away the Bards of Bacon that cover them on the Spit, and untying the Packthreads, but not taking out the Bacon that is between the Skin and

Flefh

Flefh of the Breaft; pour the Gravy hot into the Difh to them.

5. *Raggoo of Cray-fifh.*

Wafh fome Cray-fifh, and when they are well cleaned boil them in Water, pick them, take off the Tails and the reft of the Shells, and pick out the Body; let the Shells be faved for other Ufes, we have fhewn in a preceding Number their Ufe in making the Cullis of Cray-fifh.

Cut off the Ends of the Tails, and then prepare the other Ingredients of the Raggoo.

Shred fome Mufhrooms, but not fmall, cut fome Truffles into thin Slices, and add fome Artichoke Bottoms and Afparagus Tops; mix all thefe together, and add the Cray-fifh to them.

Tofs all up in a Saucepan with a Bit of Butter, and then add a little ftrong Broth.

Put in at the fame Time fome Pepper and Salt for Seafoning, fome Nutmeg, and three or four Slices of Lemon; fet the Saucepan to fcimmer over a very gentle Fire; add, after it has boiled a little, an Onion cut very fine; let it fcimmer on, and when it is thoroughly enough put in fome Cullis of Cray-fifh to thicken it; fend it up hot in a fmall Difh.

It is the beft Way of eating Cray-fifh, and is a very excellent Difh.

6. *Maiden Cream.*

Break five Eggs, fave the Yolks for other Ufes, beat up the Whites with fome Orange-Flower Water and Sugar, and add fome Milk.

Set a Plate to be warmed over a Stove with a little Cinnamon.

When the Plate is warm, and the Mixture is well beat up, pour it in, let it ftand over the Stove till it is done enough, then make a Fire-fhovel red hot, and hold it over the Plate to brown it; ferve it up as foon as well coloured.

7. *Chocolate*

7. *Chocolate Cream.*

Mix together a Quart of Milk and a Quarter of a Pound of the fineſt Sugar, ſet them over the Fire and boil them for ſome Time; beat up the Yolk of an Egg, put it in, and let it boil up two or three Times, then take it off the Fire, and put in ſome Chocolate to colour and give it a Flavour; ſend it up hot.

8. *Cutlets with Raggoo.*

Cut ſome large and handſome Veal Cutlets, beat them flat upon a Dreſſer, then lard them carefully, drudge them with a Mixture of Pepper, Salt, Crumbs of Bread, and ſhred Parſley.

Lay them in Readineſs.

Then make a Raggoo of Veal Sweetbreads, with Muſhrooms, as we have before directed, and when this is ready dreſs the Cutlets.

They are to be toſſed up in melted Bacon till they are well done and of a fine brown; then heat a Diſh, keep the Raggoo hot, lay the Cutlets handſomely in the Diſh, and pour the Raggoo over them. Send them up hot.

There is no Occaſion to make a large Raggoo, nor to put in any expenſive Ingredients; ſo that this Diſh may be made at a ſmall Price, and without any great Difficulty, and it is a very fine and elegant one, fit to come to the beſt Table.

9. *Cutlets with four Sauce.*

Cut ſome fine and moderately thick Veal Cutlets, ſet them on in a Saucepan of Water, and let them boil till they are pretty well done, then take them out, and lay them to drain and cool.

Make a Batter of Eggs and a little Flour, and let it be pretty thin.

Set on a Pan with ſome Hogs Lard, when it is hot dip the Cutlets in the Batter, and then put them into the Pan; let them fry till they are of a fine brown.

Make

Make a Sauce of Verjuice, Salt, and Pepper, mix it in a China Sauce-boat, and fend it up with the Cutlets.

This is the French Way of eating them, but it will not pleafe an Englifh Palate till ufed to it; however, the Difh need not be negleded for that. Thefe Cutlets eat very well with a good Sauce of Gravy or Cullis.

10. *Cutlets marinated*

Squeeze into a fmall Soup Difh four good Lemons, take out the Pips, and put to the Juice three Bay Leaves broken, fome Chives fhred fmall, fome Pepper and Salt, half a dozen whole Cloves, and a Glafs of Verjuice.

Cut fome handfome Veal Cutlets, beat them flat, and lay them in this Liquor to marinate; let them lie in it three Hours, turning them once in Half an Hour.

Then make a thin Batter thus:

Beat up an Egg, and mix with it fome Flour and Water, melt an Ounce of Butter and pour it in, ftir all thefe together, and keep the Batter of a due Confiftence, by adding a little Water if too thick, and a little Flour if too thin.

When this is ready, fet on a Pan of Hogs Lard.

When that is hot take out the Cutlets from the Marinade and dip them in it; when they are handfomely covered with the Batter put them into the Pan, and fry them to a fine brown.

Then heat a Difh, lay them in, and fend them up garnifhed with fried Parfley.

We in England are very fond of Sauce, fo they who chufe it may put Gravy Sauce to thefe, but they are better without.

11. *Cutlets in Hodge-Podge.*

Cut fome thick Cutlets either of Veal or Mutton, fet them on to boil in a fmall Quantity of ftrong Broth, and put on with them fome Turnips cut in Quarters; let them boil half an Hour, then add fome Pepper and Salt, fome Sweet Herbs, and a whole Leek; and lay fome Chefnuts to roaft.

When the Broth and its Ingredients have fcimmered fome Time, and the Chefnuts are cracked peel them; break them, but not very fmall, and put them into the Saucepan.

Let it continue upon the Fire fcimmering till the Cutlets are thoroughly done, and the Chefnuts well foaked through; then pour it into a warm Soop Difh, and fend it up.

12. *Cutlets with Gravy.*

Cut fome fine Cutlets of Veal or Mutton, beat them flat and make ready a Seafoning, and fome melted Bacon.

The Seafoning is to be made thus: Shred fome Parfley very fine, pick and chop to Pieces fome Savoury Herbs, and grate in a little Nutmeg; add fome Pepper and Salt, and a few Crumbs of Bread made very fine.

Set this Seafoning ready on a Plate, and then dip the Cutlets in the melted Bacon, fprinkle them immediately over with fome of the Seafoning, and make it ftick on as thick as you can: Then lay them on a Gridiron over a very clear Fire, and let them be nicely browned; ftrew fome more Crumbs of Bread over them every Time they are turned, and when they are well done, and of a good Colour, ferve them up with fome good Gravy.

There are a great Variety of Ways of dreffing a very cheap and very common Difh. We in general go on in the fame Trot Road, broiling them and nothing more, or elfe making them into Collops with various Ingredients.

Thefe

Thefe two Ways of dreffing we have in the former Part of this Work defcribed, with all the Cautions needful for doing them well; but here we fee a
Variety of other eafy Methods, by which a Man who
had nothing to eat but Cutlets, might have a new
Difh out of them every Day; all Elegant, and none
of them at all Expenfive.

13. *Veal a la Daube.*

This is a Difh intended to be eaten cold, and as
there are feveral other Articles befides Veal that may
be done in the fame Way, and the Seafon is now
coming when fuch Difhes will be very agreeable,
it is highly neceffary that the Cook be made acquainted with it.

Daube is properly a cold Ragoo; the Way of
doing it in Veal is this.

Take off the Skin from a Piece of Veal; lard it
carefully, and then fet it in Readinefs.

Put into a large Soop Difh proportioned to the
Bignefs of the Piece of Veal, a Quantity of white
Wine, and Verjuice equally mixed.

Put into this five Bay Leaves broken, ten whole
Cloves, a Spoonful of whole Pepper, and fome Salt;
ftir all this well about with a Bundle of Sweet Herbs,
then put in that alfo, and when this Marinade is ready,
lay the larded Veal into it.

Let it foak four Hours, and turn it frequently in
that Time

When it is taken out fpit it, lay it down to a moderate Fire, and pour the Liquor out of the Soop
Difh into the Drippingpan; bafte it with this as it
roafts.

When it is near enough, pour the Liquor out of
the Drippingpan into a Stewpan, and taking the
Meat from the Spit, put it into the Stewpan with it,
pour in as much Gravy as will make it fufficient to
cover the Meat, and add a Couple of Anchovies
boned, and cut fmall, a large Spoonful of Capers

chopped, a Lemon cut in Slices, and half a Dozen frefh Mufhrooms cleaned and cut to Pieces.

Let the Meat fcimmer in thefe for fome Time, and then fet it off the Fire.

It may be fent up in this Manner hot ; but the beft Way, and indeed the proper Defign of the Difh, is to be fet by to be cold, and fent up at Supper.

14. *A Green Goofe a la Daube.*

Make a large Quantity of Seafoning thus : Mix together fome Chives cut fmall, fome frefh Lemon Peel fhred, and fome Bay Leaves clipped.

Add to thefe fome Pepper and Salt, grated Nutmeg, and Cloves bruifed.

When this is ready, cut fome Bacon into large Pieces for larding. Pick the Goofe and make it very clean ; lard it carefully with thefe Pieces of Bacon, and throw over it the Seafoning juft directed ; then wrap up the Goofe carefully in a Napkin, and put it into a fmall Pot; pour upon it equal Quantities of white Wine and ftrong Broth, till the whole be enough in Quantity to boil it.

When it has boiled till you judge it is done enough, remove the Pot from the Fire, and let all be fet by together for the Goofe to cool in the Liquor.

When all is perfectly cold, take out the Goofe, unroll the Napkin, and when it is to be ferved up, lay a clean Napkin upon a Difh, lay the Goofe cold upon it ; and garnifh with frefh Parfley.

This is a very elegant Way of eating a Green Goofe cold ; and any other Fowl may be dreffed in the fame Manner. Chickens, Turkey-poults, and Pigeons, are all excellent in this Management. And as there is no Variation in the Way of doing them, we fhall let this one Receipt ferve for all.

The French drefs Partridges, Pheafants, and other Game this Way, but the Tame Fowls do better.

15. *Duck*

15. *Duck a la Braise.*

This is another of the famous Ways of dreffing in foreign Kitchens ; and as feveral Things are done in the fame Method under this Name, we fhall here make the Cook familiarly acquainted with it, under the Method of doing a Duck.

Chufe a very fine, young, but full grown and large Tame Duck : Let it be cleaned, picked, and prepared with the moft nice Care.

Cut fome Bacon into pretty thick Pieces for larding.

Mix fome chopped Parfley, Chives, Sweet Herbs, Pepper, Salt, and grated Nutmeg for a Seafoning, with the Pieces of Bacon in this ; and then lard the Duck very well with them.

When the Duck is thus ready, cut fome thin Slices of Beef, and fome thin Slices of Bacon ; cover the bottom of a large Stewpan with thefe, and ftrew over them, and among them fome Carrots, Turnips, and Parfnips cut fmall ; a Lemon fhred thin, Rind and all : Half a Dozen Cloves, an Onion cut fmall, and fome Pepper, and Salt, and Sweet Herbs picked from the Stalks, but not chopped.

When the Bottom of the Stewpan is thus covered, lay in the larded Duck, and ftrew over it what was left of the Seafoning of the Bacon for larding.

Cut fome more Slices of Beef and Bacon, and cover the Duck with thefe, and with more of the Roots, Herbs, and Seafoning : Lay fome thin Slices of Bacon over all ; then put on the Cover of the Stewpan, and fix it down clofe.

Set the Stewpan upon a brisk Fire in a Stove, and put a good deal of burning Charcoal upon it.

When it is enough, take away the upper Coals, and uncover the Pan ; take out the Duck and fet it to drain : This is the Duck a la Braife.

The French prefer a Wild Duck, but thofe who have eat this Difh frequently with me at Bath, when I have tried both, always prefered the Tame.

3 Y 2 The

The Duck being drained, is to be ferved up with fome rich Sauce.

The French ufually fend up the Ducks dreffed this Way with a Raggoo : None is better than the Raggoo of Sweet-Breads before defcribed. They never fend up a Raggoo with this Fowl but when it is done a la Braife ; but as this is an expenfive Way of dreffing, we fhall give the Reader a Method which anfwers the fame Purpofe, with much lefs Charge and Trouble, and therefore will be more agreeable to all but the greateft Families.

17. *Duck with Raggoo.*

Chufe as before a fine, tender, well grown Tame Duck.

Cut fome Bacon into large Pieces for larding, feafon thefe with the fame Seafoning of Sweet Herbs and Spices directed as before, and lard the Duck very thick with a careful Hand.

Strew the Remainder of the Seafoning over the Duck, and then drudge it well with Flour.

Set on a Stewpan with fome melted Bacon ; put in the Duck, and tofs it up to brown it : Then put it into a Pot, and make a Brown with the melted Bacon and fome Flour. Put this into the Pot with the Duck, and pour in as much good Broth as will juft cover the Duck, then feafon it, and fet it on to ftew.

When it is near done, put in Half a Pint of Mountain Wine, and then add fome Pepper, half a Dozen whole Cloves, an Onion chopped to Pieces, a Handful of fhred Parfley and fome Sweet Herbs : Laftly cut to Pieces a Lemon, Rind and all, and put that in.

Cover up the Pot again, and fet the Duck to ftew over the Fire again with thefe Ingredients : Then, when it is thoroughly done, take it out of the Pot, and ferve it up with a Raggoo of Sweet-Breads, with

with Mufhrooms, Truffles, Afparagus Tops, and Artichoke Bottoms.

If this be well managed, the Difh is hardly to be diftinguifhed from the right Way of doing it a la Braife. I have had tolerable Judges at my Table, who have been deceived by it.

We fhall have Occafion to direct fome other Difhes to be done a la Braife in the fucceeding Part of this Work, where to avoid tedious Repetitions, we fhall only name it, referring to this Place for the Receipt ; and in any of thefe Cafes, the Reader is to keep in Mind, that according to the Choice of the Family, the Difh may either be done a la Braife in the genuine Method, or in this Way that I have now named in it's Stead.

18. *Duck with Peafe.*

The Peafe are to be made into a Raggoo for this Purpofe, and therefore according to the Rule we have juft laid down, the Duck muft be dreffed a la Braife, either in the genuine or fecond Manner.

Which ever Way be preferred, a young Duck is to be chofen, and the Raggoo is to be made of fine young Peafe.

While the Duck is Stewing, this Raggoo muft be got ready thus.

The Peafe muft be toffed up with a little Flour and Butter, fome Pepper and Salt, and a Bundle of Sweet Herbs.

When this is done, pour in a little very rich Veal Gravy to moiften them ; let them ftew a Time in this ; then when the Duck is ready, beat up a Couple of Yolks of Eggs in a little Cream, and mix this with the Raggoo of Peafe.

Take out the Duck, lay it carefully in a warm Difh, and pour this Raggoo round it, and fome upon it.

If the Duck be done a la Braife in the right Way, I would advife the Raggoo to be poured into the

Difh,

Diſh, and then the Duck laid in without any of the Raggoo upon it ; but if it be done in the other Way, let the Raggoo be poured over it, when in the Diſh. There will be ſome difference in the look of the one and the other, and the Raggoo entirely hides this.

19. *To dreſs Eels a la Daube.*

This is a Diſh like the other Daubes, intended to be eaten cold, but there is a Particularity in the Manner of dreſſing it : It is to be done thus :

Chuſe three fine Eels, and a Brace of handſome Tench.

Cut open one of the Skins of the largeſt Eels, and lay it ready for the Reception of the Meat.

Pick the Fleſh of theſe Eels and of the Tench from the Bones, chop the whole together, and ſeaſon it with Salt and Pepper ; grate in three Quarters of a Nutmeg, and add three Cloves bruiſed.

This being all mixed perfectly well together, cut out the Fleſh of a Couple of other large Eels into longiſh ſlender Pieces, ſuch as are cut for Larding. Cut open another of the largeſt Skins, and lay that alſo ready ſpread flat out upon a Table.

Then begin to lay the Meat upon the firſt Skin.

Firſt lay a Layer of the Slices of Eel, then a thicker Coat of the Minced Meat, upon this put more of the Slices of Eel, and upon them more of the Minced Meat.

Thus go on till all is uſed, and there be a Heap of it together of the Shape of a Brick. Preſs this gently down with the Hand, and lay over it the other Skins, tie them round and ſecure them in ſuch Manner, that the whole may keep entire ; then wrap it up carefully in a Linnen Cloth, and put it into a large Saucepan with ſome freſh Broth.

Set it over a gentle Fire, and let it do leiſurely for ſome Time.

When it is judged to be three Parts done, pour in a Pint of red Port Wine, and put in at the ſame

Time

Time half a Dozen whole Cloves, a Couple of Bay Leaves broke, and fome whole white Pepper and Salt.

Cover up the Saucepan, and let this Stew till the Eel be thoroughly done; then fet it off, that it may all cool together.

This is the Difh the French eat inftead of our Collar'd Eel.

They cut Slices of this and fend it to Table on a fmall Difh, it looks beautiful, and eats very fine.

20. *Poached Eggs with Cucumbers.*

This is a very elegant little Difh, and as it depends entirely upon the Choice of each of the two Articles, the Eggs being new laid, and the Cucumbers young and frefh, no Time of the Year can be properer for it than the prefent.

Cut an Onion to Pieces, put it into a Soop Difh, pour upon it fome Vinegar, then add Salt and Pepper; ftir all well together and cover it up.

Get half a Dozen young and fine Cucumbers, peel them, fplit them open, and if there be large Seeds in any, cut them out.

When the Cucumbers are thus prepared, put them into the Soop Difh to the Vinegar and Ingredients; let them be there an Hour.

Then take them out, put them into a Saucepan, and tofs them up with a Piece of Butter. When they begin to grow brown, pour in fome Broth, and fet them over a gentle Fire to fcimmer for a Quarter of an Hour.

Then take off the Fat, put to them fome rich Cullis, and fet it on again, that it may be kept hot and perfectly mixed.

Chufe half a Dozen fine large and perfectly new laid Eggs; break them into a Cup one by one, and poach them in Butter: Lay them handfomely in a fmall Difh one by one as they are done; cut away all

the

the White, fo that nothing remains but the round Yolk; and pufh thefe pretty clofe together.

When they are all in, pour the Raggoo of Cucumbers over them hot, and fend them up immediately: This is a fmall, but an extremely elegant Difh.

21. *To drefs a Hare the Swifs Way.*

Set on a Stewpan with fome ftrong rich Broth; cut a Hare in Quarters, and lard them well with thick Pieces of Bacon.

Strew fome Pepper, Salt, and beaten Cloves into the Broth, ftir it together, and then put in the Quarters of the Hare.

Cover it up, and fet it over a gentle Fire; let it ftew till it is three Parts done, then add a Bottle of Red Port Wine, and fome Blades of Mace: Cover up the Stewpan again, and fet it over a gentle Fire to be thoroughly done.

When the Hare is near enough, make a Sauce thus: Mince the Liver very fmall, and having faved what Blood you could from the Hare, put thefe into a Saucepan together, duft in a little Flour, and add half a Spoonful of Vinegar: Make all thefe hot together, and while they ftand on the Fire, chop a Spoonful of Capers, and cut off the flefhy Part of a Couple of Dozen of Olives; mix all this together in the Saucepan of Sauce.

Take out the Hare, and lay the Pieces regularly and handfomely in the Difh; pour in this Sauce, and ferve it up hot.

22. *A Raggoo of Lamb.*

Set on a Stewpan with fome rich Broth, put in fome Pepper and Salt, and half a Dozen whole Cloves; and add half Dozen Mufhrooms, and a Bunch of Sweet Herbs. Let thefe heat together.

Then cut fome Lamb into moderately large Pieces; beat them flat, and tofs them up in a Saucepan to

brown

brown them, and then put them into the Broth, cover up the Stewpan, and let them stew till they are enough.

When the Lamb is done, thicken up the Sauce with some rich Cullis, and serve it up hot.

This is a cheap Raggoo, but it is a very good one.

Mutton may be done in the same Manner, but Lamb is better.

23. *To stew Lettuces.*

Cabbage Lettuces are the best for this Purpose, and such are to be chosen as are large, thick, and very well cabbaged.

Take a Dozen of these large and fine Lettuces, wash them in several Waters, and see they are perfectly clean, then put them into a Pot with a large Quantity of Water, and boil them half an Hour.

Take them out one by one with a Skimmer, and lay them in a large Hair Sieve to drain.

When they are a little cooled throw them into a large Pan of cold Spring Water, stir them about, then one by one take them up, squeeze them gently in the Hand to get out the Water, and when drained in this Manner as well as they can be, place them one beside another regularly in a small Stewpan.

Mix up a Quarter of a Pound of Butter with a Tea Spoonful of Flour; put this into the Middle of the Stewpan.

Put in three Blades of Mace whole, and a Piece of Bacon as big as a Walnut, with half a Dozen Cloves stuck in it.

When all these are in pour upon the Lettuces as much Veal Broth as will just cover them, sprinkle in some Pepper and Salt, and set them over a clear Fire.

They must be kept scimmering in this Way three Quarters of an Hour.

By this Time the Lettuces will be thoroughly stewed, and the Broth will be thick and rich like Cream.

Pour over them a little drawn Butter, and give the the Pan a Shake about, but it muft not be toffed, for that would break the Lettuces, and the Beauty of the Difh is to fee them come up whole.

All being thus finifhed, warm a fmall Difh and flide out the whole carefully fo as not to break the Lettuces; lay them regularly, and take out the Mace and the Bacon with the Cloves; place fome toafted Sippets about the Edge of the Difh, and fend it up hot.

This is not only a very pretty Difh of itfelf, but it ferves for other Purpofes.

A boiled Chicken ferved up upon a Difh of ftewed Lettuce is very elegant and agreeable.

But when it is intended for this Purpofe, it is better to thicken it up farther by mixing in a Yolk of an Egg and Cream.

24. *A Raggoo of Mufhrooms.*

Chufe fome Mufhrooms of a moderate Size, clean them perfectly, and then fet them on in a Saucepan with fome melted Bacon, Pepper and Salt, and a Spoonful of fhred Parfley; tofs them up, and then moiften them with fome rich Gravy.

When they are well done thicken them with Cullis, or if that be not at Hand thicken up the Liquor in the common Way, and ferve them up.

25. *Mufhrooms with Cream.*

Chufe fome half-grown Mufhrooms, clean them, cut them to Pieces, and tofs them up in a Saucepan with fome Butter, feafoned with Salt and fome grated Nutmeg, and with a Bunch of fweet Herbs.

Let them be toffed up over a brifk Fire, and when they are done enough pour in fome thick Cream; let all be well heated together, and fend them up in a warm Soup Plate.

CHAP.

C H A P. VII.

Of Puddings.

A R T. I. *A fine Rice Pudding.*

CLEAN fome Rice, blanch it in Water, and then fet it on in Milk proportioned to the Quantity of the Rice; put in fome Salt at firft, and when it is half boiled break in a large Stick of Cinnamon, let it boil fome Time longer with this, and then add fome fine Sugar powdered.

When the Rice is boiled tender, and the whole is thick, take it from the Fire.

Pick and wafh half a Pound of Currants, and ftone the fame Quantity of the fineft Raifins of the Sun.

Beat up fix Eggs with three of the Whites, mix thefe with the Rice and Milk, and then put in the Currants and Raifins, and ftir all well together.

Break a Pair of good Beef Marrow Bones, take out the Marrow, cut it into fmall fquare Pieces, and ftir thefe in; then put it into a Difh, and fend it to be baked.

We have in the preceding Numbers inftructed the Cook to make common or ordinary Rice Puddings; this is a very delicate one, and is fit to appear at any Table.

Suet may be ufed inftead of Marrow, but it is much inferior to it, and for a Difh intended to be elegant the Difference of Price is not worth minding.

2. *Potatoe Pudding with Orange.*

Boil two Pounds of very found and fine Potatoes, peel them carefully, and put them into a Marble Mortar, beat them to a Mafh; then melt half a Pound of Butter, pour it in by Degrees to the Potatoes, and beat all up together well, then boil it half an Hour.

When

When it is thus done, pour over it fome melted Butter and a Glafs of Mountain Wine; laft of all fqueeze over it a fine Seville Orange, and duft on fome fine powdered Sugar; fend it to be baked, and order it to be but little done.

Some eat this Kind of Potatoe Pudding boiled, but the baking gives it a very fine Relifh.

3. *A Cowflip Pudding.*

Pick the Flowers of a Peck of frefh-gathered Cowflips, chop them fmall, then put them into a Marble Mortar, pound them well, and mix with them half a Pound of Naples Bifcuit and three Pints of thick and rich Cream; put the Cream in by a little at a Time; but in the End let the whole be well beaten together.

Set this all together on the Fire in a large Saucepan.

Mix together three Spoonfuls of Cream and two Spoonfuls of Rofe Water; fet it by you in a Glafs.

Then break twelve Eggs into a Punch Bowl, beat them up with the Rofe Water and Cream, and fweeten the whole to the Tafte; mix this with the boiling Ingredients in the Saucepan, and fet it off the Fire.

Butter a Difh of a proper Size, pour this in, and when it is enough baked ftrew fome of the fineft Sugar powdered over it, and fend it up hot. It is an elegant Pudding.

4. *A Quaking Pudding.*

Take a Quart of Cream, twelve Eggs, Whites and all, beat them very well, and ftrain them into the Cream, ftrew a good Spoonful of Flour over the Cloth, pour in the Pudding, tie it up, and let it boil very faft an Hour.

5. *A Boiled Loaf.*

Let a Penny Loaf be rafped; put it into a Pan, and pour upon it a Pint of Milk boiling hot.

Let it ftand till all the Milk is foaked up, and then tie it up in a Bag, and boil it a Quarter of an Hour; this will do it fufficiently.

Take

Take it out of the Bag, lay it in a warm Difh, and pour over it fome melted Butter; throw fome fine Sugar powdered over this, and then fqueeze over it a Seville Orange : If a little white Wine and Rofe Water be mixed in the Butter while it is melting it will improve it, and if the Orange Juice be done in the fame Manner it eats well.

6. *Chefnut Pudding.*

Boil a Dozen and half of Chefnuts in fome Water for a Quarter of an Hour.

Then pour them into a Sieve; as they cool pick off the Peels, and throw them into a Mortar, beat them to a Pafte with a little Orange-Flower Water, then pour in a Glafs of Sack, and grind all together to a thin Pafte.

Beat up twelve Yolks and fix Whites of Eggs, mix this well with the Chefnuts, grate in fome Nutmeg, and then ftrew in fome Bafket Salt.

Pour in three Pints of rich Cream, and half a Pound of meltd Butter; mix all thefe Ingredients perfectly well together.

When the Pudding is thus ready cover a Difh with fine Puff Pafte, and pour in the whole.

Send it to the Oven.

When Cream is not to be had, Milk thickened up with fome Yolks of Eggs, will do in this and the before-mentioned Puddings.

In this Cafe three Eggs are to be allowed to every Quart of Milk.

7. *A Cream Pudding.*

Set on a Quart of Cream in a Saucepan, put to it two Blades of whole Mace, and grate in half a Nutmeg; let it boil up, and then fet it off to cool.

Blanch a Quarter of a Pound of Almonds, and beat them to Pafte, with a Spoonful of Orange-Flower Water.

Break eight Eggs, beat up all the Yolks and three of the Whites, mix with this the Almonds, and then by a little at a Time mix in all the Cream.

When

When the Pudding is thus ready take a thick Cloth, wet it, flour it well, pour in the Pudding, tie it up, and boil it brifkly half an Hour.

When it is taken up, melt fome Butter with half a Glafs of Sack, pour this upon the Pudding, and ftrew fome Sugar over the whole; fend it up hot. It is a very nice and elegant Kind of Pudding.

8. *Norfolk Dumplings.*

Beat up a Couple of Eggs with a little Salt, and by Degrees mix in half a Pint of Milk, then get in as much Flour as will make the whole into a pretty thick Batter.

While this is beating up let a large and very clean Saucepan be fet on the Fire, three Parts full of Spring Water.

When this boils, drop in the Batter in fuch Quantities at a Time as will ferve for a fmall Dumpling; keep the Water boiling brifkly, and they will be done in three Minutes.

Pour off the Water through a Sieve, and lay the Dumplings hot into a Difh; they are to be ferved up with a Piece of plain Butter let into each by cutting a Hole at the Top.

They are a very good Kind of Dumpling, and coft fcarce any Thing but Care; but the greateft Niceity is required that every Thing be clean, elfe they are fpoiled.

C H A P. VIII.

Of Pies.

A R T. I. *An Artichoke Pie.*

MAKE a good Puff Pafte Cruft, and fpread it carefully over a Difh, rub a Quarter of a Pound of Butter over it very evenly and regularly, then fet it ready.

While

While this is doing a Dozen young Artichokes are to be well boiled, feparate the Leaves and the Choke, cut the Bottoms clean from the Stems, and lay in as many of thefe Side by Side as will cover the Bottom of the Difh.

Strew fome Pepper and Salt upon thefe, and fprinkle in laft of all a little beaten Mace.

Lay another Layer of the Bottoms upon thefe, and ftrew fome of the fame Spice and Seafoning upon them.

Break a Quarter of a Pound of frefh Butter into fmall Pieces, and mix it carefully among the Chokes.

Set on a fmall Saucepan with a Quarter of a Pint of Water, cut to Pieces half an Ounce of Truffles, and the fame Quantity of Morels, boil them in this Water; then pour the Water into the Pie, and fcatter the Truffles and Morels over the Bottoms.

While this is doing boil twelve Eggs hard, take the Yolks clean out, and lay them regularly in the Pie.

This done pour in a Quarter of a Pint of Mountain Wine all over the Bottoms, and then put on the Lid.

Send it to the Oven, with particular Charge not to over do it : When the Cruft is baked it is enough, for the Things are all dreffed before.

It is a very rich and extremely pleafant Pie, and is to be ferved up hot.

2. *An Onion Pie.*

This, though we commonly call it an Onion Pie, is made of a Mixture of Potatoes, Onions, and Apples, and they ought to be in equal Quantities to give it a good Tafte.

It is to be made thus :

Boil about a Pound and half of Potatoes, and when they are pretty well done, peel them and cut them into Slices, peel the fame Quantity of Onions, and cut them alfo into Slices, and pare fome Apples, cut

them

them in the fame Manner into Slices, taking out the Cores.

When the Ingredients are thus ready make a good Cruft, and cover a Difh with it; break a Quarter of a Pound of Butter into fmall Pieces, and diftribute this over the Cruft; and then make the following Seafoning:

Grate down a whole Nutmeg, bruife a Quarter of an Ounce of Mace, mix thefe together, and add a Tea Spoonful of beaten Pepper, and three Tea Spoonfuls of Bafket Salt; mix all thefe together, and ftrew fome of it over the Bottom.

Then lay in a Covering of the Potatoes, Onions, and Apples interchangeably, a Slice of one and a Slice of another.

Then lay in the Yolks of four Eggs boiled hard.

Upon thefe lay in fome Potatoes by themfelves, then fome Onions, and at Top fome Apples.

Duft in fome of the Seafoning as every Parcel is put in.

Mix half a Dozen more hard Yolks of Eggs in different Parts of the Pie, and alfo half a Pound of Butter broken into Scraps.

When all is thus in, fpread over the upper Layer fome Butter, and fcatter on the Remainder of the Spices.

Cover up the Pie, and fend it to the Oven, firft pouring in a Quarter of a Pint of Water.

As the Potatoes are boiled before they are put in, half an Hour in a moderately hot Oven will do the Pie. It is to be fent up hot, and is a very good Difh.

3. *Cherry Pie.*

As Cherries are now coming in, there will be a Variety and Novelty in fending up once in two or three Days a Cherry Pie, which is beft of all made thus:

Chufe a proper Quantity of large Duke Cherries gathered in a Morning, for they are then fulleft and
fineft

fineſt flavoured, pick them from the Stalks, and ſee they be very clean.

Prepare a Quantity of Sugar, which muſt be the very fineſt Loaf Sugar beat to Powder, and make a ſmall Quantity of very good Cruſt.

All being thus ready, lay in a little Cruſt hand-ſomely round the Edge of the Diſh, then ſtrew in a thin Covering of the powdered Sugar upon the Bottom ; this done lay in the Cherries even and regular without breaking, and if there be a blemiſhed Cherry leave it out.

When half the Fruit is in ſtrew over them ſome of the powdered Sugar, then lay in the other half, and over them ſtrew more, then put on the Lid, and let it be baked in a ſlack Oven.

Some, when Currants are in their greateſt Perfection, ſtrew in a Quantity of picked Currants among the Cherries : In this Caſe there muſt be a larger Quantity of Sugar allowed, becauſe of the Sharpneſs of the Currants ; but the Cherry Pie, if made of a proper Fruit, and of a right Degree of Ripeneſs, is better without them.

It may be very proper to put ſome large Cherries into a Currant Pie, becauſe the Currants are too ſharp; but well-choſen Cherries are ſo moderate between ſharp and mellow, that they need no Addition.

4. *A Muſcle Pie.*

Clean a Quantity of Muſcles, and put them into a large Saucepan, without any Water, to ſtew.

While they are doing make ſome good Cruſt, ſpread ſome over the Sides of a ſmall Diſh, and ſet it ready.

When the Muſcle Shells are all open, and the Fiſh tolerably done, take them up, take out the Muſcles, pull away the Beards, and ſee there be no Spiders or young Crabs in them.

Put theſe picked Muſcles into a clean Saucepan, pour to them as much of their own Liquor ſtrained from the other Saucepan as will be enough to cover them; put in a Piece of Butter, and some Crumbs of Bread.

Strew in some broken Blades of Mace when they are near done, then pour the whole into the Dish, put on the Cover, and send it to the Oven. Half an Hour will do it.

It is a very pleasant Pie, and is the safest Way of eating Muscles.

A Scollop Pie made in this Manner is a very rich and excellent Dish, and a Pie may be made in the same Manner of Oisters; in this Case the largest and finest Oisters are the fittest.

5. *A rich Pigeon Pie.*

Chuse a Dozen very fine young tame Pigeons, pick them carefully, and truss them.

Cut out some good Bacon into Pieces for larding, and lard the Breasts of the Pigeons very well.

Make a Seasoning of Pepper and Salt, Nutmeg, and Savoury Herbs, and when the Pigeons are larded strew this all over them till they are well covered with it.

Shred fine some Chives, a good deal of Parsley, and some picked Leaves of Savoury Herbs; mince some Morels, and two or three Truffles; cut the Livers small, and chop twice their Weight of Beef Marrow, and half as much fat Bacon as there are Livers; mix all these together, and when they are well chopped pound them in a Mortar.

Stuff the Bodies of the Pigeons with this, but do not use it all, for there must be some to go in loose.

All Things thus ready, make some very fine Crust, lay it in a Dish of a proper Size, and spread ove it the Remainder of the Force-meat reserved for that Purpose; let this lie on it in a thin equal Layer.

Lay in the Pigeons regularly and carefully, with here and there a Bay Leaf among them.

When

When they are all in cut fome large and thin Slices of Veal, and in the fame Manner fome thin Slices of fat Bacon, cover the Pigeons in the Pie with thefe Slices, and then fend it to the Oven, with Orders that it be carefully and thoroughly baked.

When it comes home take off the Top, take out the Veal and the Bacon, fkim off the Fat, and pour in a good hot Raggoo of Sweetbreads made as we have before directed ; lay on the Lid again, and fend it up hot.

A Pie may be made of two or three Turkey Poults in the fame Manner.

6. *A Duck Pie.*

Chufe for this Purpofe a Couple of fine Ducks, wild or tame, according to the Tafte of the Company, trufs them for roafting, and then put them on in fome Water and parboil them.

While the Ducks are on the Fire, cut out fome fine fat Bacon, and fome Lean of Ham, into proper Pieces for larding.

Lard the Ducks well with this, and make a Seafoning of Parfley, Chives, fweet Herbs, Pepper, and Salt.

When the Ducks are larded, ftrew a good deal of this Seafoning over them.

The Ducks being thus perfectly ready, roll out a Sheet of Pafte an Inch thick, and raife it into the Form of a Pie.

Cut fome thick Slices of Bacon, beat them well with a Peftle, and lay them thick at the Bottom of the Pie ; then lay in the two Ducks.

Fill up the Space about the Ducks with Mutton Chops larded, ftrew fome of the fame Seafoning as was before ufed over thefe Chops, and then put the Remainder over the Pie, when they are in.

When the Pie lies even at the Top, lay upon it fome thin Slices of Veal, and over thefe fome of Bacon, then lay on a Sheet of Cruft for a Cover,

and

and fend it to the Oven, where it fhould ftand four Hours.

When the Pie is ready to come home, make a Raggoo to add to it.

This fhould be made of Sweetbreads, Livers, Cocks-Combs, Truffles, and Mufhrooms; they muft be firft toffed up in melted Bacon, and then adding fome good Gravy they muft ftand fcimmering three Quarters of an Hour.

After this the Fat is to be taken off, and if there be any Cullis of Ham and Veal in Readinefs, a little of that fhould be added, if not, the Raggo will do very well without it.

When the Pie comes home place it in a Difh, raife the Cover, take off the Pieces of Veal and Bacon, then fkim off the Fat, and pour in the hot Raggoo; lay on the Cover again, and fend it up.

7. *A Soal Pie.*

Get fome large and very fine Soals, and get alfo three or four large Eels of the right Silver Kind.

Skin and clean the Eels, cut the Flefh from the Bones and chop it fmall, then put it into a Marble Mortar, put to it half a Dozen Morels fhred fine, four Truffles fhred and chopped, four frefh Mufhrooms fhred fine, fome Leaves of fweet Herbs picked clear from the Stalks and chopped, fome Pepper and Salt, and a little grated Nutmeg; beat all thefe well together in the Mortar.

Melt about two Ounces of Butter, pour this in, and beat it all up well again together.

When all is fine and well mixed, fet this by on a Plate.

Then prepare fome Cruft for a raifed Pie, fhape it, and fet it ready.

This done, put the Soals into a Pan, and fry them till they are about half done.

Take them up, and cut the Flefh in long Slices from the Bones.

Make

Make a Seafoning of fome Leaves of fweet Herbs chopped fine, and mixed with Pepper and Salt ; and every Thing being now ready, begin to make the Pie.

Firft cover the Bottom with fome of the Eel Force-meat, then lay in nicely and carefully fome of the Slices of Soal.

Sprinkle over thefe fome of the Seafoning juft made, and then lay in the Remainder of the Force-meat and of the Soals one over another, with a little of the Seafoning always between them.

When all is in put fome fine frefh Butter over the whole, and then lay on the Cruft ; rub it over with Egg, and fend it to the Oven.

When it is about coming home make a Raggoo of Truffles, and keep it hot.

When the Pie is come in fet it in a Difh, raife off the Cruft, fkim away the Fat, and pour in the Raggoo hot, fo fend it up.

8. *A Turbot Pie.*

We have given before a Method of baking a Turbot, which is a very fine Way of eating that excellent Fifh ; this is altogether different, and by many is efteemed preferable.

Make fome Cruft, and prepare a Seafoning of favoury Herbs, Pepper, and Salt.

Thefe Things being ready, chufe a good thick Turbot, lard it carefully with fine Anchovies, and then prepare the Pie for it.

Firft lay fome frefh Butter over the Bottom, on this ftrew fome of the Seafoning, and lay in a Couple of Blades of Mace broken, then lay in the Turbot, and ftrew upon this again fome of the Seafoning ; grate over it alfo a little Nutmeg, and throw in fome broken Pieces of Mace.

Laftly, cover the Turbot with frefh Butter, put on the Lid, and fend it to the Oven.

When

When it is near coming home make a Raggoo of Cray-fifh and Truffles, and when the Pie comes home open it, get the Fat that fwims about clean off, then pour in the hot Raggoo, and fend it up.

9. *Spanifh Petty Patties.*

Cut a Piece of fine fat Bacon, a Piece of Veal twice as big as the Bacon, and the Breafts of a Couple of Pullets.

Blanch thefe together in boiling Water, and then mince them very fmall.

Prepare a Seafoning thus :

Cut to Pieces the Leaves of fome favoury Herbs, chip fome Mace very fine, bruife fome Cinnamon and a Couple of Cloves, and flice very fine fome Rocambole and half a Clove of Garlick, add fome Pepper and Salt, and mix all well together ; then mix it with the minced Meat.

Make fome fine Puff Pafte for Cruft, and make feveral Patties ; put into each a Piece of this Forcemeat and a fmall Bit of Butter, then fend them to a flack Oven, and when done fend them up hot.

C H A P.   IX.

Side and fmall Difhes.

A R T. I.   *A Raggoo of Afparagus.*

CHUSE fome fine young Afparagus, and cut off the green Tops as far as they are tender, blanch them in fcalding Water, and then put them into a fmall Saucepan ; pour upon them fome rich Gravy, and a little Effence of Gammon of Bacon, or if they be in Readinefs, fome Cullis of Veal and Ham, and fome Effence of Ham.

This laft Method is the richeft by much ; but when thefe Things are not in Readinefs the other will very well do.

Let

Let thefe fcimmer together till the Afparagus is done enough, and the Liquor is thick, and in great Part wafted.

Then roll an Ounce of Butter in a little Flour, and put it in ; fhake all about till the Butter is melted and mixed, and then add a Tea Spoonful of Vinegar. Send it up hot,

2. *A Raggoo of Shardoons.*

Set on a Pot of Water, put in an Onion ftuck with Cloves, two or three Slices of Bacon, and a Piece of Butter rolled in Flour ; when it boils throw in the Shardoons picked and wafhed very clean, and let them boil till they begin to be tender.

Then take them out, cut them fmall, and let them ftand in a Sieve to drain.

Set on a Saucepan with fome Cullis of Veal and Ham, or, if you have not that, fome good Gravy with a Slice of lean Ham in it.

Let thefe fcimmer over a flow Fire till the Shardoons are thoroughly tender, then fet it over a quicker Fire, and when a good deal of the Liquor is wafted, and the reft is very thick, put in a Piece of Butter rolled in Flour, and when that is melted fend it up hot.

3. *A Raggoo of Endive.*

Chufe fome of the fineft and beft bleached Endive, pick it very clean, and throw it into fcalding Water to blanch it.

Throw it into a Pan of cold Spring Water, then take it up, fqueeze it a little in the Hand to drain it, lay it on a Dreffer and chop it, each Head into three or four Pieces, no fmaller, and put it into a Saucepan

Pour to it fome very rich Gravy, or if it be ready fome Cullis of Veal and Ham, let it fcimmer well over the Fire, and when the Endive is tender and the Liquor thick, ferve it up ; or if you pleafe add a little Cullis, or fome Butter in Flour to thicken it, either

Way

Way will do, but if the Gravy be not put into it in too large a Quantity at firft it will come very right of itfelf.

4. *A Raggoo of Cauliflowers.*

All thefe Raggoos of Vegetables are to be made in the fame general Manner, but there are fome little Particularities to be obferved in each on which the Perfection and Niceity of the Difh depends ; wherefore we have given thefe feparate Kinds as a Direction for the others.

Cauliflowers are at this Seafon fmall, hard, and white, thefe are fit for raggooing, and the great Art of the Cook is to preferve their Colour.

This is to be done by firft blanching them in white Water in this Manner :

Set on a Pot half full of very clear foft Water, put in a Slice of Bacon and a Piece of Butter rolled in Flour ; ftir this about as it heats, and it will be white, foft, and thickifh : As foon as it boils throw in three of thefe fine fmall Cauliflowers, and let them boil till they are three Parts done.

Then take them up, fet them to drain, and when the Water is run off put them into a Saucepan with fome rich Veal Gravy, or fome Cullis of Veal and Ham ; let them fcimmer a while, then fet the Saucepan over a brifk Fire, put in a Piece of Butter rolled in Flour, and a Tea Spoonful of Vinegar ; when the Butter is melted, and all well mixed, ferve it up hot. The Cauliflower no Way eats fo well.

5, *A Welch Rabbit.*

Cut a handfome Piece of Bread and an even Slice of Cheefe, let the Bread be of the Shape of the Cheefe, but a little larger every Way.

Put a Salamander in the Fire, or a large Poker, or the Bottom of a Fire-Shovel heated red hot will do.

While the Iron is heating toaft the Bread carefully on both Sides, without making it hard or burning it.

Then

Then toaft the Cheefe on one Side, lay the Bread in a Plate, lay the Cheefe upon it with the toafted Side downwards, hold the red hot Iron over the other Side to toaft and brown that.

Put a little Muftard on it, and fend it up very hot. Two fhould go up together.

6. *A Scotch Rabbit.*

Cut a Slice of Cheefe very large and handfome, cut a Slice of Bread, without Cruft, juft of the Size of the Cheefe ; toaft the Bread on both Sides, and butter it, then toaft the Cheefe on both Sides, and lay it evenly upon the Toaft and Butter. Send it up hot without Muftard.

This fhould be made larger than the Welch Rabbit, and fent up fingle, one in a Plate, as that fhould be two.

7. *An Englifh Rabbit.*

Cut a handfome Toaft of Bread without Cruft, and fhave a good Quantity of Cheefe very fine.

Set a Tin Oven before the Fire, and have in Readinefs a Glafs of red Port Wine.

Toaft the Bread carefully on both Sides, then pour the Wine upon it, and turn it.

When it has foaked up the Wine fpread the fcraped Cheefe thick upon it, lay it in the Oven, and place it before a good Fire; the Cheefe will do very quickly and very finely. Send it up very hot.

Thefe are the three Ways of toafting Cheefe ; the firft is the genuine Method, and thofe who are fond of Cheefe prefer it to either of the others.

One would think nothing could be eafier than to toaft a Slice of Cheefe, and yet not only in private Families but at Taverns we fee nothing is done fo badly : The Directions here given are eafy to be obferved, and they will never fail to fend it up either Way mellow, hot, well done, and with the Bread crifp and foft.

8. *Stewed Cheese on Bread.*

Cut a large Slice of Bread of such a Shape as to lie handsomely in the Bottom of a Plate without filling it up; a Round of a threepenny Loaf, with the Crust pared thin off, is very proper; toast this carefully, and lay it on a Plate, pour on it half a Glass of red Wine, turn it, pour on another half Glass, and then set it before the Fire that it may keep warm while the Cheese is doing.

Rub the Bottom of a Pewter Plate with Butter, cut some Cheese in moderately thin Slices, spread these evenly upon the Plate, then pour in a Quarter of a Glass of white Wine.

Cover the Plate with another, and set it over some hot Coals in a Chaffing-dish; let it stand about four Minutes and it will be very well done.

Put a Shovel on the Fire to be red hot; stir in a little Mustard among the stewed Cheese, spread it carefully upon the Bread, and then brown it by moving the red hot Bottom of the Shovel slowly over it. Send it up hot.

9. *Buttered Loaves.*

Break twelve new-laid Eggs, beat up all the Yolks with half the Whites, and mix in among them a Quarter of a Pint of Yeast.

Pour this through a Sieve into a Dish, and add to it some Basket Salt, and a Tea Spoonful of beaten Ginger.

Make this into a high Paste with Flour, warm a large Napkin, and wrap the Paste in it, let it remain so a Quarter of an Hour, then break it into Parts, and make them up into so many little Loaves.

These may be either baked or boiled, and should have a Piece of Butter and a Glass of Mountain Wine to each.

When they are to be served up, three or four of them must be laid handsomely on a Dish, and served up with fine Sugar strewed over them.

10. *Grilled*

10. *Grilled Shrimps.*

Let a Quantity of large frefh and fine Shrimps be picked carefully ; draw them over upon a Napkin, and fee that there be ne'er a fmall or bad one, nor no Piece of the Shell hanging to any of them, for this would be perceived in the Mouth, and would difgrace the whole Cookery.

Seafon thefe picked Shrimps with Pepper and Salt, and mix in a Spoonful of fhred Parfley.

Then prepare fome Scollop Shells, put fome Butter to the Shrimps and other Ingredients, and add fome grated Bread ; let them ftew half an Hour, and then draw a hot Salamander or other hot Iron over them to brown the Surface, and fend them up.

11. *Buttered Shrimps.*

Pick a Couple of Quarts of Shrimps in the niceft Manner, and fee there be not the leaft Scrap of a Shell on any Part of them ; put them into a Saucepan, pour to them a Pint of Mountain Wine, and fet them to ftew over a gentle Fire. Break eight Eggs, beat them up with a little white Wine, and grate in fome Nutmeg.

Melt half a Pound of Butter, and by Degrees mix it with the Egg, then pour all into the Saucepan, fhake it only one Way, till the whole is thoroughly well mixed and hot together : Then toaft fome Bread, cut it into Sippets, and having warmed a Difh, lay them round the Edges ; pour in the whole out of the Saucepan. It is a very rich and very elegant Difh. Send it up hot.

12. *Afparagus Rolls.*

Take three French Rolls ; cut off a Piece of the Cruft of each handfomely at the End, that it may fit the Place again ; then take out the Crumb, leaving the Cruft entire.

Fry thefe Rolls in frefh Butter, till they are of a nice brown.

Break

Break fix Eggs, beat up their Yolks in a Pint of Cream, add fome Salt, grate in a little Nutmeg, and fet it over the Fire, ftirring it till it be perfectly mixed, and very thick.

Boil an Hundred of fine young Afparagus.

Cut off a few of the Tops, and fave them entire. Cut off the green Part of all the reft, and chop it fmall, mix it among the Cream, and then fill the Rolls with it ; put on the Piece of Cruft that was taken off, and ftick up the fine Pieces of the Afparagus Tops, faved for that Purpofe, in Holes made in the Rolls for that Purpofe, before the frying.

Send them up hot. It is a very elegant Difh, and a very fine Way of eating Afparagus.

13. *Stewed Parfnips*

Chufe fome fine fweet moderate fized Parfnips.

Boil them well, then fcrape and clean them perfectly, and cut them into thin Slices.

Put them into a Saucepan with a good deal of Cream, and a Piece of Butter rolled in Flour and a little Salt.

Let them ftew, and after a Time fet them on a brifker Fire, that the Cream may boil up ; then ferve them up hot without any Addition.

14. *Stewed Cucumbers.*

Pare a Dozen of fine frefh gathered Cucumbers ; cut them into thick Slices, and lay them on a coarfe Cloth to drain off fome of the Water.

When they are pretty dry flour them, and fry them in frefh Butter till they are of a fine brown ; then take them out with an Egg Slice, and lay them in a Plate before the Fire, that they may keep warm.

Pare another Cucumber, and cut a Slice lengthways out of it, that the Seeds may be fcooped out.

Fill this with Onions fried brown: They may be very conveniently fried with the Slices of the Cucumbers

bers

bers juft named. Strew a little Pepper and Salt over the fried Onion before it is put in ; then put the Slice of the Cucumber that was cut out into it's Place again, and tie it round with Thread to keep it entire.

Set this over the Fire with fome Butter in a Stewpan, and fry it till it be of a fine Brown all over.

Then take it out of the Pan, lay it on a Plate to keep warm alfo, and put in a little Flour into the Stewpan. Stir this carefully about, as it is dufted in ; when the Butter is well thickened, put in three Spoonfuls of Water ; then add half a Pint of white Wine, and two Spoonfuls of Ketchup.

Stir all thefe well together, then put in three Blades of Mace, four whole Cloves, half a Nutmeg, and fome Pepper and Salt.

Stir all this well together, and pour it into a Saucepan ; put in the Cucumbers, and tofs them till they are all thoroughly hot, and relifhed with the Sauce, then take out the whole Cucumber carefully, and lay it in the Middle of a Difh, put this all round it, and pour the Sauce over all : Send it up hot, garnifhed with fried Onions.

15. *Round Eggs.*

Set on a deep Fryingpan, and put into it three Pints of clarified Butter, make it thoroughly hot, then ftir it about with a Stick. Break an Egg into a Cup, hold it ready over the Pan : Stir the Butter again, till it run round like a Whirl Pool, and then drop in the Egg in the Middle ; let it remain till it is about as much done as a common poached Egg ; then take it up with a Slice. It will be as round as a Ball, this Shape coming from the Motion of the Butter.

When one Egg is taken out, do another in the fame Manner, and fo on till there be enough done. Set them at a Diftance before the Fire till all are ready, and then ferve them up, either with Gravy, or with ftewed Spinage. They will keep their round Shape, and remain hot a long Time, and an Egg eats no Way prettier; they are therefore very agreeable for a Variety, where there are feveral Difhes.

16. *Peafe with Cream.*

Shell a Quart of delicate young Peafe, put them into a Stewpan with a Piece of Butter rolled in Flour, feafon them with Pepper and Salt, and grate in fome Nutmeg: Strew in half a Spoonful of the fineft Sugar powdered, put in a Bundle of Sweet Herbs, and fome chopped Parfley; the Piece of Butter for a Quart of Peafe, fhould be about three Ounces.

When all thefe are together, pour in a Quarter of a Pint of boiling Water.

Cover up the Stewpan, and fet it over a gentle Fire to ftew a little; when all is well mixed, and the Peafe are enough, pour in a Quarter of a Pint of thick Cream, give it a boil up, and then warm a fmall Soup Difh; pour the whole in, and ferve it up hot. It is a pretty Side Difh.

17. *Fine Hafty Pudding.*

Break a new laid Egg into a Difh of Flour, and work it up into a ftiff Pafte, with as much of the Flour as it will take up.

Cut this Pafte a-crofs and a-crofs, and at length Mince it as fmall as poffible.

Set on a Saucepan with a Quart of Milk, and when it boils put in this minced Pafte; put in at the fame Time fome Bafket Salt, a Spoonful of fine Sugar powdered, and as much beaten Cinnamon as will lie upon a Sixpence.

Then add a Piece of Butter as big as a Wallnut rolled in Flour, and ftir it about one Way.

When it is all well mixed, put in fuch another Piece of Butter, and then ftir it about, and pour the whole into a Difh, ftick up fome Pieces of frefh

Butter

Butter in different Places, and fend it up immediately to Table.

18. *Hasty Fritters.*

Mix together fome Ale that is not bitter, and a little Flour; get in more Flour by Degrees, and then put in fome fhred Apple and a few Currants wafhed and picked; beat it up till all is very well mixed, and moderately thick.

Then fet on a Stewpan with fome Butter; make it very hot, and then drop in fmall Quantities of this Butter.

A large Spoonful is enough for each Fritter, and about five may very will be droped into the Pan at a Time; but Care muft be taken that they do not run together.

When they are of a fine delicate Brown, they muft be taken up with a Slice, and laid regularly in a warm Difh, and fprinkled over with Sugar.

19. *Fine Fritters.*

Pare fome fine Golden Pippins, cut them in Slices, take out the Cores, and then chop the Slices fmall; mix thefe with a rich Batter made in the following Manner.

Break four new laid Eggs, and beat them up with Half a Pint of thick Cream; add a Spoonful of Brandy, grate in a little Nutmeg, and a Tea Spoonful of beaten Ginger muft then be mixed in.

When all this is well beat together, mix in fome Flour, and make it into a good thick Batter: Put in the chopped Apples, and ftir all well together, and then fry them as before directed, in a large Quantity of very hot Butter. Currants may alfo be added to thefe, but they are as well without: They make a Variety in the Difhes, and in the plainer Kinds of Fritters, they are wanted, for they are otherwife poor, but in thefe nothing is needful by Way of Addition.

20. *Curd*

20. *Curd Fritters with Saffron.*

Mix together a Quarter of a Pound of Flour, and Half a Pound of Curd.

Beat up ten Eggs, and mix in them two beaten Cloves, half a grated Nutmeg, two Blades of pounded Mace, and two large Spoonfuls of fine Sugar powdered; when all thefe are mixed, ftir in eight Grains of Powder of Saffron, or if you have it in the Houfe, a Spoonful of Tincture of Saffron, made with Wine: This latter is the beft Method.

When all thefe are perfectly mixed, add the Curds and Flour, and then fet on the Pan.

Put in a large Quantity of Butter, and let it be made very hot; then drop in the Batter by Degrees, and fry the Fritters in it as before directed: This done, lay them in a Difh with Sugar.

21. *Fritters Royal.*

Set on a Pint of new Milk in a Saucepan; when it boils pour in a Pint of Sack, and let it boil up well.

Set it off the Fire, and when it has ftood five or fix Minutes, take off the Curd.

Break half a Dozen new laid Eggs into a large Bowl, beat them up with this, and add as much Flour as will bring the whole to the right Confiftence of Batter; then grate in a Quarter of a Nutmeg, put in a Table Spoonful of powdered Sugar, and as much beaten Ginger as will lay upon a Sixpence.

Set on a Pan with a great deal of Butter, and when it is very hot, drop in the Batter, a large Spoonful at a Time.

Set a Difh to warm, and have a Cafter of powdered Sugar ready; as they are taken up, place them regularly in the Difh, and duft a little Sugar over them. Then fend them up hot.

22. *Vine*

22. *Vine Leaf Fritters*

Mix in a Soop Plate a Quarter of a Pint of Brandy, a fmall Glafs of white Wine, fome rafped Lemon-peel, and a Spoonful of powdered Sugar.

Cut off fome fmall, frefh, and juicy Vine Leaves.

Cut the Stalks away clofe, and put the Leaves into this Mixture.

Mix up fome white Wine and Flour into a moderately thick Batter.

Set on a Stewpan with a good Quantity of Butter, when it is very hot, drop in the Fritters.

A Leaf is to be taken out of the Brandy for every Fritter, and when they are fried to a fine Brown, they are to be ftrewed with Sugar, and glazed with a red hot Salamander or Shovel : The Difh muft be very hot, and they muft be fent up quick.

23. *Clary Fritters.*

Gather a dozen Leaves of Clary from the upper Part of fuch Plants as have not come into Flower. Cut the Stalks off clofe, and wipe the Leaves very clean with a Napkin.

Lay thefe in Readinefs, and then make the Batter with Milk and Flour, and fee that it be very well mixed, and not too thin.

Set on a Stewpan with a large Quantity of Butter; when it is very hot, dip the Leaves one by one in the Batter, fee they be thick covered with it, and then drop them into the Pan. Set a Difh to be warm before the Fire, and as they are taken up, lay them in regularly; ftrew fome Sugar upon them, and fend them up hot.

Thefe are not only pleafant to the Tafte, but very cordial.

24. *Apple Fraizes.*

Chufe fome large and very fine Apples, cut them in thick handfome Slices, taking out the Cores.

Set on a Pan with a good Quantity of Butter, when it is hot throw in the Apples, and fry them to a delicate brown.

Then take them out, and lay them to drain.

Break five Eggs, beat up all the Yolks and three of the Whites, with a Quarter of a Pint of Cream and a Glafs of Sack, grate in fome Nutmeg; add two Spoonfuls of powdered Sugar, and bring in by Degrees as much Flour as will make it of the proper Confiftence of Batter, then pour in a Quarter of a Pound of melted Butter.

When this is ready fet on the Pan with Butter for frying.

Drop in a Soup Ladle full of Batter, lay a Slice of Apple upon it, then pour on more Batter, and fry it brown.

Let there be a Difh kept warm ready, and fend up the Fraizes covered with powdered Sugar.

28. *Common Pancakes.*

Break eight new-laid Eggs, beat up all the Yolks and half the Whites, and mix in a Spoonful of beaten Ginger.

Add to this by Degrees a Quart of Milk, and then as much Flour as is needful to make it into Batter of a good Confiftence: The Flour muft be put in a very little at a Time, and mixed carefully and thoroughly.

Then add a Glafs of Brandy, and half a Spoonful of Bafket Salt.

Stir all this very well together, and fet it ready for frying.

Make a Stewpan extremely clean, put in a Piece of Butter as big as a Walnut, then put in a Ladle full of the Batter, and move the Pan round that the Batter may fpread all over it.

Shake the Pan, and when one Side is done turn it.

The beft Way is by toffing it, which, to an experienced Cook who is not afraid of what fhe is doing, is very eafy; if not, it muft be done with Care by the Help of a flat Slice.

Let

Let a Difh be fet before the Fire to heat, and lay the Pancake in it when both Sides are done.

Then put in another, and fry it in the fame Manner, and when enough lay it upon the firft.

Fry feveral others in the fame Manner as the firft, lay them carefully one upon another, fee that they be thoroughly dry, and ftrew powdered Sugar over them.

⁎ *The Art of toffing a Pancake.*

This is a Thing very eafy to a bold Hand, but which a timerous Perfon will never be able to do well; for fuch a one, fhe is to know that the firft Thing to be done is to get rid of her Fear, and then a little Practice will make it quite familiar.

The beft Way to learn it is this:

Let a Kitchen Table Cloth be fpread upon the Ground at a fmall Diftance from the Fire, and when the firft Pancake is ready for turning let the Cook try to tofs it over the Cloth; if it falls in right it is very well, and if not there is no Harm done, it will be catched clean, and may do for the Servants Table.

When there is not the Danger of throwing them into the Fire the Cook will have lefs Fear, and as we have faid before, the lefs Fear the more Likelihood of Succefs.

The Way is to hold the Pan very fteady, and tofs the Pancake with a fudden Jerk.

Practice is all; for as the Children play at Bilbecket till they can catch the Ball every Time for many Minutes together, in the fame Manner the Cook will be able to tofs a hundred Pancakes without miffing once, when fhe is accuftomed to the Method of it.

29. *Rich Pancakes.*

Break a Dozen and half of Eggs, feparate all the Whites, and beat up the Yolks, with a little Salt and half a Pound of fine powdered Sugar.

When

When thefe are well mixed add half a Pint of Sack, and the fame Quantity of Cream.

Beat all thefe up, and take in by Degrees as much Flour as will give the Pancake Batter a due Confiftence to run over the Bottom of the Pan ; laft of all add two Blades of Mace beaten fine, half a Tea Spoonful of powdered Cinnamon, and the fame Quantity of grated Nutmeg.

Fry them in the fame Manner with the others.

They will not be crifp, but they are very delicate.

The Difh muft be kept warm, and Care taken to fend them up very hot.

30. *Paper Pancakes.*

Thefe are a fine Kind of Pancakes that are to be done extremely thin, and when laid one over another they have the Refemblance of a Quire of Paper ; whence their Name is given them.

Break fix new-laid Eggs, beat up a llthe Yolks and half the Whites ; mix in by Degrees a Pint of rich Cream, three Spoonfuls of Sack, and one Spoonful of Orange-Flour Water.

Grate in a little Nutmeg, and ftrew in a Spoonful of powdered Sugar.

Melt half a Pound of Butter, and let it ftand till it is near cold.

Mix by Degrees three Spoonfuls of Flour in the Batter, and then get in the Butter.

When all are well mixed, the Batter for the Paper Pancakes is ready.

Set on a Pan for frying them, and do this in the very fame Manner as the others, only making each Pancake very thin.

31. *Rice Pancakes.*

Put into a Saucepan a Quart of rich Cream and three Spoonfuls of Flour of Rice.

Set this on a flow Fire, and continue ftirring it till it mix thoroughly and be as thick as Pap.

While

While the Saucepan is over the Fire ftir in by Degrees half a Pound of frefh Butter, and grate in fome Nutmeg.

Then pour the whole into a Pan to cool.

Break nine Eggs, beat them well with a little Salt and fome fine powdered Sugar, and add three Spoonfuls of Flour.

When thefe are perfectly well mixed, and the Cream and Rice are cold, ftir all together.

The Batter is thus finifhed, and the Pancakes are to be fried carefully in the ufual Manner.

When the Cream is not thick, the more Rice is to be ufed; and this Way Milk may very well anfwer the Purpofe.

32. *Cream Pancakes.*

Take a Pint of Cream, four Eggs, four Spoonfuls of Flour, half a Pound of Butter well clarified, mix it all well together with a little Salt and grated Nutmeg; fry them by themfelves, without Butter in the Pan.

S E C T.   III.

Of PICKLING.

ART. I. *To pickle Naftertion.*

MAKE your Pickle of white Wine Vinegar, and Bay Salt a fmall Handful, for it muft not be too fharp of the Salt; let them boil very well together; then take it off, let it ftand till quite cold, and put in the Naftertion Buds as you gather them, and ftop them down clofe; when it has ftood fome Time make fome frefh Pickle, and put the Buds into it, then fet it by for Ufe.

2. *The beſt Way to pickle Cucumbers.*

Take the leaſt Cucumbers, rub them well, and put them in a Pot or Barrel, then put in a Round or Layer of Dill or Fennel Seed in Branches, and upon that a Layer of Cucumbers ſo as not to touch one another; ſtrew on them ſome Ginger, Mace, and Cloves finely beaten, ſome whole Pepper, and a little Salt; then lay in another Layer of each, and fill up the Pot with white Wine or Elder Vinegar. This Pickle ſerves for Grapes, or other Things.

Some boil the Vinegar, and pour it on hot, and Elder is beſt done this Way.

S E C T. IV.

Of CONFECTIONARY.

A R T. I. *To dry Cherries.*

WE here enter upon the Summer Part of Confectionary: It is not a great deal that can be done in it at preſent, but ſome Fruits coming in, the Houſekeeper may keep her Hand in Practice, and bring herſelf to a Readineſs for the Management of the many Things that will come in the ſucceeding Months.

Cherries, though they are now come in, are not plentiful or cheap, therefore the Work of preſerving Quantities of them may be deferred to ſome Weeks farther; but as none are more fit for theſe Purpoſes than the large, juicy, rich, and fine Kinds that come in early, we ſhall take this Opportunity of directing their Management in the ſeveral Forms, and begin with the drying them.

Let a Quantity of the largeſt and fineſt Cherries of the Duke Kind be procured.

Let

Let the Houfekeeper look thoroughly over them herfelf, that there be not an unfound one among them.

Then let them be very carefully ftoned.

To ten Pounds of Cherries thus ftoned put three Pounds of the fineft Sugar powdered ; put the Sugar to them in a Preferving-pan, and fhake that and the Cherries carefully together ; then fet it over a gentle Fire.

The Sugar will melt by Degrees, and then let the Fire be brifked up, and let them have a boil or two.

Pour the whole into an earthen Pan, and let it ftand all Night ; then put it into the Preferving-pan, and make it fcalding hot ; let it ftand to be cold again, and then fpread it upon Sieves.

After this fend them to an Oven ; let them be put in when it is not too hot and ftand all Night, then let them be turned and put in again ; and this Time, as the former, the Oven fhould be no hotter than it is after Pies.

By this fecond ftanding in the Oven they will grow very dry and firm ; put them up in Boxes, and put no Paper between them.

2. *To dry Cherries without Sugar.*

Chufe fome fine Cherries, and pick them as for the former Method.

Stone them carefully, and preferve any Liquor that runs from them in doing this.

Put them into a Preferving-pan over a gentle Fire with only this Liquor, let them boil up three or four Times, and in the mean Time fhake them feveral Times about heartily, but not violently; this done put them into an earthen Pot.

The next Day fet them over the Fire again to fcald them, and then let them ftand to be cold ; lay them on Sieves, and afterwards dry them in the fame Manner as the others in an Oven, repeating it twice : This will preferve them as well as the former, and they muft be kept in the fame Manner.

3. *To*

3. *To dry Cherries in Bunches.*

Chufe for this Purpofe Kentifh Cherries, for they are the only ones fit at this early Seafon; but toward Autumn Morellas may be dried in the fame Manner.

Tie them up in Bunches, ten or twelve in a Bunch.

Squeeze fome other Cherries, and to a Pint of the Juice put two Pounds of treble-refined Sugar; boil this once up, and it will be a rich Syrup.

As foon as it has boiled put in the Bunches of Cherries, and make it juft boil up with them, then fet them off.

The next Day fet on the Syrup with the Cherries again, and heat it enough to fcald them, but no more; then fet them off to cool; when they are cold place them on Sieves, and fet them in a flack Oven; repeat this two or three Times, turning them every Time, and they will gradually dry, retaining their Shape, and in fome Degree their Colour: They will be natural and pleafant.

4. *Cherry Jam.*

Pick fome fine Cherries as carefully as on the former Occafions, ftone them, and fet them over the Fire to boil, break them as they boil, and when they have boiled fo long that the Bottom of the Pan is eafily feen and all looks clear, put in a fourth Part of the Weight of the Cherries of fine Sugar.

To underftand this you are to weigh the Cherries as foon as they are ftoned, and to ten Pounds of them two Pounds and a half of Sugar is the proper Quantity.

When the Sugar is in them they muft have two or three boils, and then be fet off to cool.

When cold they muft be put up in Bottles, Pots, or Glaffes, and they will keep perfectly well till the next Year.

5. *To preferve Cherries with the Stalks and Leaves green.*

Gather fome fine Duke Cherries carefully, with the Stalks entire, and fome Leaves upon them.

Make

Make fome fharp Vinegar boiling hot, dip in the Stalks and Leaves, and fcald them well; then lay them on a Sieve that they may dry.

Set on a Pipkin or Silver Saucepan with two Pounds of the fineft Sugar and a Pint of Water, let this boil up, and it will be a thick Syrup.

When this Syrup is boiling hot dip the Cherries in it with the Stalks and Leaves, and when they are juft fcalded by it take them out again, and lay them on a Sieve.

Then boil up the Syrup to the Height of a Candy, and dip the Cherries into it again, then dry them on Sieves in the fame Manner as other Sweetmeats; the Cherries will thus be very fine, and the Leaves will make a pretty Appearance.

6. *To jar Cherries.*

Make a Preferving-pan perfectly clean, put into it twelve Pounds of ftoned Cherries, three Pounds of treble-refined Sugar, and a Quart of Water.

Set the Pan on the Fire till the whole is fcalding hot, then fet it off for a Time till it is fomewhat cooled, and put it on again; then let them boil till the Cherries are tender, fprinkle over them half a Pound more fine Sugar powdered, and when it is melted fkim them very clean.

Pour all together into an earthen Pan, and let it ftand three Days.

After this take the Cherries one by one out of the Syrup, and lay them regularly with the Hole downwards upon a wicker Sieve to dry; put them in a Stove, and from Time to Time remove them from one Sieve to another till they are perfectly dry.

When they are fo, lay fome fine white Paper in a Preferving-pan, and upon this lay the Cherries, cover them with another Sheet of Paper, and then with a Cloth.

Set the Pan upon a gentle Fire till they fweat, then remove the Fire, let them cool, and put them up in Jars.

N°. XX.   4 D   They

They have the fine and perfect Taſte of the Cherry, and will keep a long Time for all Uſes.

7. *Cherry Paſte.*

Stone ſome fine large Cherries, put them into a Preſerving-pan with nothing but their own Liquor, and break them as they boil.

When the Cherries have boiled ſome Time, and are growing ſtiff, put in a Pound and a Quarter of fine Sugar in Powder for every Pound of Cherries that was uſed ; let the Sugar melt perfectly, then put the whole together into a broad earthen Pan.

Set this on a Stove till it is candied.

Drop it upon Glaſs, and when it is hardened on one Side turn it, then put it up.

8. *To preſerve Cherries.*

This is a Receipt that muſt be practiſed in the later Cherries, and cannot be done but when there are ripe Currants ; however, as the Currant Seaſon is approaching, and in order to keep all the Receipts concerning Cherries together, we have thought proper to give the Method in this Place.

The moſt proper Cherries for preſerving are the Carnation Cherries.

Let them be ſtoned, and ſet ready.

Then draw ſome Jelly of red Currants, and run through a Jelly Bag.

There muſt be double the Quantity of the fineſt Sugar, as, three Pounds to a Pint and a half, and the ſame in Proportion to any Quantity; ſet this on a quick Fire, and ſcum it ; to the Quantity we have named of this add two Pounds of the ſtoned Cherries, let them boil gently, and take them off at Times.

When they are ſoft, boil them more briſkly till they jelly and are very clear, then let them cool, and put them into Glaſſes.

9. *To*

9. *To preferve Apricots.*

The early Apricot, now in its Prime, is a very fine Fruit preferved ; we fhall give here the Method of doing it, as alfo of making the other Articles for the Confectionary from it ; for there is no Kind that makes them fo fine.

We do not advife the Houfekeeper to buy this Kind of Apricot at Market for this Purpofe, becaufe being early it is dear, and the others that follow in the fucceeding Months will anfwert he Purpofe ; but where the Garden produces them there will commonly be more than are ufed for that Table, and fhe fhould always make all that can be fpared into Preferves, becaufe they exceed all others for that Purpofe.

The Method of preferving them is this :

Take four Dozen of them, and fee that they are all found, fine, and perfect.

Pare them, take out the Stones, and cover them with three Pounds of treble-refined Sugar beaten to Powder and fifted.

Let them ftand fix Hours in the Sugar, then fet them on a gentle Fire, and let them boil flowly till they are perfectly clear and tender.

Watch this very carefully ; fome will grow clear before the reft, and they muft be taken out and fet by on a Plate, putting them in again when the reft are done.

When all are thus done lay a Paper clofe over them, and fet them by till the next Day.

Then take fome of your Codling Jelly of the laft Year for thefe early Apricots, becaufe Codlings are not come in to make it for them now, boil it up, and while the Jelly is boiling make the Apricots fcalding hot, then put the Jelly to the Apricots ; about three Pints of the Jelly will be enough for this Parcel of Apricots.

Boil them flowly together ; when the Apricots rife in the Jelly, and jelly very well, put them in Pots and Glaffes for Ufe.

This

This is the Way of Preferving the fine Mafculine Apricot, which when done in this Manner, exceeds all the others by far.

The fame Method exactly is to be followed in Preferving the common Apricots that ripen in the fucceeding Months, only for them, the Coddling Jelly is to be made frefh, the Apples being fit for that Ufe at the fame Time.

In that Cafe two Pints of Jelly, and two Pounds of Sugar, anfwers the fame Purpofe, for the like Quantity of the common Apricot to be preferved then.

9. *Clear Cakes of Apricots.*

Chufe three Dozen of the fineft Apricots, pare them, take out the Stones, and put them into a Preferving-pan, with a Pound of the fineft Sugar in Powder.

Beat them gently, and by Degrees bring them to boil ; let them continue boiling till the Apricots break to Pieces.

Then put in two Quarts of the laft Year's Codling Jelly, (the Houfekeeper muft always take Care to keep a Quantity of this Jelly ready for this Ufe, otherwife fhe will lofe the Opportunity of this Preferving of the fine early Apricots,) boil thefe together for a quarter of an Hour very faft.

After this, run it thro' a Jelly Bag, and to every Pint of the Jelly, allow a Pound and Half of Sugar : It muft be the fineft Sugar, and muft be carefully fifted.

The Sugar muft be fhook in when the Jelly boils, and 'tis to ftand on the Fire till perfectly melted.

After this, it will require no more Care than once running thro' a thin Bag ; it is then to be let into a broad earthen Pan, and then filled into Pots, and fet in a Stove to dry ; when it is Candied at the Top, it muft be turned out upon Glafs, and if the Pots are big, it will be proper to cut it.

When

When it is dry on this Side, it muft be turned to dry on the other.

Often it will happen that thefe Cakes ftick to the Glafs : This very much perplexes the young Confectioner, but the Remedy is very eafy ; only hold the Glafs over the Fire a Minute, and it loofes them. As foon as they are loofe, they muft be turned and dried again on that Side where the Fire foftened them ; then put them up.

10. *Apricot Pafte.*

Pare and ftone fome fine Apricots; to two Pounds of thefe thus prepared, put a Pound of fine Sugar in Powder.

Set them over a gentle Fire; let them heat flowly that the Sugar may perfectly melt : When it is diffolved, boil them brifkly up, and break the Apricots very fmall.

Then pour in a Quart of Coddling Jelly.

Let all thus boil well together; and then to every Pound of it, add a Pound and a Quarter more of fine Sugar powdered and fifted.

The Pafte is to boil well when the Sugar is put in ; and then it is to keep on the Fire, but without boiling, till it is all melted.

It is then to be put into the Pots, and dried in a Stove, turning it till dry in the fame Manner as all Fruit Paftes are done.

11. *To preferve Green Apricots*

Gather a Quantity of good Apricots pretty well grown, but in which the Stone is not got to be hard.

Wet thefe a little, and lay them in a coarfe Cloth. Let them lie a Couple of Hours, then put in two Handfuls of Salt or more, if the Quantity be large ; rub them with this in the Cloth till all the Roughnefs of the Surface be got off.

When

When they are near clean, fet on a Preferving-pan with Water.

When this is fcalding hot, and the Apricots are perfectly clean, throw them in, let them fcald till the Water fcimmers, and is near boiling, then fet them off the Fire till the Water is cold.

Then fet them on the Fire again, and heat them till the Water begins to fcimmer, but it muft not boil up.

This is to be repeated three Times, and thus they are to be left to themfelves covered for two Days.

They will by this Time look green and fine.

Then boil them till they are tender.

Set them off the Fire, and when they are cool, take them out.

Weigh the Apricots, and to every Pound of them, allow a Pound of Sugar, and half a Pint of Water; boil this up, and it will make a thick Syrup.

Let this Syrup be almoft cold, and then put in the Apricots.

Set it by till the next Day; then heat it, and fet it off again, and repeat this every Day till the Syrup is very thick; then put it in Glaffes.

One Thing I muft here obferve, and it is of great Confequence. The green Colour of the Apricots is very much valued, and they get this by lying a confiderable Time in the Pan; it comes from the Copper, which is very unwholefome. I would therefore advife, that the Apricots be fet in a Pot of earthen Ware, and not in the Copper Pan. They will not be of fo fine a Colour this Way, but they will be more wholefome.

12. *To preferve Quinces.*

Weigh your Quinces, and to every Pound of them, before they are pared, take a like Weight of Sugar.

Pare your Quinces very thin, cut them in Halves, take out the Core very clean, and fave the Kernels.

Put a Skellet of clear foft Water upon the Fire, and when it is ready to boil put in the Quinces, let

them

them ftand half a Quarter of an Hour, ftill turning them in the Water; then take them up, lay them in a coarfe Cloth with the Holes downward, and cover them up.

To every Pound of Sugar add a Pint of Water; let it have a Boil, beat up the Whites of two new-laid Eggs and add to it; let it ftand a while, fkim it very well, then ftrain the Sugar through a Cloth and put it over again; when it is ready to boil put in your Quinces with the round Sides downwards, and keep them clofe covered.

Tie up the Kernells of the Quinces in a fine Tiffany Bag, put them into the Skellet, and they will caufe the Syrup to jelly; keep them boiling till the Quinces are very tender, and then take up the Pieces and lay them on a Plate.

Let your Syrrup boil till it will ftand to be a high Jelly, and then put them in your Pots for Ufe.

13. To preferve Oranges.

Take twelve of the frefheft Oranges you can get, with fmooth Skins; and grate off the outer Peel.

If you chufe to have them whole, with a Coring Iron take out part of the Meat; or if you chufe to have them cut in Halves leave fome of the Meat in like manner; lay them to fteep in clear Water for two Days and Nights, fhifting them Morning and Evening.

Then take them out of the Water, rub them with bafket Salt, and wipe them very dry with a clean Cloth. Boil them twice more, in two feveral Waters, till they are very tender; then take them out of the Water, with a Knife take out all the Black, and wipe them dry.

To every Pound of Orange take a Pound and a Half of Sugar; put your Sugar into a Skellet, and put in a Quart of Water to every Pound.

Take the Whites of two Eggs, beat them well, put them into the Sugar and Water in the Skellet, fet it on the Fire, and let it boil as faft as poffible,

and

and when you preceive your Syrup to thicken, put in two or three Spoonfuls of fair Water; then take it off the Fire, lay your Oranges in a Preferving-pan, and when you have ftrained your Syrup very clear pour part of it through a clean Cloth on your Oranges; give the reft a Boil, and pour it in as it boils.

Then fet the Preferving-Pan over a Chaffing Difh of very quick Fire, and let them boil up as brifk as they can; keeping them covered.

You muft have ready Half a Pound of Sugar broken into Pieces as big as Walnuts; and as it boils now and then put in two or three of them.

When they have boiled two Hours, put in a Pint of the beft white Wine, let them boil till they be very clear, and the Sugar thick; then take out your Oranges and lay them in a Bafon.

If the Syrrup be not thick enough, you may boil it a little more; put in the Juice of four Lemons, and pour it on the Oranges.

When they are cold put them in Pots.

14. *To preferve Oranges another Way.*

Take your Oranges, rub off the upper Skin with a Grater, cut a round Hole in the Top, and lay them in fair Water a Day and a Night; then boil them till they are tender, and pull the Meat out at the Hole with your Finger, if you would have it out; then put them in cold Water again, and let them lie till the next Day.

Weigh the Oranges, and take more than their Weight of Sugar. To every Pound of Sugar, take a Pint and a Quarter of Water; boil your Oranges a little while in the Syrup; pour them into a Bafon, cover them clofe with a clean Cloth, and fo let them ftand two Days.

After this drain the Syrup from them, fet it on the Fire, and when it boils pour it on the Oranges; do fo again the next Day, and if your Syrup is not too much wafted, continue to do it for three Days longer fucceffively.

When

When you have done this, fet the Syrup and Oranges on the Fire together, and let them boil till they are enough.

When you are ready to take them off, fqueze in fome Juice of Lemons, and let them boil up a few Minutes. Let them ftand a while, and then put them up.

Clofe your Glaffes with Jelly of John-Apples or Pippins, and fill the Oranges with the fame Jelly.

Lemons are done after the fame Manner, only pared thinner.

15. *To preferve Grapes Green.*

Gather them before they be ripe, four or five in a Bunch; have fome Water fcalding hot, put in your Grapes, and cover them with a Difh; let them ftand half and Hour.

Have a Skellet of Water ready to boil, take them out of the other and let them ftand in that a very little while; then take them out and peel and ftone them. Then take another Skellet of Water, put them in when it is ready to boil; and let them boil foftly for fome Time.

After this drain them for a Quarter of an Hour; then weigh them againft Sugar, and lay Sugar in the Bottom, then Grapes, then Sugar again; and let them boil half an Hour.

16. *To dry different Sorts of Plumbs.*

Take your Plumbs thorough ripe, new gathered; cut them in the Seams, take out the Stone as clean as you can, put to every Pound of Plumbs half a Pound of Lump Sugar; and put the Sugar into a Pan with as much Water as will wet it.

Then fet it on the Fire, and boil it up to the Height of refined Sugar.

Set your Plumbs on clofe by the other, the Slits downward, on a foft Fire: As they foften turn them continually; and when they are thoroughly foft take them off the Fire, and let them ftand in the fame Pan

Nº. XX.   4 E   a

a Day and a Night; the next Day fet them on again till they are thoroughly hot.

Next Day take them out of the Syrup, and fet them on the Backfide of a Sieve, with the Slits upwards, as clofe as they can ftand; and put them into an Oven at Evening where Pies were baked in the Morning.

After they are dried a little turn them; fet them as clofe as you can, and when they will bear handling take out thofe which are moft broken and fill up the Slits of the others with them, laying their Skins as fmooth as you can.

Put them into a warm Oven till they are thoroughly dry, then take very warm Water, with a coarfe Cloth hard wrung, and wipe away the Syrup very clean.

Put them into a Stove or Oven to dry them again thoroughly, and then put them up for Ufe.

17. *Another for the fame.*

Take to a Pound of Plumbs a Quarter of a Pound of Sugar, put them in a Pot clofe ftopped, and bake them in an Oven with Tarts or the like; leave them all Night, and for two Days after give them a Heat in an Oven after Bread.

When this is done take them out of the Pot, dip them one by one in fcalding hot Water, and lay them on Plates or Boards in the Sun, or over a Stove to dry.

18. *A Receipt to make Perfumes.*

Take two Ounces of red Rofe Buds, (the Leaves of them muft be ftripped off) and ufe only the red Part of the Flower.

Pound them in a Mortar, and put to them an Ounce of Benjamin: When you have pounded them fmall together, put in three Grains of Civet, four of Ambergreafe, and twelve of Mufk : Mix thefe with your Fingers, and when you have mixed them well, make them up in little Cakes.

In

In the making them up you muſt put a little Flour in the palm of your Hand, only to make them hang together; ſo let them dry in a Window.

19. *To make a Carraway Cake.*

Take a Pound of Flour dried in an Oven, half a Pound of Carraways, half a Pound of little Biſkets, half a Pint of Yeaſt, a Pound and Half of Butter, a Quarter of a Pint of Sack, half a Pint of Cream, Salt and Spices to your Taſte, and make into a Cake.

20. *Another Way.*

Take to half a Peck of Flour a Pound of Butter, mingle it with fair Water, put to it half a Pound of Carraway Comfits, and as much Sugar and Nutmeg; put to it a good Quantity of Ale Yeaſt, and a little Roſe Water. Seaſon it with Salt.

21. *To make a very good Cake.*

Take three Pound and an Half of fine Flour, a Pint of good Cream, and Yolks of Eggs well beaten, three Quarters of a Pint of good Ale Yeaſt, a Quarter of a Pound of Sugar perfumed ſome Days with Muſk, and Nutmeg and Salt.

Mingle your Flour, Sugar, Salt, and Spices together; then ſtir the Eggs and Yeaſt into the Flour; melt a Pound of Butter in the Cream, and pour it into the Flour, covering the Cream with the Flour.

Let it ſtand very warm by the Fire cloſe covered three Quarters of an Hour. Strew in three Quarters of a Pound of Currants waſhed and rubbed dry; and half a Pound of Raiſins ſtoned and cut ſmall: Let the Fruit be warmed when you put them in; then make up the Cake.

Let it be thicker in the Middle than at the Sides; cut it round the Sides, and prick it; and let the Oven be pretty hot. When it has ſtood an Hour take it out and Ice it with half a Pound of fine Sugar, wetted with Roſe Water. After putting on the Icing, ſet it in the Oven again a Quarter of an Hour.

22. *Ano-*

22. *Another Cake.*

Take a Peck of fine Flour by Weight; three Pints of Cream, or as much as will wet it: One Pound and Half of Butter, four Ounces of Sugar, four Pounds of Currants, one Ounce of Cinnamon, half an Ounce of Nutmeg, four Raſes of Ginger, and a Pint of new Ale Yeaſt.

Mix this altogether, let it be pretty ſtiff, and it muſt lie by the Fire to riſe.   Then make it up.

23. *To make a Shrewſbery Cake.*

Take four Eggs, beat them with two Spoonfuls of Roſe Water, and three of Sack; one Pound of Flour well dried, half a Pound of Sugar, and three Quarters of a Pound of Butter.

Cut your Butter in Slices upon the Flour, and put to it your Sugar; then put your Eggs to the Flour, Sugar, and Butter, and mix them all well together.

Then make it into Cakes of the Bigneſs you chuſe, as thick as a Crown Piece; Roſe them like the Lid of a Pie, and bake them in a ſlow Oven.

24. *To make Cheeſecakes*

Take a Quart of Milk, and when it boils, put in eight Eggs well beaten; ſtir them upon the Fire till it comes to a Curd, then pour it out, and when it is cold ſeaſon it with a little Salt, grated Nutmeg, and ſome Sugar; add two Spoonfuls of Roſe Water, and 12 Ounces of Currants. Then put them in Paſte.

S E C T. VI.

Of Liquors.

WE have ſpoken at large of made Wines, and we ſhall now give Directions for the firſt Fruit Wine that comes in Seaſon, and after that, add the Methods for preventing the common Accidents

dents that hurt made Wines in general; the Caufes of which we fhall explain to the Houfekeeper, that fhe may guard in time.

ART. I. *Cherry Wine.*

Gather fome ripe Cherries, and if there be any to fpare of the firft ripe Kinds, none are fo proper, for there is not any Cherry whatever that has a richer Juice for Wine than the May Duke.

Take off the Stalks and bruife the Cherries in a hair Sieve, fo as to get out the Juice without bruif- ing the Stones.

Meafure the clear Juice, and to every Gallon of it put two Pounds of Lump Sugar beat to Powder.

Stir this well together, and have a clean Veffel that will juft hold the Quantity.

Let it be lightly covered, and worked.

Watch it at Times, and when it does not make any more Noife, ftop it clofe up: Let it ftand thus for three Months, and then Bottle it off, and fet it in a good Cellar. It is a very agreeable weak Wine.

2. *Of the Keeping of made Wines.*

Cherry Wine we have obferved is but a weak Kind ; and therefore it naturally follows in Reafon, and we find it in Experience, that it is but a very indifferent Wine for keeping.

All Wines, the ftronger they are keep the better. A certain Quantity of the watery Part is neceffary to perfect their Fermentation in the making, and this in fome muft be more than in others; but this is al- ways difadvantageous to the Keeping, and confe- quently thofe Wines keep worft that have moft of it in them.

In many Cafes the evaporating a Part of the Wa- ter, is a certain Way of preferving Wines from de- caying ; and in others, 'tis proper to add fome very ftrong Spirit which gives the whole a due Strength.

For

For this Purpofe it is common in many Families, to put Brandy into their made Wines. This certainly helps to keep them, but there is a Way of anfwering the Purpofe much better.

Brandy is dear, and it has a Flavour, which tho' very agreeable in itfelf, is not proper to be tafted in the Wine, as it often is when thus ufed.

Befide that, the ftrength of Brandy being but half that of a pure Spirit, fuch as Spirit of Wine, double the Quantity muft be ufed for the fame Purpofe ; and confequently the Flavour of the Wine fo much the more over-powered.

We have in a preceding Number informed the judicious Houfekeeper fo far in the Nature of Spirits, that fhe is fenfible Brandy, and all other Spirits of that Strength, which is called Proof, confifts of half pure Spirit and half Water. Now her Bufinefs is not to add Water to her Wines, which is too Watery already, and requires Spirit to remedy that very Fault. Therefore a pure Spirit of the rectified Strength is fitteft.

We have told her how bad the common Spirit is, that is fold under the Name of Spirit of Wine at the Diftillers : It is made from Malt, and is very ill flavoured ; therefore this is very improper. It has the Strength that is requifite, but not the proper Quality.

Thus much being underftood, the Houfekeeper will not find any Difficulty in difcovering what fhe is to do, or how fhe is to do it.

She wants for the Keeping of her fruit Wines, fome Spirit of the Strength of rectified Spirit of Wine, and without the bad Flavour of Malt.

Let her make this from her Raifin Wine as we have fhewn, by a third Diftillation ; or to fave a great deal of Trouble, let her buy at the Diftillers, fome of the beft Melaffes Spirit : This is but about three and Sixpence a Gallon, and being a Sugar Spirit, it has not this odious Tafte of the Malt.

This

This Spirit is of the fame Strength with Brandy, and might be ufed inftead of it, but for the Reafons we have laid down a pure rectified Spirit is moft proper; therefore let the Houfekeeper put two Gallons of this Melaffes Spirit into her Still, and with a gentle Heat draw off one Gallon wanting half a Pint; this will be pure rectified Spirit, it will have the utmoft Strength, and will have no Tafte, Smell, or Flavour; it will therefore be the proper Spirit for giving a due Strength to poor Wines.

When any Made Wine has a good Flavour and a tolerable Body, which is often the Cafe, it will not keep of itfelf, and this pure Spirit is then the proper Addition, for it certainly fets it above all thofe Accidents that rife from its having too much of the watery Part.

A Gill of this Spirit to every Gallon of Wine will in general be fufficient, but according to the particular Condition of the Wine the Quantity is to be increafed or diminifhed.

3. *Of very thin Made Wines.*

We have under the preceding Article confidered the Condition of thofe Wines, which have a very great watery Part, and yet, from the original Thicknefs of the Juice, have a tolerable Body; in this Cafe an Addition of Spirit alone is the Remedy: But there are among the Made Wines fome that, altho' they have a very agreeable Flavour, yet want both Spirit and Body; in this Cafe we are to confider the double Defect, and to think of a proper Remedy.

When we confider what the Deficiency is, there will not be any great Difficulty in finding out the proper Remedy.

The Spirit juft defcribed is to affift it in Point of Strength, and we muft give it fome Help in the Way of Body by a richer Wine.

The Houfekeeper will remember that in the laft Number, wherein we treated of Wines, we gave her

a Receipt

a Receipt for making a Sugar Wine, which had only the Strength of Wine, without Flavour or Colour; fhe will now fee one great Ufe of that Kind of Liquor: As we want a Spirit that has neither Tafte nor Flavour for giving Strength to our poor Wines; fo we require a Wine that has neither Tafte, Colour, nor Smell, for giving them a Body.

As the Requifite for this Spirit is to be as ftrong as poffible, fo the Requifite of this Wine is to have as great a Body as poffible; all that we require in the one being Strength, and all we want in the other Body.

To get a Wine proper for this Service let the Houfekeeper make according to that Receipt fome Sugar Wine, only with this Difference, that fhe give a much larger Proportion of Sugar, allowing only juft fo much Water as is neceffary to work it.

This will be Wine for her Purpofe.

Let her always keep a Quantity of this, and of the pure ftrong Spirit by her, and affift her Wines with one or both according to the Nature of their Deficiency: If they want only Strength, let her add fome Spirit; if they want Strength and Body let her mix the Spirit and this ftrong Sugar Wine together, and put them in in proper Quantities; fhe will thus be able at Pleafure, and according to the Nature of the Occafion, to affift any of her Made Wines, and it will never be perceived in the Tafte. Thus fhe will make them at firft of a finer Body and truer Flavour than others who work at Random, and they will always keep better than thofe of fuch People.

The Sugar Wine is a natural Mixture, and therefore will produce no particular Effect, and the Spirit will not be tafted.

4. *To make Apricot Wine.*

Take to two Quarts of Spring Water a Quarter of a Pound of Sugar, boil them together, and fkim the Liquor; then add two or three Dozen of Apricots

ftoned

ftoned and quartered, and when all have well boiled together take it off, and put it into an earthen Pot or Pitcher, cover it up, and let it ftand till it is cold, then ftrain it through a Cloth without breaking the Apricots, and when it is thoroughly fettled pour it into Bottles, ftop them clofe, tie them down, lay them in a cool Place, and cover them with Sand. It may be drank in a Fortnight or three Weeks.

In like Manner good Liquors may be made of other Fruits and Flowers, and the Way to make fome of them is as follows.

5. *To make Cowflip or Primrofe Wine.*

Take three Gallons of fair Water, put into it fix Pounds of the fineft Sugar, boil them together half an Hour, or more, taking off the Scum carefully as it rifes, then pour it into a Pan or Tub to cool ; when it is almoft cold take a Spoonful of Ale Yeaft, and beat it well with fix Ounces of Syrup of Lemon, mix this with the Liquor by toffing it up and down ; then take a Gallon of picked Cowflips or Primrofes, bruife them in a Marble Mortar, and put them into the Liquor ; let them work together two or three Days ; then ftrain it off, and put it into a Veffel that is juft fit for it : Two or three Days after ftop it clofe, and and three Weeks or a Month after that bottle it off, putting a Lump of Sugar into every Bottle. If it is well corked it will keep a Year.

6. *Another Way to make Cowflip or Clove-Julyflower Wine.*

Take a Gallon of Water to a Quart of Honey, let your Water boil before you put the Honey in, then let it boil again, and fkim it carefully. After it has boiled fome Time take it off, and let it ftand to cool ; work it as in the former Receipt, and when it has half done working put in the Cowflips or Julyflowers; if Julyflowers, they muft be dried two or three Days before you put them in. When it has ftood a little tun it up in a Veffel, and let it remain a Month before you bottle it off.

N°. XX.   4 F   This

This is admirable Drink without the Flowers, and will keep half a Year; but if you would have it keep a Year put two Quarts of Honey to a Gallon of Water.

S E C T. VII.

Of DISTILLERY.

THE Houſekeeper is now ſo well acquainted with the Nature of diſtilling, and the Difference of Spirits, that a very ſhort Account of all the Waters we ſhall have Occaſion to name will ſerve.

In the former Receipts we have ſet down all the particular Methods, but theſe being now underſtood, we may write to her as the Phyſician does to the Apothecary, Take ſuch and ſuch Ingredients, and diſtil a Water *according to Art.*

A R T. I. *Strong Pepper-Mint Water.*

Cut ſome Pepper-mint at the Time when it is juſt budding for Flower, and tie it up in ſmall Bundles to dry, as we have directed in a former Number.

When it is juſt become dry and criſp, and retains its green Colour and full Taſte and Smell, cut the Tops of it till you have a Pound and half of them, rejecting the thick and hard Stalk.

If the Plant have been cut up carefully about a Hand's Breadth of the thick Part of the Bunches is to be thrown away, the reſt being to be cut ſmall and uſed.

Put this into a Still, and add to it a Gallon of Melaſſes Spirit and three Quarts of Water.

Diſtil immediately three Quarts and a Pint, and add to it a Pint of Water.

This is the perfect and fine Way of diſtilling this Water, which is the fineſt Remedy in all Phyſick

for

for a fudden Sicknefs from Wind in the Stomach : A fmall Glafs of it is to be taken alone.

It may be made from the dried Pepper-mint at any Time of the Year, allowing a little more of the Herb to the fame Quantity of Spirit, for it lofes fome Virtue in keeping, or it may be made from the frefh Plant, allowing two Pounds and a half to the Gallon ; but the other is the perfeét Way, for the Plant never has fo much Virtue as when juft dried after gathering at the proper Seafon.

No Sugar fhould be put to this Water.

It taftes extremely hot, but its Effeét is like a Charm, it cures immediately.

2. *Parfley Water.*

Bruife fix Ounces of Juniper Berries, put them into a Still, and pour upon them two Gallons of Melafles Spirit, ftir them well about, and after an Hour put in a Gallon of Water; ftir it well about again, and then put in a Quarter of a Pound of Parfley Roots cut into thin Slices, and fix Ounces of Horferadifh Root cut in the fame Manner ; add of the Tops of fharp or biting Arfefmart two Ounces, and the fame Quantity of the Tops of Saint John's-wort and of Elder Flowers, and of Fennel, Parfley, and wild Carrot Seeds each an Ounce and half bruifed ; when all are in ftir it up very well again, and then fix on the Head of the Still. Let it ftand four Days ; then diftil off feven Quarts, and add a Quart of Water.

This is an excellent Water in Cholicks arifing from the Gravel or Stone in the Kidneys ; it anfwers the double Purpofe of difpelling Wind and promoting Urine.

The Houfekeeper has already been cautioned not to depend too much upon thefe Waters, or to ufe them too freely.

Thefe Cautions fhe muft always keep in Mind, for Cordial Waters are not meant as Remedies for defperate Difeafes ; they are often an immediate Re-

4 F 2   lief

lief in flight Cafes, and they are ufeful with other Medicines in fuch as are more ftubborn.

This is to be underftood of all of them, and we give their Virtues with this Caution. We give Rules for making the beft Kinds, and fay for what they are beft.

3. *To make French Water.*

Take a Quart of Aqua Vitæ, two Pennyworth of Rofa Solis, of Clove Water and Angelica Water each two Pennyworth, a Pint of Damafk Rofe Water, and half a Pint of Cinnamon Water; add to a Pint of Spring Water a Pound of fine Loaf Sugar, let it ftand twenty-four Hours till the Sugar is diffolved, and then ftrain it through a white Flannel Bag; this done mix them all together, ftrain it again, and put it in Bottles, ftopping them clofe.

4. *To make Aqua Mirabilis.*

Take of Galangal, Cloves, Cubebs, Letwell, Cardamum, Mace, Cinnamon, and Nutmeg, of each five Grains; of Lemon and Orange Peel a Dram each; of Elecampane one Dram; Buglofs Flowers, Violets, Marygolds, and Rofemary Flowers, of each a Handful; a Pint of the Juice of Celandine, and of the Juice of Mint and Balm half a Pint each; add alfo a Handful of Melilot: Mix all thefe Powders with the Juice, a Quartern of the beft Aqua Vitæ that is diftilled from all Sorts of good Herbs, and a Quart of white Wine; let it ftand all Night, and in the Morning diftil it in a cold Still.

To make it drink pleafant you muft take a Pound of fine white Sugar, fix or feven Spoonfuls of Damafk Rofe Water, and four Grains of Mufk and Ambergreafe; fet thefe on the Fire, boil it to the Height of Candy, then take it off, and pour it hot into the Water.

If you add to this a little Leaf Gold it will be the better.

5. *An-*

5. *Another Way.*

Take Galangal, Cubebs, Setwell, and Cardamum, of each a Dram; Mace, Cloves, and Nutmeg, of each two Drams; Cinnamon fix Drams; a Quarter of an Ounce of Orange Rind, a Quart of Aqua Vitæ, two Quarts of white Wine, one Quart of Sack, a Quart of the Juice of Celandine, and two Handfuls of Melilot Flowers dried : Steep all thefe together for the Space of twelve Hours, and then diftil it in a Limbeck or cold Still; add to thefe a little Brandy, and hang two or three Grains of Ambergreafe in the Glafs your Water drops into, and let it remain till confumed.

6. *To make a Cordial Water.*

Take Rofemary, fweet Balm, red Sage, Rue, dried Mint, Myrrh, Mugwort, and Angelica, of each half a Pound ; Angelica Roots three Ounces, Dittany a Quarter of a Pound; Carduus, Betony, Scabius, Pimpernell, Agrimony, Tormentil Roots, and Celandine, of each half a Pound ; Gentian Roots two Ounces, and Rofa Solis two Quarts : Steep all thefe Herbs and Roots, being firft cut fmall and bruifed, twelve Hours in five Gallons of white Wine, and diftil it off quickly in two cold Stills.

7. *To make Milk Water.*

Take four of five Quarts of new Milk from a red Cow, add a Handful of Buglofs, a few Tops of Rofemary, and a fmall Handful of Spearmint; put thefe altogether into a cold Still, and diftil it off into a Glafs or Bottle, into which is to be put a Spoonful or two of Loaf Sugar. Drink this Morning and Evening.

8. *Another, to be given in a Surfeit or Fever.*

Take fix Handfuls of green Carduus ; of Spearmint and Wormwood three Handfuls each, and two of Balm ; fteep thefe in a Gallon of Milk all Night, and diftil it the next Day. When you ufe it ftir in a little Sugar.

9. *To*

9. *To make Surfeit Water.*

Take half a Pint of Damaſk Roſe Water, and half a Pound of white Sugar-candy, let it ſteep a Day and a Night ; the next Day take Cloves, Cinnamon, Nutmeg, and Anniſeeds, of each half an Ounce, with a Slice of Liquorice, and two Ounces of Dates ; bruiſe the Spices a little when you put them in: Then take three Quarters of a Pound of ſtoned Raiſins, half a Pint of Poppy Water, two Quarts of Aqua Vitæ, three Grains of Ambergreaſe, and one Grain and a half of Muſk mixed with Sugar-candy ; tie theſe up in a Lawn Bag, and put them in a Pot ; cover it cloſe with a white Paper, and a Plate upon that ; remember to ſtir it twice a Day : Let it ſtand three Days, and on the fourth Day put in a Sprig of Angelica, a Handful of Balm, and a Handful of dried Poppy Leaves ; then let it ſtand three Days longer. Strain it through a Cotton Bag, and keep it for Uſe.

10. *To make Sir Theodore Mikerue's Surfeit Water.*

Take a Buſhel of red Poppies, ſix Handfuls of Dragons, as much Carduus, eight Handfuls of Marygold Flowers, half a Pound of Hartſhorn, four Handfuls of Spearmint, three of Balm, and two of Strawberry Leaves ; ſteep all theſe in twelve Pints of Rheniſh eight Days, then put to it four Ounces of Mithridate, one Ounce of Mace, as much Cinnamon, and two Ounces of Nutmeg. Diſtil theſe in a Roſe Still till you have a Gallon of Water.

Give ſix Spoonfuls of this at a Time, and let the Patient lie in Bed four Hours after it.

If the Sweat take a moderate Effect, twice uſing it will cure.

11. *To make Cock or Capon Ale.*

Take two large Cocks or Capons, parboil them on a gentle Fire for an Hour or more till all the Blood is gone ; add in the Decoction the Peel of an Orange, or Citron, and a little Mace ; cut off the Shanks of

the

the Capons, and throw them away, then with a Chopping-Knife mince them, Bones and all, as fmall as ordinary minced Meat; put them into a large Boulter: Then take a Kilderkin fweet and well feafoned, put into it four or five Gallons of good ftrong Ale of the firft Running, new as it is ; make in the Kilderkin a large Bung-Hole, and thruft into it the Boulter in which the Capons are : Let them fteep in it three Days and Nights, leaving the Bung-Hole open to work ; then take out the Capons, clofe the Bung-Hole, and let it ftand a Day and a half, after which bottle it off.

You may drink it after three Days bottling; but it will keep fix Weeks if clofe ftopped.

S E C T. VIII.

Of Diforders, and their Remedies.

A R T. I. *For a violent Purging.*

SET on a Saucepan with a Pint and half of pure Spring Water, put in an Ounce of Diafcordium, and two Drams of Japan Earth in Powder; boil this till there is but a Pint left, ftrain it off thick, and pour it, without letting it fettle, into a Quart Bottle, that there may be Room for fhaking.

Add to it an Ounce of Syrup of Diafcordium, and an Ounce of ftrong Cinnamon Water.

Let four Spoonfuls of this be taken once in fix Hours, or oftener if there be Occafion.

When the Diforder is ftopped, let the Patient take a Spoonful Night and Morning to prevent a Return, always fhaking it up.

2. *For the Gravel.*

Put into a clean Saucepan three Pints of pure Water, add to it an Ounce of frefh-gathered Fennel

Root

Root cut into thin Slices, and three Drams of the Seeds of wild Carrot bruifed.

Add ftoned Raifins two Ounces, and of the picked Leaves and tender Tops of Pellitory of the Wall half an Ounce; boil this heartily for ten Minutes, then ftrain it off, and add a Dram of Salt Petre.

Let the Patient take a Quarter of a Pint of this warm every four Hours, and in the mean Time drink fome foft and fine Barley Water.

3. *A bitter Infufion.*

Cut into thin Slices half an Ounce of Gentian, fhred fmall the fame Quantity of the Tops of the lefler Centaury, and add two Drams of Seville Orange Peel.

Put this into a Jar, and pour upon it a Quart of boiling Water.

Let it ftand all Night, and then filter it clear off.

Let the Perfon take a Coffee Cup full of this every Morning fafting for a confiderable Time; it will greatly ftrengthen the Stomach.

4. *Bitters with Ginger.*

Cut half an Ounce of Gentian into thin Slices, and put it into a Stone Jar.

Add to it the fame Quantity of Orange Peel frefh pared and cut fmall, and three Drams of Ginger fliced in the fame Manner.

Pour upon thefe a Quart of boiling Water, and let them ftand ten Hours.

Then ftrain it clear off, and filter it through Paper; add a Gill of white Wine, and take a Wine Glafs full of it every Morning fafting, or upon any Occafion when troubled with Wind.

This Receipt I had from an eminent Phyfician, who told me Ginger was better than all the hot Drugs at the Apothecaries; and that the only Reafon he knew why other Doctors did not ufe it was becaufe it was fold not at the Druggifts but the Grocers.

I have

I have tried this myfelf, and given it to my Acquaintance, and from what I have feen I have great Reafon to found its Praifes : I never knew any Thing like it.

When I firft took this Medicine I had no Appetite to any Food, nor was able to digeft what I eat; I always felt full, fick, and giddy after the leaft Food, and was fubject to Belchings and cholicky Pains in a terrible Degree.

I had not taken this three Days before I was in a Manner well; my Stomach was good, and I could eat heartily, and digeft it.

At any Time when my Sicknefs or the Wind returned I drank a fmall Glafs of it, and it went away immediately: And fince that Time, if my Supper ever difagrees with me, or I perceive the Tafte of it in my Mouth in a Morning, I take a Glafs of this Medicine, and am well immediately.

Having found this good Effect of it myfelf, I have recommended it to many of my Acquaintance, and they all fpeak of it the fame Way. I never knew it fail.

It is fo cheap and fo ufeful that no Family ought to be without the Knowlege of it. This I verify from the Experience of feveral Years. *M. B.*

5. *For a continual Fever.*

Blanch four Almonds, and pound them to Pafte in a Mortar.

Rub a Scruple of Camphire in another Mortar till it is fine; add the powdered Almonds by Degrees, and when thefe are well mixed pour in by a very little at a Time four Ounces of Rhue Water; add an Ounce of Plague Water, and an Ounce of Syrup of Cloves.

Let this be fhaken up, and one Table Spoonful taken every fix Hours.

It is a very fine moderate Cordial, and it operates by Sweat mildly and gently.

6. *For a parched Mouth.*

Set on a fmall Saucepan with half a Pint of Water, put into it a Quarter of an Ounce of the Kernels of Quinces dried.

Let it boil fome Time, and then ftrain it hot thro' a coarfe Piece of Linen.

The Liquor will be as thick and roapy as the White of an Egg, and is excellent to cool and foften the Tongue when it parched up and white in a Fever.

Some ufe a Mucilage made in the fame Manner, by boiling the Seeds of Fleawort, but this is not wholfome to fwallow; nothing can be more innocent than the Kernels of Quinces, and they make as foft and fmooth a Liquor, therefore they are greatly preferable.

The ufual Way is to fpit thefe Things out, but if this be fwallowed there is no Harm.

7. *For a Diabetes.*

Set on a Saucepan with a Pint of new Milk, add to it a Quarter of an Ounce of Roach Allum in Powder.

Let this boil till a Curd is formed perfectly.

Then feparate the Curd, and let the whole ftand to cool.

Let the Patient take a little of this twice a Day: It is apt to be offenfive to the Stomach, fo that Caution muft be ufed in taking it; but it is a very powerful Medicine.

There is not any Difeafe whatfoever more difficult to be cured than a Diabetes, yet this is a certain Remedy.

8. *Spring Juices.*

Get fome frefh Brook-lime, Water-crefs, and Garden Scurvygrafs; put into a Marble Mortar two Pounds of the Scurvygrafs and one Pound of each of the others, bruife them well, and prefs out the Juice; add one third Part of the Quantity of Seville Orange Rind.

Mix

Mix all together, and let it ſtand to ſettle.

This is to be taken a Quarter of a Pint at a Time twice a Day, and is very good againſt the Scurvy.

Some add Sugar and Compound Horſeradiſh Water to theſe Juices, but that is as they pleaſe ; they are thus rendered more palatable, but the Virtues are not encreaſed by ſuch Additions.

9. *To clean the Mouth.*

Diſſolve a Dram of Salt Petre in ſix Ounces of Spring Water, add to this an Ounce of Honey of Roſes, and twenty-five Drops of Spirit of Vitriol.

This is to be uſed by Way of Gargle, and it excellently cleanſes the Mouth when furred up by any feveriſh Indiſpoſition.

It ſhould be ſpit out.

10. *Tar Pills.*

Mix up ſome fine Pine Norway Tar with fine Powder of Elecampane Root.

Let it be made as ſtiff as Paſte, ſo that it may eaſily be made into Pills.

Take four moderately large Pills twice a Day.

It is good in the Scurvy, and in Diſorders of the Lungs. It muſt be continued for ſome Time.

11. *In a Fever.*

Mix together two Ounces of Lapis Contrayerva, and one Ounce of Powder of Virginian Snakeroot, add Syrup of Oranges as much as will make it into the Form of an Electuary.

This is not ſo properly an Electuary as a Quantity of Boluſſes, for in the regular Compoſition of an Electuary there muſt always be ſome Conſerve, which there is not here.

This is an excellent Medicine, and the Way of giving it is this :

Weigh half a Dram of it, and let that be taken every ſix Hours, drinking after it a Glaſs of the following Julep.

Take

Take Spring Water a Quart, Treacle Water fix Ounces, and Syrup of Orange Peel three Ounces, mix this together by fhaking, and give a Glafs alfo fometimes alone.

12. *Againft Giddinefs of the Head.*

Take wild Valerian Root in Powder, and Mifletoe in Powder, of each an Ounce ; mix thefe in a fmall Mortar, and add to them as much Syrup of Orange Peel as will make them into the Form of an Electuary.

Let a Piece as big as a Nutmeg be taken twice a Day for a Continuance of Time, drinking after it a Quarter of a Pint of an Infufion of Mother of Thyme made like Tea.

I have feen very great Effects from this Medicine, and have known it given in the Falling Sicknefs with great Succefs after every Thing elfe has failed.

Valerian is one of the fineft Roots we know, and the Virtues of Mifletoe are much greater than is commonly thought.

13. *For the Jaundice.*

Take Caftile Soap three Ounces, Powder of Rhubarb and Species of Hiera Picra of each half an Ounce, and Syrup of Orange Peel as much as will make the whole into an Electuary.

The beft Method of mixing them up is to mix the two Powders firft by rubbing them together, then to get fome of the Syrup in, and make them into a Kind of Pafte.

Then the Soap muft be fhaved very thin, and beat up with a little Syrup. After this both will mix very well together.

This is an excellent Remedy.

The Quantity of a Nutmeg is to be taken twice a Day, and continued till the Difeafe is removed.

If after three or four Days there is no vifible Effect, let fome prepared Steel be added in the Proportion of half an Ounce to the whole Quantity of the Electuary.

R E-

RECEIPTS *from Lady* Montague's *Book.*

ART. I. *To cure the Scurvy.*

TAKE of the Tops of the Pine Tree, broken off about an Inch and a half below the Plumb or Bush, as many as will fill a Gallon; split them throughout from Top to Bottom, Plumb and all, in four Quarters.

Boil this in a Gallon of small Ale till half be boiled away; then add to it two Quarts of strong Ale, and give that a Boil.

Take of this half a Pint every Morning fasting.

2. *Another for the same.*

Gather half a Bushel of Scurvygrafs, and take Care that it be well picked, washed clean, and dried with a Cloth; bruise it well, and add to it fix Seville Oranges, Rind and all shred together, a Pound of Raifins stoned and bruised in a Mortar, and two or three Sticks of Horseradish cut in Slices.

Tie all these up in a Bag with the Juice in them, pour upon it five Gallons of Ale, stop it up close, and in four or five Days it will be fit for Ufe.

Drink half a Pint every Morning, fasting two Hours after it; and it will be proper to drink the same Liquor at your Meals, or any other Time of the Day at Pleasure.

3. *Another when the Disease is stronger.*

Take three Pints of the best white Wine and half a Peck of Scurvygrafs prepared as before directed, with a large Lemon, Rind and all, shred into it; add to this two Ounces of Long Pepper, and a Stick of Cinnamon beat small.

Put these Ingredients into a clean Pitcher, stop it down very close, and put the Pitcher into a Pot of boiling Water; let it infuse four Hours, taking Care to keep the Water boiling all the Time, and as it
wastes

waftes have a Tea-kettle of boiling Water ready to keep the Pot filled up.

Then take out the Pitcher, ftrain off the Liquor, and bottle it up for Ufe, taking Care that it be well corked.

Drink a Wine Glafs full every Morning, fafting two Hours after it, and the fame Quantity at four o'Clock in the Afternoon.

This Remedy has been found effectual in the worft Cafes, after many others have failed.

4. *To ftop Bleeding at the Nofe.*

Burn a Piece of Sponge in a hot Firefhovel till it is reduced entirely to Afhes, tie up thefe in a Lawn Bag, dip it in writing Ink, and ftop the Noftrils with it.

Some dip it in Vinegar inftead of Writing Ink, and either Way it is efficacious.

5. *For a Cough or Confumption.*

Take of Comfrey Roots clean wafhed, fcraped, and fhred, half a Pound ; of Liquorice well bruifed four Ounces ; and a Handful of Curants wafhed clean and dried in a Cloth ; to thefe Ingredients add Balm, Mother of Thyme, and Wood or Garden Sorrel, of each, one Handful ; an Ounce and a half of Annifeeds bruifed, and fixteen or eighteen broad Figs fhred fmall.

Boil thefe in two Quarts of fair Water or fmall Wort till half be wafted ; but let it boil very flow, for it will be the better for ftanding over a gentle Fire for eight or ten Hours.

Strain off the Liquor, and fweeten it according to your Palate with Loaf Sugar : Drink it Morning and Evening, or at any other Time of the Day.

6. *An approved Electuary for a Cough.*

Take of the Syrup of Horehound one Ounce, and the like Quantity of Syrup of Maiden Hair, Coltsfoot, and Liquorice ; of powdered Elecampane, Liquorice, Annifeeds, and Orice, each half an Ounce.

Mix

Mix thefe up into an Electuary, and take the Quantity of a Nutmeg the laft Thing before you go to Bed at Night, and the firft Thing in the Morning.

7. *For a Sprain.*

Take common Clay and boil it in white Wine Vinegar till it is of the Thicknefs of a Salve, fpread this upon a Linen Cloth, and apply it to the Part affected ; let it lie on till it is dry, and if the Complaint is not removed apply a fecond, and it will not fail of a Cure.

8. *A Powder for the Yellow Jaundice*

Take of Hartfhorn, Turmerick, the inner Rind of Barberry Tree, and Powder of Earth-Worms, each one Dram, and of Saffron half a Dram.

Reduce all thefe to a fine Powder, and take as much as will lie on a Six-pence in two or three Spoonfuls of Poffet-Drink every Morning fafting, and the like Dofe at four o'Clock in the Afternoon, for feven or eight Days fucceffively.

9. *A Poultice for a Swelling.*

Take of Feverfew, Herb of Grace, and red Sage, each one Handful ; beat them well together, and boil them three Quarters of an Hour in the Dregs of ftrong Ale.

When thefe have boiled fufficiently, thicken it with coarfe Wheat Flour.

10. *For a Burn or Scald.*

Take a large Handful of the yellow Mofs that grows upon Stones, the like Quantity of Sheep's Dung, and to thefe add alfo a Handful of the Bark of Elder ; fry them in Mutton Suet till you think the Virtue of the Ingredients is fried out ; then ftrain off the Fat, and it will make an excellent Ointment for the Cure of Scalds or Burns.

11. *A*

11. *A black Salve for Burns.*

Take a Pint of Sallad Oil and half a Pound of red Lead, fet it over a flow Fire in a Pan, pouring in as much Vinegar as will cover the Bottom before you put in the Lead and Oil : Let the Fire be exceeding flow, and when it is turned black add to it fix Pennyworth of Saffron, and two Ounces of Bees Wax.

When thefe are mixed together, let it fcimmer gently over the Fire to bring it to a proper Confiftence ; drop a little upon Paper, and when it does not run about it is thick enough. Put a little Oil upon a Table or fmooth Board to prevent it from fticking, pour the Salve upon it, and make it up in Rolls.

This is good for a frefh Burn, and if it is not very bad it will be fufficient to drefs it once in twenty-four Hours ; but in worfe Cafes it fhould be dreffed twice a Day.

12. *For an Ague.*

Take a Handful of Yarrow, Roots and all, beat it in a wooden Difh, and add to it a Spoonful of Bay Salt ; put this over the Fire in a Frying-pan till it is hot, and have ready a brown Paper Bag the Breadth of your Hand ; fill the Bag out of the Pan, prefs it flat, put it upon the Top of the Head, faften it on with a Night Cap, and let it remain three Days and Nights ; then take this off, and have a like Quantity ready to clap on.

Throw what was taken off into a Warming-pan of Coals, and let the Perfon hold his Head in the Smoak till it is all confumed.

This is to be repeated three Times, and it never fails of a Cure.

Receipts *from* Lady Hewet's *Book.*

ART. I. *For the Hemerroids in great Extremity.*

TAKE a Quart of white Wine, and add to it a Handful of broad Plantain fhred, and an Ounce of Cinnamon ; boil this gently to a Pint, then

ftrain

ftrain it off, and fet it on the Fire again, adding an Ounce of Annifeeds, and half a Pound of white Sugar; let it boil a little.

Take two good Spoonfuls of this Night and Morning.

2. *The Ointment to the former Drink.*

Dry fome Annifeeds in a Fire-fhovel till they be blackifh, then beat them to fine Powder, and mix it up with Honey.

Anoint the Part often with this, or dip in a Rag and apply to it.

3. *A Powder for Convulfion Fits.*

Take a Raven, pick off the Feathers, gut it, and fend it to the Oven in a clean earthen Difh. Let it be put in every Time the Oven is heated till it will rub to a fine Powder.

Of this Powder let the Perfon afflicted take as much as will lie upon a Silver Groat every Morning fafting, for nine Days together.

This is very feldom known to fail of giving Relief; but as it is a Diforder that often returns, it will be very proper to keep fome of the Powder always in Readinefs, to ufe occafionally.

4. *To cure Convulfion Fits in Young or Old.*

Take a Handful of the green Leaves of Fox-gloves, and as much of the Polypodium of the Oak, boil thefe in a Quart of Spring Water till half is confumed, and if you pleafe you may fweeten it with double-refined Sugar, or Sugar-candy.

To a Man or Woman give two large Spoonfuls the firft Thing in the Morning and the laft at Night, and continue this eight or ten Days, or till a Pint be taken: To a Child give but a Spoonful at a Time, and continue it till half a Pint be taken.

The proper Time to gather the Polypodium is when Saturn has the Afcendant, and the Fox-glove when Venus reigns; at other Times they have not half the Virtue.

N°. XXI. 4 H 5. *To*

5. *To prevent or cure the Rheumatism.*

Take Annifeeds, Sweet Fennel Seeds, and Coriander Seeds bruifed, of each an Ounce; Alehoof, Germander, Angelica, Saint John's-wort, and Heartfeafe, of each two Handfuls; tie all thefe up in a Bag, and put them into five Gallons of fmall Ale.

Drink of this three Times a Day, efpecially Spring and Fall.

6.   *For Rheumatick Pains.*

Take a Pound of Lignum Vitæ Shavings, put them into three Gallons of Spring Water, and let it boil away to two.

Let the Party drink half a Pint of this every Morning fafting, and the fame Quantity about four o'Clock in the Afternoon.

7.   *A Receipt for the Scurvy.*

Take a Peck of the beft Garden Scurvygrafs, the fame Quantity of Alehoof picked clean, a Dozen of Seville Oranges wiped clean and fliced, Rind and all; put thefe into a Kilderkin of fmall Ale: After it has done working ftop it up, let it ftand three Days, and then drink it at Meals, or any other Time.

The beft Time to drink this Beer is in the Month of March; during which the Perfon afflicted fhould drink no other.

8.   *For an Ague.*

Take Radix Contrayerva Pulvis one Dram, and fteep it in two Spoonfuls of Annifeed Water. Drink this an Hour before the Fit, and drink a Glafs of Carduus Water after it; then go to Bed, and fweat three Hours.

Repeat this twice more in the fame Manner.

9.   *An approved Receipt to cure an Ague.*

Take an Apple and cut a Hole in it, faving the Top; fill the Hole with Tobacco, put on the Top again, lay it to the Fire, and roaft it well; then chop it up together, fpread it on a double Rag, and lay it upon both the Wrifts as hot as you can bear it, juft

before

before the Fit; repeat this three Times, giving a Vomit of Carduus before the fecond Fit.

With this I have cured a third Day Ague.

10. *For the Dropfy.*

Take two Quarts of white Wine, put to it an Ounce of Elder Flowers, the fame Quantity of Afh Keys; Roman Wormwood and Hyffop one Handful each, a Dram of Saffron, and a Handful of Centaury.

Steep thefe in the Wine two Days, and then let the Patient drink the Quantity of a Wine Glafs full twice a Day, letting the Ingredients remain in till the Wine is gone.

11. *To make a Water for the Stone.*

Take Alehoof and Pellitory of the Wall, of each a like Quantity, when they are in their Prime; diftil them together till you have four Quarts of Water, pour this into a Pot, and let it ftand till Afh Keys are pretty big.

Then take Grammel, Annifeed, and Sweet Fennel Seeds bruifed, of each an Ounce, and fteep them twenty-four Hours in the above Water; put it into the Still, Seeds and all, and add thereunto a Handful of Alehoof and Leaves of Pellitory of the Wall, and as many Afh Keys as the Still will hold; then diftil it off.

12. *Another for the fame.*

Take a Pint of the ftrongeft white Wine, fet it on the Fire, put to it two Ounces of old Alicant Soap, and let it continue till diffolved; then take it off the Fire, fweeten it with Syrup of Marfh Mallows, and give it to drink.

This is an excellent and approved Remedy.

13. *A Receipt to make Daffy's Elixir.*

Take of Annifeeds, Fennel Seeds, and Coriander Seeds, each two Ounces, and the like Quantity of Liquorice; Cocheneal and Saffron of each one Dram;

Sena

Sena and the beſt Rhubarb of each one Ounce; and Raiſins of the Sun ſtoned one Pound.

Bruiſe the Seeds and Liquorice, and ſtew the Rhubarb; then put the whole into a Stone Jug, and pour upon it three Quarts of the beſt Brandy.

It may be made uſe of in ten Days, but it is better after ſtanding three Weeks.

Two Spoonfuls ſhould be given at Night, and two in the Morning; and ſo more or leſs, as there may be Occaſion.

14. *A Remedy for the Evil.*

Take two Quarts of Spring Water, and put to it two Handfuls of Archangel, two Ounces of Liquorice in Slips, and the ſame Quantity of Sweet Fennel Seeds bruiſed.

Put theſe in a Pot, ſet it over a gentle Fire, and let it ſcimmer till a Quarter be waſted; then take it off, let it ſtand to cool, and when cold ſtrain it thro' a Sieve, and ſqueeze the Herbs.

Let the Patient take a Quarter of a Pint of this every Morning faſting, the ſame Quantity at Four in the Afternoon, and repeat it again at going to Bed.

15. *For the Cholick.*

Take a Head of Garlick, bruiſe it well, and put it into a Pint of Sack, then ſet it over the Fire, and boil it away to half a Pint.

Drink this going to Bed, keeping yourſelf warm; and repeat it two or three Nights.

16. *To force away Pains.*

Take half an Ounce of Marſh-Mallows, a Quarter of an Ounce of Cummin Seeds finely beaten and ſifted, and a Quarter of an Ounce of the Oil of Sweet Almonds; mix theſe together, and then put ſome into a Spoon, warm it, and anoint the Place afflicted with Pain, rubbing it in with your Hand for half an Hour; then wrap over it a Piece of Flannel to keep it warm.

17. *To*

17. *To make Charity Oil.*

Take a Handful of blue Valerian, and the fame Quantity of Lavender, Camomile, Rofemary, and Sage; fhred thefe fmall, and put to them a Quart of the beft Sallad Oil.

Let this ftand in the Sun nine Days, ftirring it frequently; then boil it till the Herbs are blackifh.

After this take it off, let it ftand to cool, ftrain it, and put to it again the like Quantity of all the above Herbs except the Valerian, and fet it in the Sun nine Days longer.

Repeat this once more, then ftrain it off, and put it in a Bottle; ftop it clofe, and keep it for Ufe.

It is good for any green Wound, old Sore, Bruifes inwardly or outwardly, Swellings, Strains, Blafts, or Burns.

The Quantity to be given for an inward Bruife is feven or eight Drops in Poffet-Drink going to Bed, and fweat after it.

18. *To cure the Itch.*

Take Half a Pound of Butter, a Quarter of a Pound of Brimftone, and a Quarter of an Ounce of Cloves beat fine; Rofe Water and white Wine Vinegar of each a Quarter of a Pint; and Bay Leaves and Dock Roots of each one Handful. Boil thefe all together half an Hour, ftirring it all the while; then let it ftand to cool.

The next Day fkim off the Top, leaving all that is clear; clarify the Top, and fet it by for Ufe.

It muft be ufed only at Nights going to Bed, when you muft anoint every Part where it is come out, and particular Care muft be taken to rub it well in all down the Back Bone; taking every Morning as much Flower of Brimftone as will lie upon a Shilling in fome warm Milk.

19. *An approved Receipt for the fame.*

Take fix Ounces of frefh Hog's Lard, and four Ounces of Elecampane Roots made very clean, and fliced as thin as you can; boil the Roots in ftrong Beer or Vinegar till they are tender, then drain them from the Liquor with a Spoon; put them in a Mortar, and beat them to a Poultice.

Then take half an Ounce of Barberries, an Ounce of Salt Petre, and an Ounce of common Brimftone, all finely powdered; mix all thefe Things very well together by beating them in a Mortar, and immediately before the Party goes to Bed let his Body be anointed all over with this, efpecially in every Joint, and rub it in well by a good Fire three Nights together.

The Patient muft put on clean Linen at his Anointing, and have clean Sheets; both which he muft make ufe of for three Weeks without Change.

This Remedy, with God's Blefling, hath never been known to fail.

20. *A Receipt for fore Eyes.*

Take Conferve of red Rofes two Ounces, the fineft Bole Armoniac half an Ounce, and Sugar of Lead a Dram; then add as much Frogs Spawn Water as will make it of a proper Confiftence, and with this anoint the Eyes when going to Bed.

21. *An Eye Water.*

Take an Ounce of Lapis Lafulæ, and an Ounce of white Sugar-candy; fteep thefe twelve Hours in half a Pint of red Rofe Water; then ftrain it through a fine Cloth, and put it in a Bottle. Shake it when you wafh your Eyes with it.

22. *A moft precious and fafe Water for a hot Rheum in the Eyes.*

Take a Pint of white Wine as it comes from the Grape; it muft be very clear; (this Wine Coopers can help you to, but it connot be had at Taverns) put it in a Pewter Pot with a Cover; then heat a Stone called Lapis Calaminaris, about the Bignefs of an Egg, red hot in a Wood Fire, and put it into the

Wine,

Wine, shutting the Lid down after it; repeat this twice, then take it out, and put in half an Ounce of Camphire, pure, white, and clear as Glass; let this stand in the same Pot fourteen Days, then pour it into a Bottle, Camphire and all; stop it close, and keep it for Use.

Drop a little in the Eye Morning and Evening, or dip a little Cotton in it, and apply it to the Corner of the Eye next the Nose.

23. *An approved Receipt for a Blast of the Eyes or Face.*

Take half a Handful of Houseleek, shred it small with a Knife, and put it into half a Pint of Cream; set it on the Fire in a Saucepan, and let it boil gently till it comes to an Oil. Anoint the Place affected often with this.

24. *To make a Water for the Face.*

Take three Quarters of a Pound of bitter Almonds, and blanch them; put half of them into a Mortar, and beat them very fine; then put to them half an Ounce of Mercury and an Ounce of Camphire: Beat these well together; then put in the rest of the Almonds, and pound them once more exceeding well.

Add to this a Quart of running Water, the same Quantity of white Wine, and three Quarters of a Pound of Loaf Sugar; let it stand all Night, and the next Morning strain it off. Put it in Bottles, and set it by for Use.

25. *A Wash for the Face.*

Take half a Pound of French Barley, and boil it in Spring Water; shift the Water three Times, and the last Time let it boil away from three Quarts to one; then strain it off, and put to it a Quart of white Wine, an Ounce of Rosemary Flowers, a third Part of a Pound of bitter Almonds blanched and beaten, and two Lemons cut in Slices, but without the Peel.

Let this stand two Days, then strain it off, and put to it four Pennyworth of Camphire, an Ounce of

Venice

Venice Talk, an Ounce of white Sugar-candy, two Ounces of white Lilly Roots clean wafhed and fliced, and a Shillingfworth of Spermaceti.

Keep out two or three Almonds to beat up with the Camphire and Spermaceti, or elfe they will not diffolve.

Wafh your Face every Morning with this Water, and at Night ufe the following Ointment.

26. *An Ointment for the Face.*

Take a white Lilly Root or two, wafh it, and boil it in Milk till it is foft; then take it out, fkin it, and beat it to a Pulp.

Get a hundred Snails, break the Shells, ftrew Salt upon them to purge them, and then boil them in Water; when they have boiled fome Time take them off to cool, and when cold fkim off the Fat.

To a Spoonful of this Fat add an Ounce of the Lilly Root, two Ounces of the Fat of Sheeps Guts laid in Water, and wafhed out in Rofe Water twice; twelve bitter Almonds blanched and beaten fine, half an Ounce of Oil of Tartar, fix Pennyworth of Spermaceti, the Whites of two Eggs beaten to a Froth; half an Ounce of Oil of fweet Almonds, and one Ounce of double-refined Sugar: Beat all thefe well together.

27. *To cure the Canker in the Mouth or any other Place.*

Take three Pints of Ale, fet it over the Fire, and when it boils fkim it carefully; then put to it a Handful of Selandine, and half a Dozen Leaves of Sage; boil it well till it taftes ftrong of the Herbs; then take them out, and fharpen it with Allum.

Boil this again till it comes to a Pint, and when cold put it up in a Bottle. Stop it clofe, and it will keep good a whole Year.

28. *A Poultice for a Swelling in the Neck or elfewhere.*

Take Melilot Flowers, Linfeed, and Althæa Roots, of each two Drams; boil them in a little Water till

it

it is confumed; then add a Quart of Milk, and two Pennyworth of white Bread, and boil them to the Confiftence of a Poultice.

To this add ten Grains of Saffron, and the Yolks of two Eggs beaten up in Oil of Rofes or Camomile, and mix them all well together.

Apply fome of this Poultice once a Day.

29. *To make black Salve.*

Take two Quarts of the beft Sallad Oil you can get, and add to it one Pound of red Lead, an Ounce of Turpentine, an Ounce of Caftile Soap, an Ounce of Burgamy Pitch, an Ounce of black Rofin, an Ounce of Bees Wax, and a Pound of white Lead.

Boil thefe together four Hours, ftirring it all the while.

It muft be made in an earthen Pan.

30. *To make a green Salve.*

Gather in the Heat of the Day young Bay Leaves and Wormwood of each Half a Quarter of a Pound, and red Sage and Rue of each a Quarter of a Pound; do not wafh them, but pick them clean, and beat them fmall in a Mortar.

Then take three Quarters of a Pound of the Suet of a Sheep juft killed, pick it clean, and fhred it fmall; add this to the Herbs in the Mortar, and pound them again till they are well mixed; then add a Quart of Oil, and work it all up with your Hands till the Oil is well incorporated; this done take it out of the Mortar, put it into an earthen Pan; cover it up clofe, and fet it by in a clofe Place for eight Days.

This done fet it over a Charcoal Fire, and let it boil gently four Hours; then add an Ounce of the Oil of Spike, and let it boil four Hours longer, or till it turns green, ftirring it frequently; then ftrain it through a new Canvas. Put it in a Gally-pot, ftop it clofe, and keep it for Ufe.

31. *A Salve for a Green Wound or Burn.*

Take a Pound and a Quarter of Oil, and half a Pound of red Lead, boil them together a little, and then take them off the Fire.

Then add by Degrees five Ounces of Bees Wax, two Pennyworth of Camphire, and as much beaten Chalk as will lie upon a Shilling.

When it is near cold spread some Oil thin upon a Sheet of white Paper, turn up the four Corners, and pour in the Salve; then roll it up in little Balls, and keep it for Use.

32. *A Salve to cure any Green Sore.*

Take Half a Pound of Rosin, a Pound of the best Venice Turpentine, a Pound of unwrought Wax, a Pound of Sheeps Suet fried, and eleven Spoonfuls of Sallad Oil; mix all these together, and melt them over the Fire in an earthen Pan.

Then take Smallage, Plantain, Orpin, and Buglofs, of each one Handful, and a large Handful of Mugwort; chop these small, grind them in a Mortar, and put them into the Liquor on the Fire.

Let them all boil together half an Hour, then take it off, and squeeze it through a new Canvas Strainer into a Gally-pot. Cover it up, and set it by for Use.

33. *Serjeant Pyle's (Serjeant-Surgeon to King Charles the Second, and King James) Limmentum Arces for Green Wounds and Wounds on the Head.*

Take of Gum Elemi an Ounce and a half, Venice Turpentine an Ounce and a half, Sheeps Suet two Ounces, and an Ounce of Hog's Lard; melt and mix these in an earthen Pipkin, and make it up as before directed.

34. *The Breast Salve.*

Take a Quart of Sweet Oil, half a Pound of white Lead, half a Pound of red Lead in fine Powder, and five Ounces of the best Castlle Soap cut in Pieces;

mix

mix them very well together, then fet it on the Fire in
an earthen Pipkin or Pot that holds a Gallon.

Let the Fire be fmall when you firft fet it on, and
let it fcimmer an Hour and a half, ftirring it all the
while with a Stick; then increafe the Fire, and boil
it till it comes to an Oil, taking Care to ftir it as before to prevent its boiling over.

When it is fo ftiff as not to ftick to your Fingers
oil a Difh, and pour it out by Degrees into the Difh,
work it up with your Hands into Rolls, and lay it
by for Ufe.

It muft not be too cold when you pour it out; and
it will be five Hours in doing.

This Salve is good for fore Breafts, Bruifes, Sprains
in the Back, the Dropfy, Gout, Boils, Impofthumes,
Green Wounds, and old Sores.

35. *The approved Gripe Water.*

Take an Ounce of Rhubarb, flice it thin, and dry
it by the Fire, then powder it very fine, and put it
into a Quart of the beft Brandy.

The Quantity to be given at a Time is, to a Man
four Spoonfuls, to a Woman three, and to a Child lefs
according to its Years and Strength.

Repeat this every fix Hours, firft fhaking the Bottle,
and it will foon drive away the Complaint.

36. *A Powder for the Worms.*

Take Wormfeed, Fennygreek, Aloes, St. John's-
grafs, burnt Hartfhorn, and Sea-wort, of each an
equal Quantity finely powdered; Flour of Brimftone
half the Quantity of the reft, with three Times the
Quantity of the whole of powdered Sugar.

To a Child of two Years old may be given half a
Dram, and to one that is older the Quantity may be
increafed.

It muft be given the Day before the Full of the
Moon in a Spoonful of Sack, and the two Mornings
following; drinking an Hour after it a Pint of thin
Water-gruel.

37. *An-*

37. *Another for the same.*

Take prepared Coraline, Hartſhorn, Wormſeed, and Rhubarb, of each a like Quantity, finely powdered.

Let as much of this be given as will lie upon a Six-pence three Mornings together faſting.

38. *To ſtop a Looſeneſs.*

Let there be a Quarter of an Ounce of Cloves boiled in two Quarts of Water till it comes to three Pints, with a Cruſt of white Bread in it; then ſtrain it off, and ſweeten it with double-refined Sugar.

Drink half a Pint at a Time, and repeat this as often as you pleaſe.

39. *To preſerve Roſes to purge.*

Take a Quantity of Damaſk Roſe Buds, and clip off the white Part; then take to every Pound of Roſes three Pounds of fine Sugar, and one Quart of Roſe Water.

Have ready upon the Fire a Pot of boiling Water; put the Roſes and Water into a Pitcher, ſtop it down cloſe, and ſet it in the Pot; let it remain there till the Roſes are boiled tender, then take out the Pitcher, unſtop it, and put in half the Sugar; ſtop it up again, put it into the Pot, and let it boil a little longer.

When it has boiled ſome Time put in the reſt of the Sugar, then give it another boil, and when you take it up ſqueeze in the Juice of ſome Lemons thro' a Sieve.

A ſmall Quantity of this in a Morning will be ſufficient for a Doſe, which operates without occa-ſioning Sickneſs.

40. *A Remedy for Giddineſs in the Head.*

Take three Drops of Oil of Lillies of the Valley, roll it in a little fine Sugar, and make it into Pills.

Take

Take three or four of thefe when you find it coming on.

41. *Another for the fame.*

Take half an Ounce of Mofs Powder, two Nutmegs baked in a Loaf and powdered, a little Orrice
Powder, a Quarter of an Ounce of Benjamin, half as
much Frankincenfe, and the fame Quantity of Brud
Seed; beat all thefe together, and ftrew them on the
fore Part of the Head every Morning and Evening.
When the Dizzinefs comes on air your Cap over Benjamin, and with a Funnel let fome of its Smoak up
your Noftrils.

42. *A Medicine for a Cold.*

Take a few Raifins of the Sun, and ftone them; add
a little Conferve of red Rofes, fome white Sugar-
candy, four Drops of Oil of Vitriol, and as much Oil
of Sulphur; beat all thefe in a Mortar till they come
to an Electuary.

Take the Quantity of a Nutmeg every Night going
to Bed.

43. *Lozenges for a Cough.*

Take a Pound of brown Sugar-candy and a Pound
of Loaf Sugar, beat them well, and fift them through
a very fine Tiffany Sieve.

Then take an Ounce of the Juice of Liquorice, mix
with it three or four Spoonfuls of Hyffop Water, and
fet it over a gentle Fire to fcimmer a little.

Then take the Sugar-candy and Sugar, one Dram
of Orrice Powder, and half a Dram of Gum Dragon
beaten very fine; add a Dram of Powder of Elecampane, a Dram of the Spirit of Annifeed, and two
Grains of Mufk.

Mix all thefe well together with the Juice of Liquorice and Hyffop Water, and add as much more
of the latter as will make it into a ftiff Pafte.

This done roll them into little Balls, and keep them
in a dry Place for Ufe.

44. *For*

44. *For the same by Dr. Beaufort.*

Take two Ounces of the Oil of Sweet Almonds, three Drams of Hail's Powder, a Dram and a half of Gum Arabick, a Dram and a half of Diacodium, and three Drams of Aquamirabilis.

Mix all thefe very well together, and make them into a Linctus.

A Spoonful is to be taken frequently when the Cough troubles you.

Take Milk Water two Ounces, compound Rofe Water two Drams, and Diacodium fix Drams; mix all thefe together for a Draught, and when afflicted drink it at Night going to Bed.

45. *For a Chin-Cough.*

Roaft what Quantity of Eggs you pleafe till the Whites begin to be hardifh; then break the Tops of the Eggs, pour out the Yolks, and fill up the Vacancies with white Sugar-candy powdered very fine.

This done cover the Holes again with Pieces of the Whites, put them in a clean earthen Difh, and fet it in hot Wood Afhes for fome Time.

Be careful to fave all the Liquor that runs from them, and give a Spoonful of it at a Time to the Child thus afflicted.

46. *Another for the fame.*

Take a Quarter of a Pound of brown Sugar-candy, and beat it fmall; put to it a Quarter of a Pint of Aqua Vitæ, fet it on the Fire in an earthen Pipkin, and boil it to a Syrup.

Then take it off, and add to it half a Pint of the Juice of Alehoof.

Give the Child a Spoonful of this four or five Times a Day.

SECT.

S E C T. IX.

Of Diforders of Cattle, and their Re-medies.

A R T. I. *For the Meazles in Swine.*

MIX together a Quart of ftale Urine, and Half a Pound of Derbyfhire Reddle, which they fell at the Colour-Shops, and many call Red-Oaker.

Stir this well together, and when it is perfectly mixed, pour upon it a Gallon of fweet and good Whey made warm.

Keep the Hog fafting all Night, and give him this in the Morning.

The Sweetnefs of the Whey will make the reft go down, and it is a certain Remedy. The Hog will leave fome of the Grounds at the Bottom, but that is no Matter; it is not defigned that he fhould fwallow all the Reddle that is mixt in the Urine, only the fineft and lighteft Part of it: And this never fails to go down, for the whole Liquor keeps of a thick red to the laft.

2. *For the Sleep or Evil.*

This is a Diforder which affects Swine in the Summer Months, and has very bad Confequences if not taken in Time; for they always neglect their Food when they are troubled with this Diforder; and confequently they ftarve and pine.

They are known to have it not only by their continual fleeping in the Middle of the Day, but by their Droufinefs and poor look at all other Times.

The Method of Cure is this:

Pick

Pick a good Quantity of the fmall Stone Crop which grow on old Walls; it has yellow Flowers, and is very fharp to the Tafte. Let the Farmer take Care to gather the right, for there are feveral Sorts, and this is the only one that has the right Virtue.

Bruife a good deal of this, and fqueeze out the Juice; mix it with fome warm Mafh, and give it the Hog early in the Morning, after he has been fhut up all Night without Victuals.

He will eat this freely, and it will prefently make him very fick.

He will Caft very much, and his Stomach being cleanfed, the Diforder will leave him.

If once does not do, let him have the fame again the next Day; and it rarely fails.

SECT. X.

Of the Garden and Orchard.

IN the beginning of this Month, we gave the Houfekeeper an Account of what would be the Produce of the Garden in its feveral Kinds: we are now to mention the proper Work to be done in it toward the latter Part of this Month, to prepare for the Products of the next: For according to that Care, they will be both in Quantity and Quality.

The Kitchen Garden being the moft material, in refpect of our Plan, we fhall confider that firft.

The Crop is in a Manner all in the Ground, and every Thing is growing a-pace.

The Gardiner muft remember that the fame Heat and Moifture which fet his Beans, Peafe, and other Products fo faft into growth, will have the fame Effect upon the Weeds. Thefe are a Kind of Hydras, or many headed Monfters, that till very

thorough

thorough Care is taken, rife the fafter for being cut up.

The Reafon is this : Many of the Roots and Fragments of Roots of the Perennial Kind remain ; fome of which have been dug in deep, and lain long quiet; but in the frefh Digging of the Borders, come near the Air again, and grow ; for Weeds are not like ufeful Plants that require Care and Attendance : The leaft Piece will fhoot, and fcarce any Thing deftroys them.

Befide thefe, the Wind brings in the Seeds of the Red-Nettle, Groundfell, the Wild-Oraches, and many others, which taking Advantage of the new dug Ground, fhoot up inftantly, and grow quick.

Thefe muft be hoed up as faft as they grow ; and in this let the careful Gardiner obferve, that he may at the fame Time, give a great deal of Strength to his Plant, by breaking the Surface of the Ground : Therefore inftead of fhaving the Weeds off as too many do, let him always cut with a Stroke flanting downwards, and thus he will more effectually deftroy them ; and in this Ground made rich already, by Digging and Manure, he will cut in two or three Inches, and make a fine new Surface ready to receive the Dews.

When he has got all his Borders clean, and in Order, let him think of *fowing*, *planting*, and *tranf-planting*.

As to Sowing, we have obferved already, that what he has to do on that Head, is not very much.

A fecond Crop of Brocoli may be very well fown now ; and if the Weather be not too hot and dry, fome Turnips in a fhady Place, will come up quick, and very foon grow for the Table.

A Crop of French Beans, fhould be fown alfo at this Time, and all the Kinds of Lettuces ; for there will thus be a Succeffion of them ripening for the Table, one after the other.

Young Salleting may be ftill fown, but few much regard it at this Seafon.

'Tis very valuable when there is little elfe for the Supply of the Table ; but that is not the Cafe now, there is a Plenty of every Thing of the large Kind. The Middle of *June* is a very good Time for the Planting out thofe Sweet Herbs, which have been fown for the Ufe of the Kitchen.

They are now of a Bignefs to bear removing ; and there will be the Summer before them for Encreafe.

They fhould be planted at a good Diftance from one another, and fhaded from the Sun, and watered in Evenings, till they have taken Root.

The Cabbage and Savoy Plants, fown in the early Months, will now be fit for removing ; and there will be very proper Places for them.

The Gardiner has cleaned all his Ground, and there will be the Intervals between his Beans, and fome other early Crops very happily ready to receive his Plants of this Kind.

They will do better thus, than if tranfplanted into a clean Bed ; for the Stalks of the Beans and other Plants, will fhade them till they have taken Root ; and then by that Time they want any Share of Nourifhment, thefe will be ready to come up.

The pulling up the Bean Stalks will be like digging the Ground about thefe Plants ; for every Thing that breaks the Ground anfwers this Purpofe, and they will flourifh upon it greatly, and get into a fine Forwardnefs for fupplying the Kitchen in Winter.

The early fown Endive will now alfo be ready for tranfplanting, and there muft be a chofen Piece of Ground for this Purpofe : It muft be fomewhat fhaded, and moift. They muft here be planted at a moderate Diftance, and they will be quickly fit for blanching.

Toward

Toward the End of *June* alfo, is the proper
Time for planting out Chardoons for the laft Time ;
and in this, regard muft be had to the Nature of the
Plant, and the particular Management it requires.

It is very large, and it is to be blanched to a great
Height. For this Reafon, it muft ftand in a Bed of
rich and light Mould, and muft be placed at a great
Diftance, one Plant from another.

Four Foot is the proper Diftance, and as it rifes
the Earth muft be carefully hoed up to cover the
Stalks ; on this will depend their fine Colour, and
their delicate Flavour. When Chardoons are not
well blanched, they look Dirty, and eat Coarfe.

If we caft our Eye from the profitable Garden
to that for Pleafure, we are to tell the Gardiner, that
a great deal is to be done there this Month.

All the Annual Flowers that have not before been
removed from their Seed Beds, are now to be fet out
into the Places where they are to remain.

The Evening is the propereft Time of the Day for
this Purpofe ; and the Gardiner fhould always con-
trive his Work fo that the laft Hour of the Day be
employed on this Bufinefs.

Let him make good Holes for the Reception of
thefe Plants ; remove them with good Balls of Earth
about them, and place them carefully in. Then let
him give them a gentle Watering, to fix the Earth
to their Roots ; and if the Sun be powerful the next
Day let them be fhaded at Noon.

A little Care at this Time, gives the Garden a
great deal of Beauty in the fucceeding Months. Thefe
Plants are tender, fo that a little Matter hurts them ;
but this is the laft Accident to which they are expofed ; if they efcape Damage upon their removing,
they will grow very faft : They are very apt to droop
for a Time if not well managed ; but if this be too
much, they will never recover it afterwards.

The fibrous rooted Plants have now made their
Shoots from the Root, fo this is the beft Time for
making Layers for propagating them.

Carnations

Carnations are propagated this Way ; as alfo Sweet Williams, and all that Kind of Plants.

Carnations are now coming into Flower, and a great deal of Care is to be taken of the finer Kinds, for no Flower is fo fubject to Injuries.

Nothing is fo common as their being deftroyed by Earwigs; therefore let the Pots be carefully fearched for Vermin. Ants are very common about them, and will do a great deal of Damage.

As the Florift obferves them coming into Bloom, let him fnip the Ends of the Flower-Cup, which the vulgar Gardiners call the Pod, in about five Places at equal Diftances; this will make the Flower open regularly.

When Carnations are left to themfelves, they often open all on one Side, and never difplay themfelves properly afterwards.

They are naturally a Flower that continues a good while, but they may be made to ftand twice their natural Time by good Management.

To this Purpofe they muft be defended from Wet, and from the extreme Violence of the Sun. The common Contrivance for this Purpofe is a Covering of Glafs : This very well defends the Flower from Rain ; but inftead of preferving it from the Sun, it gives that greater Power, the Heat of the Noon Sun in *July*, through a Glafs being fcorching.

I have feen many a fine Flower that would have ftood a great while if left to itfelf, burnt up prefently by this Defign to preferve it. Some Years fince Mr. Willis who was famous for his Carnations, at Bath, invented the eafy Method of ufing oiled Paper inftead of Glafs, and feveral here followed it. 'Tis fo commodious, cheap and eafy, and anfwers both the Purpofes fo well, that I wonder every one does not follow it.

This oiled Paper perfectly well keeps off the Wet, and is not fubject to fcorch up the Plants with the Sun.

Thofe

Thofe Flowers which are propagated by Cuttings, are now to be put into the Ground. The Perennial Afters, Scarlet Lychnis, and fuch others, are to be raifed this Way. They muft be planted in a rich Soil, and a Situation not too much expofed ; and they muft be fhaded at firft, and after that watered at Times, till they have taken good Root.

All the Spring Flowers are now paft, and their Roots fhould be taken up.

Some of thefe will not bear to be kept out of the Ground any long Time, as the Futillary, Dogs Tooth, Perfian Iris, and the like ; thefe fhould be now taken up, and foon put into the Ground again where they are intended to Flower the next Spring ; and the others are to be taken up and preferved out of the Ground, till the Time of Planting them again in the End of Autumn. The Tulips, and fuch others, muft be carefully cleaned from Filth ; and hung up in Bags in a fhady Place.

Many keep them in Boxes and Drawers, but there is Danger in this Practice, for Rats and Mice are extreamly fond of them, and often get at them.

Toward the End of this Month, the Gardiner muft again go over his Fruit Trees with a careful Eye: Whenever he fees the Fruit ftand too thick, he muft thin it again, always keeping it in his Mind that one good Peach is worth two ftarved ones, either for the Table or the Market ; and that it is much more to his Credit to have a fmall Number of Fruit, than his Trees crowded with fuch as are not worth gathering.

Let him rub off the firft Rudiments of all ftrait forward Shoots, and of any others that grow irregularly ; but this is all he muft do : It is a bad Time of the Year to do any Thing with the Knife.

Where the Fruit upon the Wall Trees ftands too much expofed to the Sun, it will be proper to draw over fome Leaves by Way of a Covering for them. This was their Intent in Nature, and as we fpread

out

out Wall Trees unnaturally to the Sun, we fhould have a regard to this, where we leave them too much expofed.

Care muft be taken to keep the Ground about the Roots of the Trees clear from Weeds, as well as that where ufeful Plants or Flowers grow.

We have explained the Occafion, and the Nature of this in the Directions for laft Month, and the fame holds good here.

Some pull them up by Hand, but hoeing is the better Practice; becaufe it anfwers the Purpofe of a flight Digging about the Roots at the fame Time.

Whenever there happens a fhower this Month, let the Gardiner be fure to vifit his Wall Fruit, and look carefully after Snails; as alfo Mornings and Evenings, in the fame Manner as in the preceding Month.

Particular Care muft be taken this Month, of the new planted Trees.

They muft have fome Water given them at Times, and Mulch fhould be laid about their Roots, that they be always kept in a Condition of growing, by the moift Temper of the Ground.

The Vines are fuch luxuriant Growers, that they muft be looked after carefully. All fide Shoots, and ill placed Branches muft be taken off. If any of their long Branches be got loofe from the Wall, as they frequently will be, they muft be nailed up; and Regard muft be had to the Bunches, to give them all the Advantages of Ripening.

Thefe require a great deal of Sun, and the Leaves of the Vine are fo large, that often they too much fhade them. It is frequently neceffary to clear thefe away in fome Places, as it is to draw the Leaves of other Fruit Trees over the Fruit.

The Grapes if they are not favoured in this Manner by the Art and Conduct of the Gardiner, not only ripen poorly, but never attain to their full rich and Winey Flavour.

THE

THE
COOK, HOUSEKEEPER's,
AND
GARDINER's COMPANION.

J U L Y.

SECT. I.
Of Provisions.

A Bill of Fare for the Month of July.

Fish, Flesh, and Fowl, as in the last Month.

CHAP. I.
Of Garden-Stuff.

ART I. *Of Greens and Roots.*

THE Garden at this Season affords in a Manner all its Stores ; Cauliflowers are in great Perfection, and there are fine Cabbages.

Lettuces are in their great Perfection, and they are plentiful ; the Cos and other fine Kinds for Sallads, and the Cabbage and the like of that Sort, for Soops and Stewing.

Small Salleting is to be had, but it is lefs regarded, becaufe the fine Cos Lettuce of this Season is fo much more efteemed ; indeed the young Salleting is not only

best

beſt in Spring from its Novelty, but in its Nature; it may be had all the Year round by Hot-Beds and other Arts, but it is never ſo fine, tender, and delicate, as at the natural Seaſon.

With Care the Table may be ſupplied in *July* alſo with Celeri and Endive; and for thoſe who have the Italian Manner of eating, there is Trinachia: There is alſo Spinach, and in general the ſweet Herbs for Soups and Seaſoning are at this Time in their greateſt Perfection.

The Roots in Seaſon are Carrots and Turnips, Onions, Garlick and Rocambole, Scorzona and Salſafie, and the Red Beet; which laſt many eat in the Manner of a Carrot, to boiled Beef and other Meats, and tho' inſipid, it is not unpleaſant, and makes a Variety.

Horſe-Radiſh is fine at this Time, and there are Potatoes very mealy and delicate; and thoſe who chuſe to continue the Spring Products in their Gardens, may have Radiſhes.

The Fruits of the Kitchen Garden we ſhall alſo ſpeak of under this Head; thoſe of the Orchard come in ſeparate. Beans, Peaſe, and Kidney Beans are now in their prime Perfection, and make a very good Appearance at Table. Artichokes continue in perfect good Seaſon, and Cucumbers and Mellons are in great Perfection.

There is alſo another Fruit that juſt comes in Seaſon in *July*, this is the Tornato, uſed by many in Soups, and very well deſerving to be brought into univerſal Practice.

2. *Fruits for the Deſert.*

There is no Month in which the Deſert may be ſo largely or ſo well furniſhed as *July* with fruits, nor any in which they come ſo plentifully into the Service of the Kitchen or Confectionary.

Cherries are in their great Perfection, the large Dukes, the Heart, and the Carnation Cherries are in
their

their Perfection, and the Black Cherries begin to come in. The Kentifh Cherry is alfo now very fine, and excells many of the others for various Ufes ; and for curious Deferts, the Amber Heart and White Spanifh are now to be had in their prime Order.

Apricots are come in now, and the common Kind is getting to its Ripenefs. This, to be eaten in its Perfection, fhould be gathered juft as it begins to mellow ; before this Time it is hard and four, and after this it grows mealy ; no Fruit is fo particularly fixed to a Time of gathering. For thofe who are curious in Fruits, the Algier and Turkey Apricot may be had alfo now, and the Buda Kind is a very fine one.

The early Peaches are alfo come in now, the Nutmeg Peach may be had in Plenty, the brown and the white ; and there are fome other of the early ones that juft now begin to ripen.

This is an early Seafon for Nectarines, but there is one Kind that toward the End of *July* may be had, it is called Fairchild's early Nutmeg Nectarine.

Plumbs are coming in, and fome Kinds will fhew their beautiful Bloom upon the Table, and be fit for eating The Orleans Plumb, which our People call the Arline, begins to ripen, the Violet Plumb is well ripened, and the Morocco Plumb, may be had in good Perfection from a favourable Situation.

Strawberries are yet in Seafon, and particularly the nicer Kinds ; the white and green are now in their Perfection ; and the Chili Strawberries are alfo at this Seafon ripe ; thefe are not very common, but they deferve to be more introduced into Gardens ; they will ftand very well, and their Fruit exceeds the Hoboy very much in Size.

Laftly, to name Apples and Pears ; they are now to be had of feveral Kinds as they come in Succeffion. The Codling is now in fine Condition, the white Juneating continues very fine, and the Summer Cofting, and the Summer Pearmaine. The John Apple is yet fine, as are alfo the Stone Pippin, and the Oaken Pippin.

N°. XXII.   4 L   For

For Pears, the Jargonelle and Orange Musk are now in their fine Season; as also the Primitive Pear, the Robin Pear, and the Muscade, a small but very agreeable one. These serve the Desert, and there may be even till this Time, some of the Winter Pears preserved for baking, if the Housekeeper have been careful; the most likely Kinds are the Worcester Pear, and that which the Gardiners call Lord Cheynes Green.

SECT. II.

Of COOKERY.

CHAP. I.

Of Roasting.

ART. I. *To roast a Chicken the Polish Way.*

CUT a Quantity of fine fat Bacon for larding, and cut also four Anchovies, taking out the Bones.

Chuse a fine Chicken, and when picked and drawn lard it carefully with the Bacon and Anchovies, a Piece of one and a Piece of another; and when this is done, strew over the whole a Quantity of Sweet Herbs, and Spices shred and mixed together.

Cut the Liver of the Chicken small, and mix with it some Parsley, three Truffles, a Slice of Bacon minced small, the Yolks of two Eggs, and a Blade of Mace pounded; mix all this well together, then strew in a very little Pepper and Salt; when all is perfectly well mixed, fill the Body of the Chicken with it, and lay it down to roast at a moderate Distance from a very good Fire.

When

When the Chicken is half done heat a clean Fire-ſhovel till it is juſt red hot, then let it cool till the Redneſs is gone off, and put into it three or four ſquare Pieces of fat Bacon; the Heat of the Shovel will make the Bacon run, and this is to drop over the Chicken by Way of baſting.

A great deal of Care muſt be taken in this Article; if there be the leaſt Foulneſs on the Fire-ſhovel it will come off with the Bacon and black the Chicken, or if the Shovel be too hot it will make the Bacon run too thin, and burn: The Intent is, that the Heat of the Shovel be juſt enough to let the Bacon melt for the dripping upon the Fowl, and when well managed it gets this Way a very peculiar and fine Flavour.

When it is well done, ſend it up with the following Sauce:

⁎ *Sauce for the Poliſh Chicken.*

Chop two Spoonfuls of Capers very fine, then chop a large Spoonful of young Parſley, ſome Chives, and a ſplit Anchovy boned.

Strew over theſe ſome Pepper and Salt, grate on a little Nutmeg, and mix the whole perfectly well to-gether.

Squeeze into a ſmall Sauce-boat a good Lemon, take out the Pips, put in a Tea Spoonful of Baſket Salt, and two large Spoonfuls of Oil; beat theſe well up together, then put in the Capers and the reſt of the minced Meat; ſtir all well together, and ſend it up with the Chicken.

Some pour this over the Chicken, but it is beſt ſent up ſeparate.

2. *To roaſt a Partridge larded.*

Pick and draw a Brace of Partridges; cut ſome very fine Bacon for larding, and having gently blanched the Partridges lard them carefully with thin Slices of the Bacon.

Cover them with Paper after they are ſpitted, and lay them down to a gentle Fire: Let them continue

at

at fome Diftance till they are foaked well, and then ftir up the Fire, take off the Paper, and brown them handfomely.

This is the Way they eat Partridges in France, and they have a Mellownefs and Flavour much beyond ours.

3. *To roaft Plover.*

Plover are to be dreffed as Woodcocks, without drawing, and the Method now ufed by the beft Cooks is this:

Pick them clean, blanch them, and lard them with fine Bacon cut very fmall for that Purpofe; lay them down to a moderate Fire, and make a Toaft of a Round of a Three-penny Loaf with the Cruft cut off, lay this in the Dripping-pan, and when the Plover are done fend them up with the Toaft.

4. *To roaft a Turkey Pout larded.*

Chufe a fine, well-grown Pout, not too young, and yet not fo large as for the Flefh to be hard; let it be picked, drawn, and truffed: Cut out fome fine Bacon into pretty large Pieces for larding, lard the Turkey Pout carefully with this, and fpit it; cover it with Paper, and lay it down at a Diftance before a good Fire to foak well.

When it is near done take off the Paper, brown it, and ferve it up hot.

5. *To roaft young Rabbits.*

Let a Couple of nice, well-grown, but young Rabbits, be fkinned, gutted, and blanched; then rub them over with a Piece of fat Bacon warmed for that Purpofe, and lard them handfomely with thick Pieces of fine Bacon; fpit them together double, and roaft them before a very good Fire, and fend them up brown.

Few People would imagine the Difference there is between a Couple of Rabbits done in this Way and a fingle one; there is a Mellownefs in them when

roafted

roafted double that they have not otherwife, and many People prefer them this Way to a fingle Leveret.

6. *To roaft Larks.*

Pick a Dozen of Larks, and trufs them, but do not draw them, finge them carefully with white Paper, and put them upon Skewers with Bacon round them cut in thin Slices.

Tie them to a Spit, and lay them down to a good Fire: When they are near done throw over them fome very fine Crumbs of Bread.

7. *To roaft Venifon the Italian Way.*

Put into a large Soup Difh fome Vinegar, fweet Herbs, and Spices, with a Bay Leaf and a Stick of Cinnamon both broken. Set this by.

Lay the Venifon that is to be roafted upon a large Gridiron placed high over a very ftrong and clear Fire, turn it till it is well blanched, then throw it into the Soup Difh hot from the Fire; turn it about three or four Times while it is cooling, and when thoroughly cold take it out for larding.

While the Venifon is in the Liquor cut fome Bacon out into large Pieces for larding, and when it is taken out lard it all over very carefully, then fpit it, and cover it with large thin Slices of fat Bacon, and wrap Paper over the whole.

Thus prepared lay it down to the Fire, and bafte it well with the Liquor out of the Soup Difh.

When it is done fend it up with Powrade, a Sauce made with Pepper, as we have before directed; but for thofe who like fweet Sauce fome fhould be fent up alfo in a Bafon.

8. *To roaft a fmall Kid.*

Chufe for this Purpofe a fmall fat Kid, let it be fkinned and truffed, then throw it into warm Water to blanch it.

While this is doing cut out a good Quantity of fine Bacon for larding; when the Kid is blanched

and

and cold lard it all over, and fpit it, lay it down to a found good Fire, at a moderate Diftance, covered with Paper.

When it is near done take off the Paper, and ftrew fome very fine Crumbs of Bread all over it; brown it up, and ferve it in hot with fome Green Sauce, garnifhing the Difh with a good Quantity of frefh-gathered Water-creffes.

9. *To roaft Ortolans with Eggs.*

Beat up half a Dozen Yolks of Eggs with a very little Bafket Salt.

Pick the Ortolans, cut off the Claws, and take out the Eyes; this done put them upon a Silver Skewer, tie them to the Spit, and lay them down to a very brifk Fire at a moderate Diftance; fprinkle them from Time to Time with the beaten Eggs, and let them get a very good Colour.

See the Difh be hot, and that they be fent up quite hot.

10.   *To roaft young Pigeons Ortolan Fafhion.*

Chufe four very young tame Pigeons from the Neft before they have Feathers for flying, cut off the Heads, pick them, draw them, and blanch them; and let all this be done fpeedily, fo that they may be upon the Table within an Hour after they are out of the Neft.

Beat up the Yolks of four Eggs with a little Salt; cut off the Ends of the Feet, and then wrap every Pigeon quite round in a thin Slice of very fat Bacon.

Round this wrap a Couple of frefh-gathered Vine Leaves, and then fpit them, and lay them down to a good Fire, tying the Leaves on when they are fpitted.

When they are near done take off the Leaves and the Bacon, fprinkle the Pigeons well feveral Times over with the beaten Eggs, and brown them up. Send them to Table hot without any Sauce, and they will be very much approved.

11. *To*

11. *To roaſt Chickens ſtuffed.*

Chuſe a Couple of fine fatted and well-grown Chickens, pick them, draw them, ſinge them, and lay them ready for ſtuffing.

Cut the Livers into ſmall minced Meat, chop two large Spoonfuls of Parſley, and grate two Ounces of Bacon; cut a Dozen young Onions as ſmall as the Parſley, mix all theſe together, then ſtrew on a little Pepper and Salt; grate over all ſome Nutmeg, and add a few Leaves of ſweet Herbs picked clean off and not cut, half a Blade of Mace, and one Clove bruiſed.

When this is all well mixed together, ſtuff the Bodies of the Chickens with it.

Then ſet on a large Stewpan, put in ſome freſh Butter, ſome whole Parſley, a Bunch of young Onions, and ſome ſweet Herbs cut; throw in the Chickens ready ſtuffed, and roll and toſs them about.

Then take them out, ſpit them, and cover them with thin Slices of fat Bacon, lay them down to a good Fire covered with Paper, and when they are well done make a rich Sauce of Gravy, or cover them with a rich Raggoo, which is the true Way.

12. *To roaſt Chickens with Anchovy Sauce.*

Chuſe a Couple of fine large Chickens perfectly tender and young, pick them, draw them, truſs them, and ſinge them.

Cut the Livers to Pieces, and mix ſome Bacon and ſweet Herbs with them, and adding a Piece of Butter ſtuff the Bodies with this.

Then lay them down to roaſt.

Waſh eight right Gorgona Anchovies, for if they be not of the fineſt Kind the Diſh will be ſpoiled, cut two of them very ſmall, ſplit the reſt, take out the Bones, and lay them in Readineſs.

Set on a Saucepan with ſome rich Gravy, ſqueeze in a large Lemon, and throw in a Roll of the Peel of another

another Lemon, not that which was fqueezed, for the Flavour of that will be loft by the fqueezing; when thefe are hot together throw in the minced Anchovy, and let the whole ftew a few Minutes.

When the Chickens are done lay them in a Difh, lay the Slices of Anchovy upon them, and pour carefully over them the Sauce: If the Slices be wafhed off by pouring on the Sauce, lay them handfomely on, and fend it up.

C H A P. II.

Of Boiling.

A R T. I. *To boil a Pike crimp'd.*

CHUSE a very large Pike, take it directly from the Water, fcale it, gut it, cut off the Head, and crimp it.

All this muft be done in a few Minutes after it is out of the Water, or it will not be worth any Thing.

The Crimping is to be done with a fharp Knife in the following Manner.

Cut the Flefh, and cut through the back Bone firft of all at an Inch below the Head; cut the Body thro' except a very little at the lower Part, that when all is done the whole may hang together.

The firft Cut being thus made, do the fame at an Inch Diftance, and the like at every Inch till within a Hand's Breadth of the Tail.

Every Cut muft be made like the firft, going thro' the Back Bone, and through all the Flefh of the Fifh, only leaving enough entire at the Bottom for its holding together.

This being done, throw the Fifh into a large Veffel of Well Water juft drawn.

The whole Crimping may be done in two Minutes by a fkilful Hand, and on this depends the Excellence of the Fifh, for being cut thus quick, and hardened

by

by the cold Water, it will eat as firm as the Kernel of a Nut.

Set on a Pot with a great deal of Water, throw in a Handful of Bay Salt, and a Quarter of a Pint of Vinegar.

The Head and the Tail of the Fifh, which were cut off, when it was crimped are to be put into the Water as foon as it boils and has been fkimmed, and the Head is to be fplit open.

When thefe have boiled five Minutes put in the Crimp, either entire, or cut into feparate Slices, by going through the Piece that was left to hold them together.

Put in the Melt with the Crimps, and let it boil a Quarter of an Hour.

Then warm a large Difh, take out the Head and Tail, and drain them, then lay them in the Middle of the Difh.

Take up the Slices, and drain them, and lay them round the Head and Tail.

While the Fifh is laying in the Difh let the Sauce be got ready.

Draw a Pound of Butter with a Spoonful of Water, and let it be as thick as Cream, then fqueeze in a Lemon, and drop in a few Pieces of Horferadifh fcraped very fine, and juft wetted with Vinegar; pour this over the Fifh, and take Care to fend it up hot.

This is one of thofe elegant Difhes which we recommend to the genteel Tables, becaufe it cofts no more than the plaineft Way of doing the fame Fifh; and we can affure them, thofe who never tafted Pike this Way do not know how excellent a Fifh it is.

There are in Whitlefea Moor, and fome other Places, very large Pearch, which I have ordered to be dreffed in the fame Way, and there is hardly any Fifh, River or Sea, that comes up to them.

We owe the Invention of crimping of Pike to the Dutch, but few here would approve their Sauce; it is only oiled Butter; they melt it gently over the

N°. XXII.   4 M   Fire,

Fire, ftir it about with a Ladle, and fo pour a Quart of it over the Fifh.

Thofe who have eat Pike in Holland, and diflike this Method, yet allow the Fifh tafted to a Miracle.

The proper Garnifh for this Difh is raw Parfley wafhed and chopped a little, but not cut very fmall.

2. *To boil Salmon crimp'd.*

There is little Difference in the Method of doing this from that we have defcribed for the Pike ; but the leaft Things muft be obferved in this Art, or the Cook will find her Difhes fpoiled, and not know what does the Mifchief.

This is only to be done in the Salmon Countries to Perfection, but if a good frefh Salmon be chofen in London, it will be found much preferable to the common Way.

Let the Fifh be fcaled and gutted, cut off the Head and the Tail, and cut the Body through at once into Slices an Inch and half thick ; have a large Pan of Pump Water fet by you, and as the Slices are cut throw them in ; then when they are all in ftrew a Handful of Bay Salt over the Surface of the Water, ftir it about, and take out the Fifh.

Set on a large deep Stewpan, boil the Head and Tail, but do not fplit the Head, put in fome Salt, but no Vinegar ; and when thefe have boiled ten Minutes fkim the Water very clean, and put in the Slices ; when they are boiled enough take them out, and while they are draining make fome Shrimp Sauce to fend up with them.

The Head and Tail are to lie in the Middle of the Difh, the Slices are to be placed regularly round them, and the whole is to be garnifhed with whole Leaves of Parfley.

3. *To boil Plaife au Court Bouillon.*

Plaife are at this Time in the Height of their Perfection ; they are a cheap Fifh, and being dreffed in
the

the Way of the Court Bouillon they are an excellent and an elegant Diſh.

The Reader is not to be frighted at the Name of this French Method, for we ſhall, as in other Inſtances, ſhew how it is to be done at a moderate Expence: We ſhall not ſpare our Cook any Trouble, but we ſhall ſhew that the beſt Diſhes, with due Care, may be dreſſed with little Coſt.

Chuſe four large and thick Plaiſe, waſh them, gut them, and wipe them dry.

Strew over the Bottom of a Stewpan ſome ſhred Parſley, and a few Slices of Onion.

Upon this lay the Plaiſe, then ſtrew ſome Pepper and Salt upon them, and put over them ſome more Parſley and Onions, a Couple of Bay Leaves broken, ſome Chives, and ſome Slices of Lemon cut very thin with the Peel; laſt of all ſprinkle over them ſome Leaves of ſweet Baſil cut very ſmall, and a ſmall Piece of a Blade of Mace ſhred fine with a Pair of Sciſſars.

Upon theſe Ingredients gently pour half a Pint of white Wine, the ſame Quantity of Vinegar, and as much Water as will make this cover them moderately.

Set them over a Stove with a gentle Heat, and let them ſtew till they are enough; then take off the Stewpan, but do not at firſt take out the Fiſh, let them lie in the Liquor that they may be well reliſhed with it, and the mean while prepare the Sauce.

Split and bone a Couple of waſhed Anchovies, and ſhred them ſmall; melt ſome Butter with Pepper and Salt, and two whole Chives; add the Anchovies, take out the Chives, and put in a little Flour to thicken it: Turn it over the Stove.

Take the Fiſh out of the Liquor, let them drain, and lay them in the Diſh; then pour the Sauce over them.

They are thus a very high-flavoured Diſh.

The

The expenfive Way is to add a large Quantity of Cullis of Cray-fifh to the Sauce ; but this is not needful ; the Sauce we have directed is very good alone, and if any chufe to enrich it, fome good Gravy will do very well in the Place of it.

We have directed the Manner of doing this Crayfifh Cullis in a former Part of this Work, fo that fuch as chufe the expenfive Way will there find the Method of doing it in the greateft Perfection ; but we here propofe what will anfwer perfectly well without fuch Charge.

4. *To boil a fmall Turbot au Court Bouillon with Caper Sauce.*

This is another of thofe Difhes that are elegant in their Kind, and yet come within the Compafs of a moderate Table.

A fmall Turbot is to be bought cheap, and this Way is very fine.

Gut it, wafh it, and dry it in a fine Napkin, then cover the Bottom of a Stewpan with Thyme, Winter Savoury, Parfley, and an Onion fliced ; lay the Turbot upon this, and let the Stewpan be a fmall one ; it fhould only be juft big enough to hold the Fifh, becaufe when larger more Wine is required, which creates an Expence, and anfwers no Purpofe.

The Fifh being laid in, ftrew over it a good Quantity of the fame Herbs, with fome Chives, and fome fweet Bafil ; pour in equal Quantities of Vinegar and white Wine till the Fifh is covered, then ftrew in a little Bay Salt, add a few Corns of whole Pepper, and fet the Pan over a gentle Heat in a Stove, increafing it by Degrees.

Let the Fifh ftand thus till it is done, then fet the Stewpan off the Fire, but do not take the Turbot out of the Liquor till the Sauce is made, for the fame Reafon that the Plaife were ordered to lie in it, which is, that the Fifh gets more of the Tafte of the Liquor

when

when it is done and ftands in it cooling a little, than it did all the Time of the doing.

When the Stewpan is taken off, prepare the Sauce in this Manner:

Set on a Saucepan with a good deal of Butter, put in two Anchovies wafhed, fplit, and boned; add two large Spoonfuls of Capers cut fmall, and fome Chives whole; then fprinkle in fome Pepper and Salt, grate in a Nutmeg, and add a Pinch of Flour, a Spoonful of Vinegar, and a little Water.

Keep turning the Saucepan over a Stove, and when it is done pour it over the Turbot, which muft be put dry into a warm Difh ready, and fent up very hot, garnifhed with Horferadifh.

5. *To boil a Turbot with Gravy.*

Chufe for this Purpofe a middling-fized Turbot, and gut it, wafh it, and wipe it dry.

Prepare a deep Stewpan wide enough to hold it, and put in the Fifh, with two Bay Leaves, a Handful of Parfley, a large Bunch of fweet Herbs, and an Onion ftuck with Cloves; add fome Salt and Pepper, and fet this by in Readinefs.

Clean out a Saucepan perfectly, and put into it two Pounds of Veal from any coarfe Part, and next lay a Quarter of a Pound of Bacon cut into thin Slices.

Cover the Saucepan, and fet it over a flack Fire; let it ftand till the Meat begins to ftick, then put in a good Piece of Butter, and a large Spoonful of Flour; ftir this all up with a wooden Spoon, and let it be well browned.

Then put in a little ftrong Broth, or, if that be not in Readinefs, fome Water will ferve the Purpofe; ftir all well about again, and when it is mixed ftir and fcrape off all the Brown that fticks to the Sides of the Saucepan, then let it mix well together, and ftand hot fome Time.

This being done cut fome Slices of fat Bacon, lay them over the Turbot, then heat a Pint of ftrong

white

white Wine boiling hot, pour this upon the Turbot, and then ftrain in the Veal Gravy ; fet it over a Fire to be done, and when near enough remove it to a flack Heat that it may ftand to take the full Strength and Relifh of the Ingredients.

When it is thoroughly foaked take it out, lay it on a warm Difh, and pour the Gravy into a Saucepan, thicken it up, and put it over the Turbot by Way of Sauce.

The French throw away the Gravy, and ferve up the Fifh with a Raggoo made for this Purpofe of Sweetbreads, Cocks-Combs, Truffles, and Mufh-rooms. This may be the more elegant Method, but it is not fo well as the cther.

There are fome who value Things only for being expenfive, and to fuch this Method may be fuited, but the Confufion of Taftes fpoils all ; the Turbot with a Sauce of its own Liquor is fufficiently rich for any Table, and in that Condition it is much lefs expenfive, and will better pleafe a critical and judicious Palate.

C H A P. III.

Of Broiling.

A R T. I. *To broil Pearch with Anchovy Sauce.*

CHUSE for this Difh Pearch of a moderate Size, and if that can be done have them brought frefh from the Water, fcale them, gut them, wafh them, and dry them in a Napkin.

Melt a good Quantity of Butter with fome Salt, let it be thick, and when it is cooled a little dip the Pearch into it, roll them about till the Butter fticks well to every Part of them.

Then fet a Gridiron over a very clear and brifk Fire, but let it ftand at a great Height above the Fire, for the Pearch muft be foaked well before they are browned up.

While

While the Pearch are broiling, make the Sauce in the following Manner :

Set on a Saucepan with fome Butter, a Pinch of Flour, and a whole Leek; add two Spoonfuls of Vinegar, a little Water, fome Pepper and Salt, and a third Part of a Nutmeg grated; wafh and bone three Anchovies, put them into the Saucepan cut into fmall Pieces, and keep fhaking it over a Stove while the Fifh are doing.

When they are near done move the Gridiron a little nearer the Fire to brown them, then lay them in a hot Difh, and pour the Sauce carefully over them, keeping back the Leek.

2. *To broil Bream with Caper Sauce.*

A Bream is a common and neglected Fifh ; it is but a very indifferent one till it grows to a great Size, but then dreffed in this following Manner it is excellent.

Chufe the biggeft Bream you can get, gut it, but do not fcale it, wafh it, dry it in a Napkin, and rub it over with a little melted Butter.

Set a Gridiron at a good Diftance over a clear and brifk Fire, and on this lay the Bream ; when it has been on fome Time turn it, and then prepare the Sauce.

Melt fome Butter with a little Flour, Vinegar, and Water, add fome Chives chopped fmall, a Spoonful of Capers alfo chopped, and fome minced Parfley, with Pepper, Salt, and a little Nutmeg; tofs this up over a Stove, and when the Fifh is enough take it off the Gridiron, lay it on a heated Pewter Difh, and raife the Skin about the Middle of the Back. It will rife eafily, for it is very loofe, and following the Courfe of its rifing it will all be ftripped clean off without the leaft Difficulty.

When the Bream is perfectly well cleaned of it lay it in a China Difh warmed, and pour the Sauce over it.

3. *To*

3. *To boil a Pike.*

Chuſe for this Way of Dreſſing a middle-ſized Pike, and get it as freſh from the Water as poſſible.

Melt ſome Butter, with Pepper and Salt and a little Flour; pour it into a Soup Diſh, and let it ſtand a little to cool.

While this is doing, gut and ſcale the Pike, waſh it very clean, and dry it; then with a ſharp Pen-knife ſcore the Back and Sides croſs and croſs, and lay it in the Butter; roll it about that the Butter may come at every Part of it, and then ſet on a Gridiron faſt, let it ſtand high over a clear Fire, lay the Pike upon it, and let it be well done.

When it is near enough, bring it near the Fire, and turn it once, that each Side may be browned. Then ſend it up hot with Anchovy Sauce.

C H A P. IV.

Frying.

A R T. I. *To fry Lampreys with Capers.*

GET freſh Lampreys full of Life, and not ſuch as have been kept out of Water till they can ſcarce ſtir, for this makes them good for little: Bleed them, and ſave the Blood.

Then make ſome Water ſcalding hot, and throw in a little Salt, pour it into a Pan, and put in the Lampreys to clean them, rub them and waſh them thoroughly to get off their Slime, then cut them into Pieces; waſh theſe over again, and dry them in a Napkin. When this is done, ſet on a Stewpan with ſome clarified Butter; add a little Flour and ſome Pepper and Salt, a Bunch of Sweet Herbs and a Bay Leaf: Grate in a little Nutmeg, and laſt of all pour in a Glaſs of white Wine.

Put in the Pieces of Lamprey, and fry them carefully; when they are pretty well done, take out
the

the Herbs, and put in the Blood ; add at the fame Time two Spoonfuls of chopt Capers, and then thicken all up. Heat a Difh and pour in the whole together, and fend it up hot.

2. *To fry Pearch plain.*

Chufe middle-fized Pearch, gut them, fcale them, and wafh them very clean.

Then with a very fharp Pen-Knife fcore them on the Sides, but not very deep, nor very clofe ; drudge them with Flour, and then fry them in oiled Butter.

When they are well done and brown, ferve them up garnifhed with fried Parfley, and fend up with them plain melted Butter. This gives the Pearch its true Flavour, and many for that Reafon prefer it to any other Way of dreffing that excellent Fifh. But as there are others who are fond of Sauce of more Relifh to every Thing, we fhall add the following Receipt for the fame Fifh.

3. *To fry Pearch with Caper Sauce.*

Chufe larger Pearch for this Way of dreffing, and having fcaled and gutted, wafhed and dried them, cut them deep into the Sides and Back, and drudge them with Flour, with a little fine Bafket Salt among it.

When they are well prepared in this Manner, fry them as before directed, till they are thoroughly done and perfectly brown.

When the Fifh is ready, make the following Sauce : Melt in a Saucepan two Ounces of Butter, put in fome Flour, and brown it, then put in fome Chives chopped fmall, fome Parfley chopped fine alfo, and a few frefh Mufhrooms fhred fine ; add a little boiling Water, lay the Pearch taken out of the Pan into a fmall Stewpan, pour this over them, and let them fcimmer in it two or three Minutes ; then take them out, lay them on a warm Difh, and put to the Sauce two large Spoonfuls of Capers cut fmall, thicken it up, and then pour it over the Pearch.

There is no Way in which the Pearch eats better than this. The frying gives it a Firmnefs and Crifpnefs, and all this foaking in the Sauce does not take it off, altho' it mellows the Flefh very finely, and gives the whole the Flavour of the Ingredients that are put into the Sauce.

C H A P. V.

Of Baking.

A R T. I. *To bake Tench.*

CHUSE a Brace of Tench of a good Size, a fine Violet Coppery Colour and Olive; kill them by a Blow on the Head, and immediately gut them and clean them, wafh them perfectly in Water with a little Vinegar and Salt in it; cut off their Heads, and dry them in a Napkin.

Rub the Infide of a Silver Difh with Butter, or in Want of a Silver Difh, any Tart-Pan will ferve. Shred an Onion very fine, chop fome Parfley fmall, cut fome Chives in long Pieces, and ftrip the Leaves of fome Savoury Herbs; mix all thefe together, then ftrew over them fome Pepper and Salt, grate in a quarter of a Nutmeg, and add two Cloves bruifed. Strew this Seafoning all over the Infide of the Pan upon the Butter.

Save a Part of this Seafoning, and lay in the Tench; and ftrew the faved Seafoning over the Fifh. Then melt fome Butter very thick and fine, and rub fome Bread to very fmall Crumbs; fprinkle the Tench with the Butter, and drudge the Crumbs well over it; and then fend it to the Oven.

While the Tench are baking, prepare the Sauce for them in the following Manner: Shred fmall fome Parfley, fome Chives, and half a Dozen Mufhrooms frefh gathered; fet on a Saucepan with a little Butter, and when it is melted put in thefe Ingredients: Sea-

fon

fon it with Pepper and Salt, pour in a little boiling Water, and leave it to fcimmer over a gentle Fire.

Add to this at laft fome rich Veal Gravy, and when the whole is hot and ready, and the Tench are come home from the Oven, warm a Difh, pour in this Sauce, and then lay the Fifh in : Serve them up hot, and they will both look and eat very well.

2. *To bake a Fowl with Oifters.*

Chufe a large fine Fowl, let it be picked, drawn, and truffed, as for boiling : Stew a Pint of Oifters with fome Blades of Mace, a little Pepper and Salt, and a Glafs of white Wine ; pour thefe into the Fowl, tie up the Ends, and lay it in a Difh buttered on the Infide, lay over it fome Pieces of thin fat Bacon, and pour in a little Gravy ; fend it to the Oven, and when it comes in ferve it with a rich Gravy Sauce.

C H A P. VI.

Of Sauces.

A R T. I. *Italian Ramolade.*

THIS is a cold Sauce made without any heating, and is very fafhionable in Italy, for Fifh which are to be eat cold, or any other cold Difh ; it is to be made thus : Squeeze into a China Bafon a large Lemon, and a third Part of a China Orange of the fame Size ; add to this a fmall Quantity of Bafket Salt, a little Pepper, and as much Oil as there is of the other Liquor together.

Shred a good deal of Parfley very fine, wafh and bone a couple of Anchovies, and fhred fome Chives ; mix all thefe together, and put them into the Liquor ; then cut very fmall two Spoonfuls of Capers, put them in, and when all is well ftirred about, and of a moderate Thicknefs, fend it up to Table.

We

We want a cold Sauce of this Kind oftener than People in general are aware, and this is an exceeding good one for a Multitude of Occasions.

In Summer a cold Fowl, a cold Turkey, or a cold Piece of Lamb, are very agreeable to those who love plain light Suppers; but they are too dry with Salt alone, and our English Cookery does not afford any Method of eating them otherwise without heating them up, by which they lose a great deal of their Sweetness. This Sauce is not too sharp, for the Oil softens the Vinegar, and it is very finely relished with a mixed Flavour by the other Ingredients.

2. *Rich Sorrel Sauce.*

Gather a good Quantity of fine fresh and large Leaves of Sorrel, pick them clean from the Stalks into a Dish, set on a good Quantity of Water, and when it boils, throw in the Sorrel; stir it about, and let it scald, then take it off. Strain away the Water, and squeeze the Sorrel in the Manner of Spinage.

When the Water is all got out, put it into a Saucepan, and pour to it some Veal Gravy, and if it be at Hand, add some Essence of Gammon of Bacon, as we have before directed it to be made ; put in some Pepper and Salt, and a little bruised Mace, scimmer it well together, and when it is done, pour it into the Dish, and lay in the Fowl, Meat, or whatsoever it is you use it for.

This is a rich Sauce, but it is proper in all Cases, when the common Sorrel Sauce is required ; and it eats well with almost any Thing roasted.

3. *Rich Celeri Sauce.*

Set on some Meat in a large Saucepan, and put in a Piece of Butter, and a little Flour, let this heat, stirring it now and then together.

While it is heating, clean and wash some Celeri, cut it into small Pieces, and throw it into the Water ; when it is boiling, let it boil till it is tender ; then

pour

pour it into a Seive, and fet it to drain, it will be very foft, well tafted, and beautifully coloured.

Set on a Saucepan with fome good Gravy, when it is hot put in the Celeri: Add fome Pepper and Salt, fome grated Nutmeg, and a little Mace bruifed, let it fcimmer for fome Time over the Fire, then put in a Piece of Butter rolled in Flour, and a Spoonful of Vinegar; when it is all well mixed, ferve it up with the proper Difhes. 'Tis excellent with a roaft Fowl, Turkey, or Duckling.

4. *Onion Sauce with Gravy.*

Peel two Dozen of Onions, taking off a great many of the outer Skins, fet them over the Fire in a Saucepan with a good deal of Water, boil them till they are thoroughly foft, but not mafhed, then pour them into a Sieve to drain.

Set on a Saucepan with fome good rich Gravy, feafon it high, and while it heats chop the Onions to Pieces, then put them into the Gravy, and let them ftand fcimmering fome Time, that they may thoroughly mix with the Gravy, and perfectly receive its Flavour; then thicken it with a Piece of Butter rolled in Flour, and add a very little Muftard, and half a Spoonful of Vinegar: Serve it up hot with roaft Meat, Fowl, or Rabbets.

5. *Lettuce Sauce.*

Pick half a Dozen Imperial Lettuces, throw them into a Pan of cold Pump Water, and fet on a Saucepan with a good Quantity of common Water, with a Piece of Butter, and a little Flour; when this is hot and white, throw in the Lettuces, and let it once boil up with them.

Melt fome Butter in a large Saucepan, pour to it fome Eel Broth, and put in fome Flour, and a Blade of Mace, a little Pepper and fome Salt: Let this be heating while the Lettuce is boiling. When it has boiled fome little Time, pour it off into a Sieve, and as foon as drained, put it into the Saucepan with the

Sauce,

Sauce, firft chopping it a little to make it lie the clofer; heat all well together, and pour it into the Difh with boiled Fifh of any Kind.

This is the Method of making Lettuce Sauce for Lent; but on other Occafions, it may be done with Gravy in the Manner of the others.

The French cook up thefe Sauces into a Kind of Raggoos, by their ferving them up with fome of their Culliffes; but they make but very flight Difhes that Way; it is much better to ufe them in this plain Way off Sauces.

Our Englifh Sauces in general are too plain and grofs. Thefe which we have here mentioned are what our People admire fo greatly in France and Italy, and in the Houfes of Foreigners here; the Charge of them is little or nothing, and they will give a great Grace to the plaineft Difhes of the folid Kind.

C H A P. VII.

Of Soups.

A R T. I. *Cucumber Soup.*

THIS is a cheap Soup very univerfal among the the poor People of France, but very worthy to appear at better Tables.

Clean and wafh a Dozen Cabbage Lettuces, pare a Dozen Cucumbers, and take out the Cores: Cut the Lettuces and Cucumbers to Pieces, and fcald them in Water, with a Piece of Butter and a little Flour in it.

Set on another Saucepan with fome good ftrong Broth; when the Greens are tender, pour them into a Sieve, and when they are drained well, chop them lightly to Pieces, and ftir them into the Broth, and fet them on to fcimmer. Pour the Water of the Lettuce and Cucumber back into the Saucepan, and boil in it an ordinary Fowl till it is tender, while the

other

other is fcimmering ; and when it is near done, put into it a Pint of Green Peafe.

Take out the Fowl, lay it handfomely upon the Difh, put fome Sippets of Bread round, and then pour in the Soup, Herbs and Peafe together, after feafoning it to the Palate. Garnifh with Cucumber and Lettuce.

2. *Green Peafe Soup.*

Cut a fmall Piece of Bacon, Fat and Lean together, and lay it in a Soup Plate in fome Vinegar, with a couple of bruifed Cloves, a Blade of Mace, and fome Pepper-Corns ; turn it from Time to Time, and let it lie two Hours. A very fmall Piece of Bacon thus prepared will feafon a vaft Quantity of Soup.

When the Bacon is ready, chop to Pieces a fmall Knuckle of Veal, put it into a large Saucepan, and pour on it a Gallon and Half of Water.

Let it boil up, then put in the Bacon ; but not the Vinegar it was fteeped in. At the fame Time put in a Bundle of Sweet Herbs, a Handful of Parfley, and the fame of Mint, half a Spoonful of whole Pepper, and the upper Cruft of a Three-penny Loaf, or a like Quantity of any other upper Cruft toafted brown and hard, but not burnt.

Cover this up, and fet it on to boil ; let it ftand over the Fire till half the Liquor is wafted ; then ftrain it off, and put into it in another Saucepan a Pint of Green Peafe, a couple Imperial Lettuces minced, and a Head of Celeri cut down into thin Slices. Cover this up, and let it ftand two Hours over a gentle Fire.

While this is fcimmering, boil a Pint of old Peafe in a Saucepan of Water till they are perfectly tender, then pour them out into a Sieve, force the Pulp thro', and put this to the Soup in the other Saucepan : Let all boil well together to mix thoroughly.

When the whole is done, fet a deep Soup Difh to heat, and fry a French Roll quite brown ; lay this in

the

the Middle of the Dish, and then pour the Soup all about it.

There should be about two Quarts of the Soup when it is finished.

A few Afparagus Tops cut short are a very agreeable Addition to this Soup, and give it a Look of Richnefs.

3. *Portable Soup.*

This is a Receipt that may be of fome Value to thofe who have this kind of Soup; or who should chufe to deal in it, for a great deal of Money is got by what is fold under this Name. Whether the Receipt here given be exactly the fame in all Refpects with that which is ufed by thofe who make a Trade of Portable Soup, we cannot fay, for the Thing may be done various Ways. This we can affure the Reader, as will be found by Experience, that a very fine Soup of a proper Confiftence may be made thus, and that it will keep and bear Carriage, and be always ready for Ufe, and wholefome and pleafant.

Take a couple of the largeft and fineft Legs of Beef that can be bought, clean them well, firft pick away the Skin and Fat, and throw it afide, then get all the Meat and all the Sinews as clean as poffible from the Bones.

Put this Meat into a fmall Copper, and pour to it three Pails of foft Water ; add a large Veiny Piece of Beef beat tender; make a gentle Fire under the Copper, that the whole may heat gradually, and at length boil.

When it has once or twice boiled up, fkim it; and then put in a Dozen Anchovies, wafhed, fplit, and chopped into two or three Pieces. Add an Ounce of Mace fhred fmall, but not bruifed, an Ounce of whole Pepper, and a Quarter of an Ounce of Cloves whole.

Let thefe boil up together ; then peel half a Dozen large Onions, and cut them croffwife in two ; put thefe in, and add a Bundle of Thyme, a Bundle of

Sweet

Sweet Herbs, and the dry Cruft of a Three-penny Loaf, cover this up clofe and keep a moderate Fire under it, and laying on a Weight to keep the Cover firm, let it boil for nine Hours.

Then open it, and with a wooden Ladle or a ftrong clean Stick, ftir and work all very well together.

Cover it up again and make it boil gently.

When it has been boiling an Hour open the Copper, take out a little of the Liquor and let it cool, obferve whether it come to a thick ftrong Jelly, if it do, it is enough; but if the Jelly when thoroughly cold be poor and thin, it is not enough, and muft boil longer.

When it is boiled enough; that is when the Jelly is thick and fine, take all up, pour the Liquor thro' a thick Hair Bag, and put the Remainder in the Bag into a ftrong Prefs, prefs it very hard, and get out every Drop that will come.

Then mix this prefling with the ftrained Liquor, and ftir all well together; pour it thro' a Hair Sieve into an earthen Pan, and fet it by to cool.

The next Morning examine it, and it will be found a Mefs of vaftly ftrong Jelly, with fome Fat and Foulnefs at the Top, and fome coarfe Settlings at the Bottom. Take off the Fat at Top, and cut away the thick Bottom, leaving only the clear Body of the Jelly.

Put this fine thick Jelly into a Stewpan well tinned, fet it over a Stove and ftir it carefully, that it do not ftick to the Sides or Bottom of the Pan. When it has ftood fome Time over the Fire, and is perfectly well boiled up, get a Number of large deep Cups, or fmall earthen Pans ready, and pour out the whole into them, not filling them up, but only covering the Bottom an Inch deep, or more or lefs according to the Shape of the Cup or Pan.

Set on a Stewpan of Water, about a third Part of the Depth full; and in this fet the Pans and Cups of

Jelly, taking Care that the Water does not reach up within two Fingers Breadth of the Tops of the Cups, that no Drop of it may poffibly get in.

Boil this gently, but be careful that none gets near the Rims of the Cups or Pans.

This is the only Way of bringing the Jelly to the defigned Thicknefs: It was before boiled up as high as it could be over a naked Fire without burning ; but that was not enough, and in this Method, which is the fame the Chemifts call the Balneum Mariæ, and is fit for all delicate Operations ; the whole will be reduced to the Thicknefs of a ftiff Glue while it is hot, and it is then fure to be of a due Firmnefs when cold.

When the Jelly in the Cups and Pans is of this proper Thicknefs, take the Cups and Pans out of the Water, and fet them to cool.

While this is cooling in the Cups, ftretch a Piece of clean Flannel over the Top of a great Hair Sieve, wipe it carefully, and then turn out the hard ftiff Jelly upon it, and let it lie on it eight Hours in a dry airy Place ; after this fpread a Piece of Flannel upon a Table, and turn the Jelly, and lay it upon that ; let it lie as long upon this as on the former, and in the fame Manner fhift and turn it till it is perfectly dry and hardened.

It will now refemble a thick and hard Glue, and will keep a long Time ; but 'tis beft to be careful in preferving it dry.

The moft proper Method is to put it up in Stone Pots firft wiped perfectly dry, and to fet them in a dry Place.

This is Portable Soup, it may be caft into Cakes of any Size, Shape, or Thicknefs, and may be carried to Sea, or in the Pocket upon the Road. Such as is intended for long Carriage is beft made in thin Cakes, and fhould be the more carefully dry the more Accidents it may be expofed to ; it may then be put up in Balls.

This

This Kind we have defcribed is the ftrongeft, and hardeft that can be made ; but Beef is not the only Meat of which it may be compofed : A Soup of the fame Kind and Confiftence may be made of Mutton, Veal, or even Fowls, with the Addition of Ifinglafs. The Jelly will retain all the Richnefs and Strength of the Ingredients, and will get a due Degree of Firmnefs from the Ifinglafs, but it is preferable when made of Beef alone : The Sinews boiling down to a tough Jelly, and fupplying the Place of fuch Addition ; this is the more natural, and proper ; Ifinglafs mixes very well with the others, and has but little Tafte, but what it has is fifhy, which is not fo natural or fo proper.

The Ufes of Portable Soup are numerous, and it is on many Occafions very convenient.

Whenever it is to be ufed, it is to be melted in fome boiling Liquor, and nothing does this fo readily as plain Water. When a Mefs of Broth is intended to be made of it alone, pour fome boiling Water upon a Cake of it, ftrew in a little Salt, and ftir it about in a Bafon or Punch-Bowl, till it is thoroughly melted. In general half an Ounce will do very well for a Pint of Water, but this is only fpeaking in general Terms, for it may be made ftronger or weaker according to Fancy.

This Way it makes alone very fine and rich Broth.

If a plain Soup be required, let a French Roll be fried crifp, and ftir about the Cake in the Water ; when diffolved, let it once boil up, and laying the Roll in the Middle of the Difh, pour in the Soup.

This is the plain Way, but any kind of Soup may be made with it at Pleafure, for it ferves as Gravy, and any Thing ftewed or boiled may be mixed in with it.

An Ounce of this melted in a Quart of Water is juft the fame that a Quart of the Gravy was before it was fo boiled away ; and the Cook will remember

we

we have informed her in what Manner to make the feveral Kinds of Soups with this Kind of Gravy.

4. *White Pea Soup with Gravy.*

Boil a Leg of Pork in the ufual Way, and fave the Liquor: The, next Day boil a Leg of Mutton, and fave this Liquor alfo; mix them together, and when they have ftood to be thoroughly cold, take off the Fat; fet this over the Fire with two Quarts of White Peafe, and add a Bunch of dried Mint; let the whole boil till the Peafe are perfectly tender, and the whole is of a proper Thicknefs.

Then cut fome Bacon that is Fat and Lean togegether in Dice, or fmall fquare Pieces; cut fome Bread in the fame Manner into Dice, and fry them together till they are brown and crifp; pour this into the Soup, and at the fame Time add a Quart of frefh Beef Gravy, let all be made thoroughly hot together, and then pour it into a Difh, rub fome dry Mint over it, and fend it up hot.

C H A P. VIII.

Of Made Difhes.

ART. I. *Bain Marie.*

THIS is a Difh made by ftewing in that elegant Way we have juft named for finifhing the Portable Soup, the boiling in Water, fo that the direct dry Heat of the Fire never comes at it. This Difh is named from the Manner of Dreffing; we obferved that the Chemifts ufe this Way of boiling in nice Operations, they call it Balneum Mariæ; and this Bain Marie is only a Tranflation of that Expreffion.

Cut three Pound of lean Beef into Slices, cut in the fame Manner three Pound of Veal, and one Pound of Mutton, take off all the Fat.

Skin

Skin a good large Fowl, and fill the Body with Rice, and you may, if you happen to have it, add a Partridge: The Diſh will be very good without, but that will give it a Flavour very agreeable.

Scald a large earthen Pan that will hold all this Meat, ſtick an Onion full of Cloves, and ſeaſon the Meat with a little Salt, and then put all into the Pan; pour to it two Quarts of Water, and put on the Lid of the Pan, faſten it down with Paſte, and tie it over with Paper.

Set on a Kettle of Water, and put into it this Pan, taking Care that the Water do not come ſo near the Edge as to get over it when it boils

Set on a large Tea Kettle of Water to be hot, ready to fill up the Kettle to a proper Height as it boils away.

In this Manner let it be kept boiling five Hours, then take up the Pan, open it, and you will find it full of an exceeding rich Broth or Gravy; ſtrain this through a Napkin, and let it ſtand a little that the Fat may riſe and be taken off, then ſcimmer it with ſome Cruſts of Bread, and ſerve it up in a Soup Diſh. There is no Soup whatſoever that equals this in Cleanneſs of Taſte.

2. *Breaſt of Veal in Galantine.*

Make a Seaſoning with Parſley, Thyme, Sweet Marjoram, Winter Savoury, and Marygolds, ſhred all very fine together, and ſprinkled with Pepper, Salt, and grated Nutmeg.

When a good Quantity of this is ready take out the Bones of a Breaſt of Veal, beat it quite flat, and ſeaſon it all over with this Mixture.

Roll it up as tight and hard as poſſible into a round Lump, and tie it up in a Napkin.

Put it into a ſmall Porridge-pot with ſome good Broth, and throw in a Bunch of ſweet Herbs; let it boil two Hours, and then when the Liquor is well waſted put in a Pint of Mountain, and ſome Mace
bruiſed,

bruifed, boil it up once or twice, then fet it off, and let it cool in the Liquor.

When it is entirely cold take it out, take off the Napkin, and fet by the Veal.

Some fend it up whole, garnifhed with Parfley; but the better Way is to cut it out in Slices, and fend half a Dozen of them up on a Napkin fpread over a China Plate, garnifhing with Parfley, and for fuch as like Sauce the Ramolade before mentioned will be very proper; but this is one of thofe Things that carries its own Sauce with it, for it is highly and finely relifhed with the Ingredients and the Wine.

3. *Portugal Beef.*

Chufe a fine Rump of Beef, cut out the Bone as well as may be, and divide it into two Pieces; the fmall End cut acrofs in feveral Places, and flour it well, then fry it brown in Butter.

The large End is to be ftuffed in the following Manner:

Boil two Dozen of Chefnuts till they are foft, cut very fine a Quarter of a Pound of Beef Suet, cut a large Onion very fine, and wafh and bone a large right Anchovy, hafh this very fmall, and then mix all thefe Ingredients together; fprinkle over them a little Pepper and Salt, and ftuff the thick End of the Beef well with the Mixture.

Put this and the fried both in a Pan of ftrong Broth, and let them boil gently four Hours; when they are very tender take them out.

Warm a large Soup Difh, lay the large Piece in the Middle, and cut the other into Bits of a proper Size to lay round it.

Strain off the Broth, which will be now very rich, pour this into the Difh, and put in half a Dozen chopped Gherkins, and a Spoonful of Capers chopped alfo very fine. Send it up hot, garnifhed with quartered Gherkins and large Capers whole.

Some

Some fry the thin Part of the Beef enough, and do not ftew it at all ; but this, though it gives a Variety in the Look of the Difh, makes it coarfe, the fried Part being nothing but a fried Beef Steak, which is but a coarfe Thing ; in this Way of ftewing both the Liquor is browner for the fried, and the whole has a better Relifh.

It is no very expenfive Difh, and it is fingle and exceeding pleafant.

4. *Stewed Neats Tongues.*

Chufe a Couple of Neats Tongues of a moderate Size, clean them, and fet them on in a fmall Pot with as much Water as will juft cover them well ; fet them over a flow Fire to fcimmer, and let them ftand fo two Hours ; then take them off, and let them cool a little, take them out of the Water, peel them, and put them into a fmaller Pot, pour over them as much Beef Gravy as will juft cover them, and let them ftew fome Time over a gentle Fire ; then put in a Bundle of fweet Herbs, half a Spoonful of whole Pepper, one Blade of Mace whole, and a little Salt ; let thefe ftew together half an Hour longer, then put in a Pint of ftrong white Wine ; white Port is beft, otherwife Madeira or Mountain.

After thefe have again fcimmered fome Time put in a Spoonful of chopped Capers, fome boiled Turnips and Carrots cut into thin Slices, and a Piece of Butter rolled in Flour ; let it all ftew longer, and then take out the Tongues, lay them carefully in a Soup Difh, and pour all the Liquor over them ; take out the Herbs, and with a Spoon fkim off the Pepper and Spices, put fome Sippets toafted, and fend it up.

It is a Cuftom with fome to boil the Spices in a Muflin Rag tied up ; but in this Cafe they do not give their Virtue fo well as loofe, and there is no great Trouble in fkimming them off before it is fent to Table, nor any Harm in a Piece by Accident being left behind.

I have

I have heard many declare a Diflike to ftewed Tongues, and have perceived it was owing to an Article among the Spices: Moft put in Cloves, and thefe have an over-bearing and very difagreeable Tafte: I have for that Reafon omitted them entirely in this Receipt; and I can affure the Reader that many have eat it in my Houfe, and have been pleafed to praife it, who were Judges of fine eating.

However, thofe who chufe it may put in a Clove or two, but it fhould not be more than a Couple to the two Tongues, left they have this over-bearing Heat.

5. *Mutton Venifon.*

When a Sheep is killed let all the Blood be faved, and when the Carcafe is cut up let there be a Leg cut Venifon Fafhion; put this into the Blood, and let it lie foaking in it till thoroughly moiftened and impregnated with it in every Part; then take it out.

Wrap it up in four or five Sheets of Paper, and roaft it.

Let the Paper be well buttered on the Infide, and tied on to keep it faft, and let the Meat be carefully bafted all the Time it is doing with frefh Butter.

Two Hours will do it well, and about five Minutes before it is to be taken up let the Paper be taken off, and let it be bafted naked with a Piece of Butter, and then drudged with Flour to give it a good brown Froth.

When it is done fend it up laid like a Haunch of Venifon, and without any Garnifh.

Send up with it two Sauce-boats, one of the richeft drawn Gravy that can be made, and the other of fweet Sauce.

6. *A Shoulder of Mutton with a Raggoo of Turnips.*

Chufe a fine middle-fized Shoulder of Mutton, and fet it in Readinefs.

Cut

Cut into fine Shreds a Veal Sweetbread, cut in the fame Manner a Quarter of a Pound of Cocks Combs, and half an Ounce of Truffles; bruife two Blades of Mace and put to the reft, add a little Pepper and Salt, and then put the whole into a Saucepan with a Quarter of a Pint of good Gravy.

Let them ftew together till they are done pretty well, then thicken it up with a Couple of Yolks of Eggs, and when it is thus finifhed pour it out into a Bafon to cool.

While this is cooling open the flefhy Part of the Shoulder of Mutton with a Knife, and take out the Blade Bone, and into the Hollow that is made by it put the Raggoo, when it is cold few up the Slit, and fet it ready.

Cover the Bottom of a deep Stewpan with thin Slices of Veal and Slices of Bacon, put to thefe fome Pepper and Salt, a Blade or two of Mace, a Couple of Cloves, a Bundle of fweet Herbs, and an Onion; pour in a little thin Gravy juft to wet the Ingredients, and fet the Pan over the Fire: When it is hot put in the Shoulder of Mutton, pour a little more Gravy over it, and then cover the Pan; let it ftand ftewing in a fcimmering Heat two Hours, and after that boil up a little.

While this is doing pare fome fmall fine Turnips, fet them on in a Saucepan of clean Water, and boil them till they are tender, then pour them into a Sieve to drain, and let them ftand over the Water to keep hot.

Take up the Mutton firft, lay it in the Difh, and cover it up to keep hot.

Strain off the Gravy that it was ftewed in, and fkim off all the Fat; then put to it a Glafs of red Wine, two Spoonfuls of Catchup, and a Piece of Butter rolled in Flour; ftir this together, and when the Butter is melted, and all is well mixed, pour in the Turnips; let it fcimmer together to keep all of the fame Heat, then uncover the Mutton, pour this Raggoo over it, and fend it up hot.

7. *Veal Rolls.*

Make fome common Force-meat, as we have directed in the preceding Part of this Work ; when this is ready cut half a Dozen thin Slices of Veal, lay fome of the Force-meat upon each of the Slices of Veal, and roll them carefully up, rolling in the Force-meat, tie. them round the Middle with a coarfe Thread.

When they are thus prepared put them upon a Bird Spit, and rub them over when they are fpitted with Yolks of Eggs.

Flour them, and lay them to the Fire, and as they roaft bafte them with a Piece of Butter.

Half an Hour at a moderate Fire is about the Time they take doing, then ferve them up with good Gravy, garnifhed with Lemon.

If fome Truffles be ftewed in the Gravy it adds to the Flavour.

8. *A Difh of Chitterlings.*

Cut a Calf's Nut into long Slices of the Thicknefs of a Finger.

Cut fome of the lean Part of a Ham in the fame Manner ; cut alfo fome Bacon of the fineft fat Part, and fome White of Chicken. All this being ready fet on a Stewpan, and put the whole in together, feafoning it with Pepper and Salt, fome Leaves of Thyme and Winter Savoury, and fome Mace bruifed.

This being all prepared take the Guts, cut them into proper Lengths, fee they be perfectly cleaned, and fill them with this Stuffing, not cutting the Slices at all, but putting them in whole, fome of one and fome of another into each Piece of the Gut.

Set the Chitterlings thus ftuffed on a Difh in Readinefs, and cover the Bottom of a Stewpan with Slices of Veal and thin Slices of Bacon. Set this on, and
when

when it has juft been heated put in the Chitterlings ; lay them evenly in the Pan, and lay in with them an Onion cut in Slices, ftrew over them fome Pepper, Salt, and bruifed Mace, and then lay over all fome more Slices of Bacon and Veal.

Pour in a Pint of ftrong white Wine, and then cover up the Pan clofe, faftening down the Edges with Pafte.

Set it on a Stove, and put fome Fire over as well as under it, and thus let it be ftewing foftly till it is well done.

Then open the Pan, and lay the Chitterlings in a Difh. Put on a Gridiron, butter a Sheet of Paper, and lay it on the Gridiron, the buttered Side upwards ; lay the Chitterlings on this, and broil them, turning them frequently, then fend them up.

We have given the Receipt for this, becaufe it is a Difh many polite Tables are very fond of; but there is fomething ridiculous in the Nature of it, to be at fo great Expence to drefs one of the triflingeft Things that can come into a Kitchen, and that when all is done is the leaft Part of the Difh itfelf.

9. *Bifque of Fifh.*

Chufe a large male Carp for this Purpofe, gut it, fcale it, and get the Flefh as clean as can be from the Bones.

Blanch fome frefh Mufhrooms ; hafh the Flefh of the Carp and fome of the Mufhrooms together, and put them into a Stewpan with fome Butter, Salt, Pepper, fweet Herbs, and a little Fifh Broth.

Let this ftew till it is enough.

Then get out the Flefh of the Tails and Claws of half a Dozen Cray-fifh, mince this fmall, and mix with it the Liver of a Pike, if in Readinefs, and the Melt of the Carp ; fet this on in another Stewpan with fome Gravy, and feafon it with Spices. When this is ready fet it alfo off.

Warm

Warm a China Difh, and lay in it fome Crufts of Bread that have been dried in an Oven, foaked firft in Fifh Broth.

When all is thus ready pour in the whole from the firft Stewpan, which fhould be nearly of the Thicknefs of Cream, and garnifh it with the other.

This is a very rich, and is accounted a very elegant Difh.

10. *Larks raggooed.*

Draw a Dozen Larks, and having prepared them for the dreffing tofs them up in melted Bacon, with fome Truffles, fome Mufhrooms, and the Liver of a large Fowl, adding fome Spices, and an Onion with about five Cloves ftuck in it ; drudge it with a little Flour, and moiften it with rich Veal Gravy.

Let it ftand over the Fire till properly wafted, then add to it an Egg beat up in Cream, and a Spoonful of chopped Parfley beat up among it.

When this is poured into the Stewpan let it have a Turn or two over the Stove to thicken it, and then take off the Fat, fqueeze in the Juice of half a Lemon, and ferve it up.

There is no Way of eating Larks that is at all comparable to this.

11. *Livers with Mufhrooms.*

Take the Livers of eight fine Fowls, clean away the Galls, and then lay them ready.

Cover the Bottom of a fmall Tart Pan with Slices of Bacon, lay the Livers upon them, feafon them with fome Pepper, Salt, and bruifed Mace, cover them with more Slices of Bacon, and then fend them to a Paftrycook's Oven, or bake them at home.

Great Care muft be taken that they do not dry or parch.

Clean and wafh fome frefh Mufhrooms, lay them to dry over the Stove, and then lay them in a Difh, with a little Bacon and a very fmall Quantity of Vinegar.

Tofs

Tofs up fome Slices of Ham, with a Bunch of fweet Herbs and a little Flour, in melted Bacon, and add to this fome Veal Gravy without Salt.

When this is ready put in the Livers and the Mufhrooms, boil all well together, and when it is perfectly mixed and done enough take off the Fat, pour it into a Soup Difh, and fend it up.

C H A P. IX.

Of Side and Small Difhes.

A R T. I. *Rofolis of Marrow.*

BOIL three or four Eggs hard, and feparate the Yolks; lay thefe in Readinefs.

Pare three or four found and good Apples, take out the Cores, and mince them very fmall.

Mince fome very fine Marrow, and mix together an equal Quantity of that and of the minced Apples.

Then mince as much Yolk of Egg as about half the Quantity of the Marrow. Mix all thefe together.

Pare a fine Lemon, and mince about a Tea Spoonful of the Ends, grate fome Nutmeg upon this, then add fome Pepper and Salt, duft over it a little fine powdered Sugar from a Sugar-Caftor, and ftir all well about.

Pour into a Bafon fome thick and fine Cream, mix thefe Ingredients with it, and then mix in the Marrow and other Things among them, and fet it ready.

Make fome Pafte in the following Manner:

Beat up two raw Eggs with two Spoonfuls of Milk, throw in a little Salt, and two Tea Spoonfuls of the fineft powdered Sugar, and when all thefe are mixed put in Flour by Degrees till there is enough in to work up for Pafte.

When

When this is made roll it thinner than for Tarts, then cut it into fquare Pieces of the Bignefs of Cards, and lay upon each of them a Lump of the mixed Ingredients as large as will conveniently lie upon them to be covered in; a fmall Spoonful is about the proper Quantity for each.

Turn over the thin Cruft upon the Ingredients, and make the Edges faft in Shape of a little Pafty or a Half Moon, clofe it very well, otherwife it will be liable to open in the Dreffing, and finifh the Rofolis by cutting off the Edges of the Pafte with a Jagg or Runner.

Set on a Stewpan with fome Water, when it boils carefully put in the Rofolis one by one, fet it over a Stove, and keep it juft boiling, and no more, that the Cruft may not break: About a Quarter of an Hour will do them.

Some chufe the Rofolis fried, and in that Cafe it is to be done in Butter clarified, in the Manner of Fritters.

They are as well one Way as another, and therefore the judicious Houfekeeper will confider the Reft of her Table, and chufe either Method accordingly.

2. *Rofolis of Spinach.*

This is beft made of the tender young Spinach that is raifed from Seed the fame Spring, and has not ftood to be hardened in the Stalk.

Boil fome of this in the common Way, and take a Lump of it of the Bignefs of two Eggs, fqueeze the Water very clean from it, and then chop it exceeding fine.

Put to it a Table Spoonful of Sugar, a Piece of Butter as big as a fmall Wallnut, and two Spoonfuls of Cream.

Stir and mix thefe very perfectly together in a Bowl.

Mince very fine an Ounce of candied Citron Peel, and the Yolks of two Eggs boiled very hard; add to
this

this a Tea Spoonful of Salt, half a Tea Spoonful of powdered Cinnamon, and a little grated Nutmeg.

Mix the other Ingredients with thefe, put them into a fmall Saucepan, fet them over a Stove, and let them heat gently : When they have been well heated fet them off to cool, and make a Pafte of Eggs, with Salt, Sugar, and Flour, as directed for the Marrow Rofolis, and cutting it out into Pieces of the Bignefs of your Hand, make Turnovers of them, with a large Spoonful of the Ingredients in each.

Thefe are to be boiled in Water, and fent up plain. Some grate Bread and a little Cheefe over them, but this is an odd Fancy. Or they may be fried in cla- rified Butter, in the Manner of Fritters, and then there muft be a little fine Sugar dufted over them; either Way they are a cheap elegant Difh.

3.   *Spinach and Eggs the French Way.*

Chufe fine young Spinach, pick and wafh it very clean, and then blanch it a Quarter of an Hour in boiling Water.

Drain away the Water in a Sieve, fqueeze the Spi- nach to get it well dry, and then chop it very fine.

A Quantity of this fqueez'd Spinach as big as one's Fift is enough for a pretty fmall Difh.

When it is very fine chopped mix it with half a Pint of Cream, and then pour in a Quarter of a Pound of melted Butter; put to this fome Pepper and Salt, and a little grated Nutmeg; fet this over the Fire to ftew.

While it is doing cut a French Roll into Pieces of the Bignefs of a Finger, and fry them brown.

Poach four Eggs, and then all is ready.

Pour the ftewed Spinach into a fmall Difh, ftick up the fried Bread in it, and lay the poached Eggs at the Top; fo ferve it up hot.

4.   *Roman Afparagus.*

This is a new Difh reftored from a very antient one, and, though a great Favourite at the moft ele- gant

gant Tables, has never yet been made publick; we therefore hope it will recommend the prefent Number of our Work to the Readers particular Notice.

Chufe fome very fine young Afparagus, clean it perfectly well, wafh it in feveral Waters, and then cut off the Tops two Inches and a half long, throwing away the reft.

Let a large Pan of Water ftand by with a little Salt in it, and let it be Pump Water, the hardeft and coldeft that can be got.

As the Ends of the Afparagus are cut off let them be thrown directly into this, and when they are all in let them be ftirred about.

Then let there be more of the fame Water drawn, put it in another Pan, and put to it an Ounce of Salt and a Pint of Vinegar; this Quantity is fufficient for a Gallon of Water.

As foon as thefe are mixed pour off the other Water, and put the Afparagus into this, ftir them once about, and after five Minutes lay them on a Sieve to drain: This hardens them, keeps in their Juices, and preferves their Colour.

Set on a Stewpan with fome foft Water, throw in a very little Flour, and ftir it about till it is mixed and the Water looks whitifh; when it is fcalding hot throw in the Afparagus, and make it boil quickly, but it muft not boil up violently; after a few Minutes ftrain away the Water.

The Afparagus will thus be foftened, and of a delicate Colour, whitifh on the rifing Part, and green within.

While thefe are draining fet on a Stewpan with fome rich Gravy; when it is as warm as the Afparagus put that carefully in.

Set it over a Stove not covered, and let it ftew gently till the Afparagus is juft tender enough for eating.

When it is near done put in fome Pepper, a fmall Quantity of powdered Coriander Seeds, fome Leaves

of

of Wild Marjoram, and fome Leaves of Coftmary, chopped as fine as poffible ; let thefe do a few Minutes.

Then heat a Soup Difh. Set on half a Pint of white Wine for a moderate Difh ; fet it on the Fire in a Saucepan by itfelf, and put to it a little Sugar, and a Stick of Cinnamon ; make it very hot, but not boiling, then take out the Stick of Cinnamon, lay fome Sippets of toafted Bread round the Difh, and then pour in the Wine ; upon this pour carefully all that is in the Stewpan, having firft thickened it up with a Piece of Butter rolled in Flour, and thus fend it up hot to Table, garnifhed with frefh-picked Leaves of Wild Marjoram and Borage Flowers.

This is the famous modern Difh in France. It is properly enough called Roman Afparagus, for it is a Piece of the old Roman Cookery, and it is very much to the Credit of the Inventors of it.

Afparagus is no Way fo fine, nor is there any great Expence ; and there is another Article worthy Confideration, which is, that it is more wholfome this Way than any other ; the Ingredients they added being fuited to correct the Crudity of the Afparagus.

We fee they underftood all the real Art of Cookery as well as the modern French, for there is nothing in their Made Difhes of this Kind the Rudiments of which are not laid down here ; we fee only this Difference, that they ufed fome very good Ingredients neglected at this Time, but very worthy to be brought into Ufe again.

Coriander Seed, in a fmall Quantity, is a very agreeable Ingredient, and not one of all our Pot-Herbs is equal either in Flavour or Virtue to the Wild Marjoram : It is of the Pot Marjoram Kind, but warmer and more aromatick. It is a wild Herb under our Hedges, and is to be had always in Summer at the Phyfick Shops in Covent-Garden.

5. *Stewed Barble.*

Chuſe Barble of a good Size, ſcale them, gut them, and waſh them in Vinegar and Salt, and afterwards in Water.

Put them into a Stewpan with Eel Broth, juſt enough to cover them, then ſet them over a ſlow Fire to ſcimmer: When they have been ſome Time doing add to them two Sticks of Cinnamon broken, four Cloves, a Bunch of ſweet Herbs, and a Pint of white Wine; throw in ſome Corns of whole Pepper, and a Piece of Butter rolled in Flour.

Let them continue on the Fire till the Fiſh are done, and the Sauce is thickened; then take them carefully up, lay them in a Diſh, and put the Gravy to them.

The French add a Raggoo of Truffles and Muſhrooms, but the Fiſh eat extremely well in this Manner.

6. *Eggs a la Tripe.*

Boil half a Dozen new-laid Eggs hard, take off the Shells, and cut the Eggs in Slices lengthwiſe, the Whites and Yolks together.

Melt ſome Butter in a Saucepan over a Stove, and in the mean Time ſhred ſome Parſley very fine.

When the Butter is melted put in the Eggs, toſs them up carefully, then put in the Parſley, and ſome Pepper and Salt; this done, add when all is well mixed half a Pint of Cream, and having given it one more heating, warm a ſmall Diſh and ſerve it up hot, garniſhed with Pieces of Egg.

7. *Sour Eggs.*

Break half a Dozen Eggs into a Punch-bowl, and beat them up well with five Table Spoonfuls of Verjuice.

Seaſon this with Salt, and grate in a third Part of a Nutmeg; then ſet it all over the Fire in a ſmall Saucepan with a little Butter.

Stir

Stir them one Way, and when the whole is thoroughly heated, and is well mixed, and of the Thicknefs of Cream, ferve it up in a fmall Difh, with Sippets and Quarters of Lemon.

8. *Eggs in Gravy.*

Put into a Saucepan three Quarters of a Pint of the richeft Veal Gravy, and if you have any Cullis of Veal and Ham mix with it about three Table Spoonfuls ; if not, it muft be thickened up with a Piece of Butter rolled in Flour.

Break eight or ten Eggs, feparate the Yolks, and beat them up with fome Pepper and Salt, and a Glafs of white Wine ; mix this with the Gravy, and fet it over a Stove, heat it gently, and ftir it all one Way continually, that it may be perfectly well mixed.

When it is done enough grate in fome Nutmeg, and ferve it up.

9. *Eggs in Cream.*

Blanch a Quarter of a Pound of Sweet Almonds and eighty bitter ones ; put thefe together into a Marble Mortar, beat them to a Pafte with a little Sugar, and by Degrees get in a little Milk among them.

In this Manner beat them very well.

Then put to them a Pint of the richeft Cream, and the Yolks of eight new-laid Eggs beat well together ; add half a Tea Spoonful of Cinnamon finely powdered, and fqueeze in a little of the fine Zeft of fome frefh Lemon Peel.

When all is mixed ftrain it through a Sieve again and again, at leaft four Times, to keep it well united, and to feparate any Kind of Lumps or Foulnefs.

Set a Silver Difh over fome hot Embers, put a Tart-pan Cover over it, and throw fome hot Coals carefully upon that, taking great Care that nothing get in ; let it continue in this Heat till it is done enough, and then fet it by to cool.

There

There are some who eat it hot, but that is not the Intent of it: It should be sent up cold in small Dishes.

10. *Stewed Plaise.*

Chuse a Brace of fine moderately large Plaise, and clean and wash them very well; then cut off the Heads and Tails and Fins, and put them into a small Stewpan; put in with them some Morels, Truffles, Mushrooms, Sweet Herbs and Parsley. Pour to these as much white Wine as will just cover the Plaise, and add a little Pepper, and a Piece of Butter rolled in Flour; set them over a gentle Fire, and when they are near half done, turn them very gently and carefully, for fear of breaking them; and then let them continue till enough.

Take them up with great Care, for the Beauty is to have them whole; lay them regularly in a Dish, just big enough to hold them, lay the Melts by them, and pour over the whole that is in the Stewpan.

The Melts are to be stewed with the Fish, and Care must also be taken to keep them whole.

C H A P. X.

Of Puddings.

A R T. I. *An Oat Pudding.*

THE Oats to be used for this Purpose are what we commonly call Grits, or Grouts; it is the Oat stripped of the Husk, and ready for Grinding into Oatmeal; in this Condition it mixes very well with the Ingredients for a Pudding, and is like Rice, but every Way preferable.

Put into a large Punch-Bowl two Pounds of Oats, pour upon them as much Milk as will thoroughly moisten them, stir them well about, and laying a Plate over them, set them by.

Stone a quarter of a Pound of Raisins, and pick and wash the same Quantity of Currants.

Shred

Shred a Pound a Suet as fine as poffible.

Then break fix new-laid Eggs and beat them up; bring in by Degrees all thefe Ingredients into the Bowl of Oats and Milk, and when they are thus together, grate in Half a Nutmeg, put in two Tea Spoonfuls of beaten Ginger, and add as much Salt as will make it palatable.

Send it to the Oven in a proper Difh, and let it be well baked.

2. *Pith Pudding.*

This is a very rich and elegant Kind of Pudding, and Care muft be taken to do every Thing with the greateft Exactnefs in the making of it.

Take the Pith of an Ox, and lay it all Night in Spring or Pump Water; this will foak out the Blood, and loofen the Skin.

In the Morning change the Water twice, moving it gently, and pouring it off.

When the Pith is thus freed from the Blood and other Foulnefs, carefully pick off the Skin.

Throw the clean Pith as it is picked into a Punch-Bowl, and when it is all in, pour in one Spoonful of Orange-Flower-Water; work it well together with the Back of a Table Spoon, till it is as foft and mellow as Pap.

Set on three Pints of the richeft Cream in a Saucepan, quarter a fine Nutmeg, and put into it; break in a Stick of fharp Cinnamon, and tear to Pieces three Blades of Mace, and put them alfo in; let it boil up and ftrain it off.

Blanch Half a Pound of Sweet Almonds, and beat them to a Pafte in a Mortar; put in by Degrees a little, and a little, of the Cream, till the whole is in, then work all well together; pour off the Cream thro' a Sieve, and put it to the Pith, beaten up with the Orange-Flower-Water.

Break ten new-laid Eggs, take the Yolks of all, and the Whites of two of them; beat thefe up very well, and put them to the reft of the Ingredients.

Break

Break four Marrow-Bones, take out the Marrow, and cut it to Pieces, mix this with the Ingredients; then grate two Table Spoonfuls of Naples Bifcuit, mix it with Half a Pound of the fineft Loaf Sugar pounded, and add as much Salt as will feafon the whole. Mix all perfectly together.

Make fome fine Puff-pafte, cover the Bottom of a Difh with it, and make a Rim round the Edges: Pour on the Ingredients, and let it be worked with great Care. There is no Pudding fuperior to it, fcarce any equal.

Some make thefe Ingredients into a Kind of White Pudding, filling Guts with them; and this Way they are very good.

We have in a former Chapter given the compleat Method of making thefe Kinds of Puddings, therefore need not repeat it here.

3. *Neats Foot Pudding.*

Boil four Neats Feet very tender, take the flefhy Part from the Bones, mince it very fmall, and fet it by; cut into very fmall and fine Mince Meat half the Quantity of Suet that there is of the Neats Feet minced; ftrew fome Sugar over this, a little Salt, and fome powdered Cinnamon; when thefe are mixed in, put the Neats Feet to it, and add a Quarter of a Pound of candied Citron-peel minced alfo very fine.

Break into a Bowl eight Eggs, beat them up Yolks and Whites together; add to thefe Half a Pound of Currants wafhed and picked, and a large Handful of grated Bread, when thefe are well mixed together, put in the reft of the Ingredients, and having mixt up the whole, butter a Pudding-bag on the Infide, and put it in; boil it well for two Hours, and ferve it up with Sweet Sauce, or Wine, Butter and Sugar.

From

From Lady Montague's *Book.*

A R T. I. *To make an Oatmeal Pudding.*

TAKE three Quarters of a Pint of great Oatmeal, pick it very clean, and beat it in a Mortar, but not too fmall; then put to it a Quart of cold Cream or thick Milk, and add a Blade of Mace.

Set this over the Fire in a Saucepan, and let it boil gently till the Oatmeal has fucked up all the Cream; then take it off, and let it ftand till cold.

Break eight Eggs, beat up all the Yolks and four of the Whites with fix Spoonfuls of Rofe Water; put this to the reft in the Saucepan, and feafon it with Salt, Sugar, Nutmeg, and Cinnamon.

Melt a Pound of Butter, and put to it a little grated Bread, and if you have no Marrow add fome Beef Suet minced fmall.

Mix all thefe perfectly well together, then butter a Difh, put in the Pudding, and fend it to the Oven to be baked.

2. *Another Way.*

Take a Quart of Milk and boil it; then ftir in a Pint of Oatmeal Flour, boil it to the Thicknefs of a Hafty Pudding, and ftrain it through a Cullander to keep back the Lumps.

Stir in half a Pound of Butter well clarified, the Yolks of fix Eggs and two Whites, well beat with a little Salt, a little grated Nutmeg, and as much Sugar as will fweeten it to your Tafte.

Put it in a Difh garnifhed with Pafte. The Oven muft not be too hot; and three quarters of an Hour will bake it.

3. *A Bread Pudding.*

Take a Penny white Loaf, or three French Rolls, flice them, boil a Quart of Milk, and pour it boiling hot upon the Bread; cover it up and let it ftand to cool.

Beat

Beat the Yolks of five Eggs, and three Whites, with a little Salt, fome grated Nutmeg, a little Ginger, and two Spoonfuls of Sack ; fweeten it to your Tafte : Mix it in a Bafon or Bowl, tie it in a Cloth, and let it boil an Hour : The Rind of a Seville Orange or two grated into it makes a good Addition.

If you like it beft baked, omit the Sack, and melt a Quarter of a Pound of Butter in your Milk. Butter your Difh, and garnifh it with Pafte.

4. *An Orange Pudding.*

Boil two Seville Oranges, fhifting the Water four or five Times, till they are fo tender as to thruft a Straw through, and all the Bitter gone.

Then cut and take out all the Seeds, and all the Strings and inward Skins.

Beat all the reft both Rinds and Juice together in a Stone Mortar ; fqueeze in the Juice of a frefh Orange, fix Yolks of Eggs, three Whites, and half a Pound of fine Sugar : Mix all well together, and then ftir in half a Pound of melted Butter.

5. *A boiled Carrot Pudding.*

Take a Penny white Loaf and grate it, and grate as much Carrot as Bread ; beat feven Eggs, the Whites of three left out, with a little Salt, and a Spoonful of Orange-Flower-Water.

Put two large Spoonfuls of Flour, a Pint of Cream, and as much fine Sugar as will fweeten it to your Tafte.

Laftly, put in a quarter of a Pound of melted Butter ; mix all well together, flour your Bag, and tie it up ; let it boil an Hour.

6. *A Marrow Pudding, or Whitepot.*

Seafon your Marrow with beaten Nutmeg, Sugar and Salt, then take a Penny Loaf cut in Bits like Dice ; pick fome Raifins clean, put in a Difh a Layer
of

of Raifins, and a Layer of Bread, then a Layer of Marrow; let them lie in fix feveral Parts.

Then take a Pint and an half of Cream, and when it boils, put in the Yolks of four Eggs, with the Whites of two beaten with a little Nutmeg, Sugar and Salt; ftir all well together : Pour it into the Difh upon the Layers, fet it in the Oven for half an Hour, it being not over hot.

7. Judith Poyntingdon's *Receipt to make Cream Cheefe.*

Take about five Quarts of the Morning Milk, a Pint and Half of raw Cream, mix both together, and run it very hard, then flice it up with a Skiming-Difh as thin as you can, and put a fine thin Cloth wet in a deep large Vat, and fill up the Vat as full as it can hold, and let it ftand till Night.

Then turn it into another fuch Cloth, wet upon a Pie Plate, fo turn it into the Vat again.

This do twice a Day till it be hard. About three Days in the Vat will be enough.

Then lay it in a half-dry Cloth, two or three Days more, according as you fee it harden ; then put it into Rufhes pretty Thick on both Sides, and in two or three Days it will be ready for your Ufe, according as the Weather is hot or cold. You muft change the Rufhes once a Day.

C H A P. XI.

Pies.

A R T I. *Of Chicken-Pie.*

PICK and draw a Couple of young Pullets, lay by the Livers, trufs them, and then with a Rolling-Pin beat them over the Breaft to break the Bones.

Cut out fome Bacon for larding, and feafon it well with Pepper and Nutmeg, Mace and Sweet Herbs, cut and bruifed together.

Lard the Chickens very well with this, and ftrew over a little of the Seafoning when it is done.

Bruife the Livers, and add to them fome Chives chopped fmall, fome Parfley, a few Truffles and Mufhrooms, and fome of the fame Spices that were ufed for the larding Bacon: Laft of all, add fome grated Bacon, and mix up all well together.

Slit the Chickens on the Backs, and dividing this Stuffing into two equal Parts, put one Part into each; then feafon them again with Pepper, Salt, and pounded Mace, and lay them ready.

Raife fome Pafte, and lay in the Chickens: Put in with them fome Mufhrooms, Truffles, and fome Bay Leaves; cover the whole with Slices of Bacon, and then put on the Lid, and fend it to be baked.

When it comes from the Oven, take off the upper Cruft, take out the Bacon, fkim off the Fat, and pour in a Raggoo of Sweet-Breads made as we have before directed, with Mufhrooms and Truffles. Send it up hot.

2.   *Duck Pie, to be eaten cold.*

Chufe a Couple of fine Ducks, and when picked and drawn, let them be truffed for Roafting.

Put them into a Pot with fome Water, and a Bunch of Sweet Herbs: Parboil them, then take them off.

While the Ducks are in the Water, cut out fome Bacon, and fome of the lean Part of Ham into Slices, feafon it very well with Pepper, Salt, and Nutmeg.

When the Ducks are cooled, lard them well with this.

Make fome good Pafte; roll out fome of it of the Bignefs the Pie is to be, and let this be an Inch thick; flour over a Table, rub a Sheet of Paper with Butter, lay that upon the Table, and upon it raife the Pie.

Mince a good Quantity of Chives and Parfley, pound them in a Mortar with fome Butter, add fome Pepper and Salt, and ftuff the Ducks with this.

Lay

Lay Slices of Bacon on the Bottom of the Pie, and feafon them with Pepper and Sweet Herbs; add a Blade of Mace broken, and then lay in the Ducks ; fill up the Space between, and about the Ducks, with pounded Bacon: Lay one Bay Leaf a-crofs over them, and cover up all with Slices of Bacon ; then put on a Lid to the Pie of the fame Pafte, rub it over with an Egg, and fend it to the Oven.

When it is well heated, it fhould be taken out, and a Hole made in the Lid ; then a Paper is to be laid over it, and it is to be put into the Oven again, and remain there four Hours.

When it comes out of the Oven, fill up the Hole in the Lid ; let it ftand till it is about half cold, then turn it Bottom upwards, and fo let it ftand till it be perfectly cold.

It is to be ferved up cold, placing it on a Difh covered with a Napkin.

3. *Partridge Pie.*

Cut out fome fine Bacon for larding, and fet it in Readinefs.

Pick and draw eight Partridges, and trufs them, then beat their Breafts flat ; finge them with white Paper, and broil them a little upon fome very clear burning Charcoal.

Lard them as foon as they are cold.

Beat fome Bacon in a Marble Mortar, and put to it the Livers ; bruife and mix them very well together, and with this ftuff the Bodies of the Partridges.

Make a Seafoning with Sweet Herbs, Pepper and Salt, Nutmeg, Mace, and fome Lemon-Peel fhred very fine.

Raife fome Cruft for a Pie, and fhape it according to the Number of Partridges that are to be ufed ; then lay in a little of the Stuffing, made of the Livers and Bacon at the Bottom : Over this ftrew a little of the Seafoning, and then lay in the Partridges. Strew fome more of the Seafoning over them ; and then put

among

among them a little Butter, and a little pounded Bacon interchangeably.

Then put in fome Leaves of Sweet Bafil, two or three Bay Leaves, and a few frefh Truffles.

Lay all thefe between, and among the Partridges; and over them lay a Covering of Slices of Bacon.

Then put on the Lid of the Pie, and fend it to the Oven. It will require about three Hours baking; after which it is to ftand to be cold.

This is the famous Partridge Pie of France; it is often brought over to England, and very well may, for it will keep three Weeks very good, or in a proper Seafon longer. We pay in London for this Pie, at the Rate of ten, fifteen, or twenty Shillings a Bird.

It will be eafy to make it here, but we muft not expect to equal the French, for they have a natural Advantage over us in the Bird itfelf: Our Partridges are fmaller than theirs, for theirs are the red-legged Kind, and very fine.

They ufually make thefe Pies of the young Flight, juft when they are full grown; but fome Times of fuch as are older. When older Birds are ufed, they allow an Hour longer baking, and we fhould obferve the fame Caution.

4. *Woodcock Pie.*

This is a Pie for eating cold, and is to be made in the fame general Manner with the Partridge; only that the Entrails of the Woodcocks, as they give it a Superiority over the other, fo they demand a particular Treatment.

Let two Brace of Woodcocks be picked, then draw them, and put the Entrails into a China Soup Plate.

Trufs the Woodcocks as for roafting, beat their Breaft Bone flat by gentle Blows of a Rolling-pin, and then broil them a very little over fome clear Charcoal.

Cut

Cut out fome of the fineft Bacon for larding, and when the Woodcocks are cold, lard them all over carefully.

Then pound a good Quantity of Bacon in a Marble Mortar : Put to it the Livers of the Woodcocks, bruife and mix them perfectly well, and beat in two or three Leaves of Sweet Bafil.

Chop the Entrails fmall upon a Trencher, pre-ferving every Thing that comes out of them in the Chopping : When thefe are well cut to Pieces alone, they muft be put into the Mortar with the Livers and Bacon, and very well worked together.

This makes a proper Bottom and Stuffing ; and this being ready, and the Birds larded, the Pie is to be raifed.

We here fpeak of a fmall one only with two Brace, but when they can be had in Plenty, three, four, or fix Brace may be ufed much more properly at a Time.

Whatever be the Number, the Pie muft be pro-portioned in Size accordingly ; and the Cruft being raifed, they are to be put in. Firft there is to be laid over the Bottom, a thin Layer of the Stuffing ; then the reft is to be put into the Bodies of the Wood-cocks, and they are to be laid in regularly, and evenly, putting in between them fome pounded Bacon and frefh Butter mixed together, with a little Seafoning of Mace, Pepper and Salt.

When the Pie is thus filled up, lay over the whole, a very thin fingle Slice of Veal, from the whole Round of the Fillet ; over this lay a Covering of Slices of Bacon cut alfo very thin, and then put on the Lid. This done, fend it to the Oven, where it fhould ftand two, three, or four Hours, according to the Quantity of Birds ; and when it comes home, it is to be fet by to cool.

The French are very fond of thefe rich cold Pies, and with great Reafon : They are excellent, and

many

many more Kinds than are here named, may be made the fame Way.

A Pigeon Pie made purpofely to ftand to be cold, will very well anfwer this Purpofe; and the Larding of the Pigeons, and Stuffing them in this Manner, will give them a great Richnefs, and Mellownefs. If the fine full grown young Tame Pigeons be ufed for this Purpofe, few Birds will make a richer or finer Pie.

5. *A Veal Pie.*

Chufe a moderately large Fillet of Veal, and let it be a very fine one.

Take out the Bone, and then without cutting it into Pieces, beat it flat with a Rolling Pin.

Cut out a good Quantity of Bacon for Larding, and as the Meat is large, let the Pieces of Bacon alfo be of the largeft Kind ufed for this Purpofe.

Make a Seafoning of Pepper, Salt, Mace, and a little pounded Cinnamon, with fome Leaves of Sweet Bafil, and a few Leaves of Parfley, and Winter Savoury, all chopped as fine as poffible.

Seafon the Bacon well with this; then lard the Fillet of Veal all over, very thick with it; and feafon it again with more of the Seafoning.

Put into a Mortar a Handful of the picked Leaves of Sweet Bafil, and two Bay Leaves chopped fmall, beat thefe to a Mafh, put to them a Pound of the Fat of Veal, and the fame Quantity of fine fat Bacon; pound thefe together with the Leaves, till the whole come to be a Pafte.

When this is ready, and the Veal larded, raife the Pie of a proper Size for the Fillet; cover the Bottom of it with a good thick Layer of the Bacon, and other Ingredients from the Mortar: Then lay in the Fillet, fpread over it another good Coat of the fame; and thruft in fome of it between the Meat and Cruft at the Sides, and wherever there is any Crevice.

This done, lay fome thin Slices of Bacon over the whole; and when it is entirely covered with them, put on the Lid. Send

Send the Pie to the Oven, and let it be there four or five Hours.

When it comes home, fet it by to cool, and ferve it up in the Manner of the others, cold; covering a Difh with a clean Napkin, and fetting the Pie upon it. Thefe cold Pies ferve in many Courfes.

6. *Partridge Pie to be eat hot.*

For this Purpofe chufe three Brace of Partridges juft full grown in the right Seafon, draw them, pick them, and let them be truffed in the Manner of a Fowl for boiling.

Then put into a Marble Mortar fome Shalots, fome Chives, and fome Parfley cut fmall; bruife thefe well together, and then put to them the Livers of the Partridges, and twice that Quantity of fine Bacon; beat all thefe together, and feafon them with Pepper and Salt, and cut in a Blade or two of Mace.

Let all thefe be pounded to a Kind of Pafte, and when they are thus beat add fome frefh Mufhrooms.

When this is ready raife the Cruft, and form the Pie; cover the Bottom of the Pie thick with this Pafte, and then lay in the Partridges, but put no Stuffing in them; when they are in put in the Remainder of the Pafte about the Sides and between the Partridges, and then ftrew over the whole fome Seafoning of Pepper and Salt; break a Couple of Blades of Mace and put it in different Parts, and alfo lay in between the Partridges fome Shalots, fome frefh Mufhrooms, and fome Parfley.

When all this is in, and the whole is well packed together, pound fome Bacon alone in a Marble Mortar, and put a Layer of it over the Tops of the Partridges, over this lay fome Slices of Bacon.

The whole is now done, and the Lid is to be put on; then let the Pie be fent to the Oven, and baked about two Hours and a half.

When it comes home take off the Lid, and take away the Slices of Bacon; fqueeze an Orange in, and fend it up.

The

The French, who never think they make a good
Difh if they do not put into it every Thing that ever
was eaten, pour into a hot Partridge Pie thus made a
Raggoo of Cocks Combs, or of Veal Sweetbreads.
There is no Reafon for this, becaufe the Partridges
make an excellent rich Pie, and the Confufion of
Taftes is bad.

If when the Pie comes home, and the Bacon is
taken out, and the Fat fkimmed off, there is not Liquor enough, it will be very proper to pour in half a
Pint of rich Veal Gravy fcalding hot: But this is only
in Cafe it is not moift enough of itfelf; if it be, it is
better let alone.

As this Pie is beft when made of the young Flight
of Partridges, we have directed the Time of baking it
to be two Hours and a half, but if they be older Birds
they will require in Proportion half an Hour or an
Hour more.

7. *A Rabbit Pie hot.*

Skin and draw two Couple of young Rabbits, fave
the Livers, and prepare the Cruft for the Pie.

Put a Quarter of a Pound of Bacon into a Marble
Mortar, and bruife it to Pieces; add to this the
Livers of the Rabbits, beat them up well together,
then put in fome Pepper, Salt, and a Blade of Mace;
fome chopped Parfley, fome Chives, and a few Leaves
of Sweet Bafil.

When thefe are all beat fine take it out, and fet it
on a Plate.

Cut the Rabbits into Quarters, and feafon them with
Pepper and Salt, and with fome Sweet Herbs.

Cover the Bottom of the Pie with the Seafoning,
and then lay in the Rabbits; pound fome more Bacon
alone, and when well beaten add a little Butter to it;
when thefe are beat to a Pafte cover the Rabbits in
the Pie with it, and then lay over all fome Slices of
Bacon; put on the Lid, and fend it to the Oven; let
it be baked two Hours.

When

When it comes home take off the Top, take out the Bacon, and fkim off the Fat.

If the Pie have been properly managed there will be Gravy enough in it; if otherwife, fome very rich Gravy of Veal or Mutton muft be made fcalding hot and poured in; then ferve it up.

8. *A Pigeon Pie with Lettuces.*

Chufe for this Purpofe half a Dozen large and young Pigeons, and about a Dozen of the fineft Imperial Lettuces.

Let the Pigeons be drawn, picked, and truffed, as if for boiling.

Lay them for a few Minutes upon a Gridiron at a good Height above a clear and brifk Fire, turn them frequently, then lay them on a Difh ready for the Pie.

Throw the Lettuces, after they are carefully wafhed and picked, into a Pot of boiling Water, let them lie a few Minutes, ftirring and turning them once or twice about; then throw them into a Sieve to drain.

Beat up the Livers of the Pigeons in a Marble Mortar, with fome Bacon, and fweet Herbs and Spices: Then raife the Pie.

Cover the Bottom of it with fome of this Stuffing.

Put fome Stuffing in the Body of each of the Pigeons, and then beat them flat with a Rolling-pin, and lay them into the Pie: They muft be laid in one by one, and each as it were wrapped up in a Parcel of the Lettuce.

This done cram in what remains of the Lettuce any where between them, and fprinkle over them fome Pepper and Salt, and a little Mace cut fine with Sciffars, then ftick in between them fome Pieces of Butter.

Lay all fmooth and level at Top, and then cover the whole with fome Slices of Bacon.

Put

Put on the Lid, and fend the Pie to be baked. It will require two Hours and a half.

When it comes home take off the Top, remove away the Bacon, fkim off the Fat, pour in a little Effence of Gammon of Bacon, and if there want Moifture, fome rich Veal Gravy; laft of all fqueeze over it a very little Lemon Juice, and fend it up hot.

This is an excellent Kind of Pigeon Pie.

C H A P. XII.

Of Fritters.

A R T. I. *Pats de Putain.*

SHRED very fine fome candied Lemon Peel, fet on a Stewpan, pour in fome Water, and put to it a little Salt, the Bignefs of a Wallnut of frefh Butter, and this fhred Lemon Peel.

Let this boil fome little Time over a Stove, then put in two good Handfuls of Flour, ftir it immediately with the utmoft Strength of Arm to make it into good Pafte : This done take it off, and work in a Dozen Eggs, two and two at a Time. When this is well wrought fet it by in a Difh.

Set on a large Stewpan, with a good Quantity of Hog's Lard.

When it is melted and very hot dip the Handle of the Skimmer in, and then with it form the Fritters. Fry them brown, then put them into a hot Difh, pour fome Orange-Flower Water over them, and then duft on fome Sugar. Send them up very hot.

This is an excellent Kind of Fritter, and worthy the Houfewife's beft Notice.

Some inftead of the Water ufe Milk, and it makes the Fritters rather better.

2. *Chicken*

2. *Chicken Fritters.*

Set on a Stewpan with fome new Milk, and put in as much Flour of Rice as will be needful to give it a tolerable Confiftence; break three or four Eggs, beat them up, Yolks and Whites together, and then mix them with the Rice and Milk; add a Pint of the richeft Cream.

Set all over a Stove together, ftir it well, and put in fome powdered Sugar, fome candied Lemon Peel, and a little frefh Lemon Peel rafped.

Cut off all the white Meat of a roafted Chicken, cut it into fmall Shreds, and put this in; then ftir all well together, and take it off.

It will be a rich Pafte. Roll it, and cut it out into little round Morfels.

Set on a Pan with a good Quantity of Hog's Lard, when it is very hot put in fome of thefe Buttons.

Heat a China Difh, ftrew the Bottom with the fineft Sugar powdered, and when that is ready lay on the Fritters as they come hot out of the Pan, ftrew fome Sugar upon them, and fend them up hot.

Some pour Rofe and Orange-Flower Water over thefe Fritters before they fend them up, but they are better without.

3. *French Cream Fritters.*

Set on a Quart of the richeft and fineft Cream that can be got, with a Stick of Cinnamon broke, a Blade of Mace, and a fmall Piece of Ginger; let this boil up, then ftrain it off through a Sieve.

Make this into a thick Batter with fine Flour and four Eggs, then add more Flour to make it ftiff like Pafte.

Set on a Stewpan with a large Quantity of Hog's Lard, and when it is very hot begin to cut the Pafte; it is to be cut into Pieces as broad as a Half-Crown, and three Times as thick, and thefe are to be dropped into the hot Lard.

Set

Set by the Fire a China Difh to be very hot, duft fome fine Sugar into it, and then as the Fritters come hot out of the Pan put them into the Difh; when there are as many as will lie handfomely in it, for the Difh fhould not be full, duft fome more Sugar over them, and fprinkle a very little Orange-Flower Water over them juft fo as to give them a Flavour, but not to run in the Difh or melt the Sugar.

4. *Bilboquet Fritters.*

Put into a China Difh two Handfuls of the fineft Flour, break five Eggs into it, and add fome Milk, juft enough to make it work well together, then put in fome Salt, and work it again: After it is well made up, add a Tea Spoonful of Powder of Cinnamon, a Tea Spoonful of grated frefh Lemon Peel, and half an Ounce of candied Citron fhred very fmall with a Pen-knife.

Set on a Stewpan rubbed over with a little Butter, put this Pafte into it, and fet it over a very gentle Fire in a Stove that the Pafte may be done gently in the Manner of baking, without burning to the Bottom or Sides of the Stewpan.

When this is done enough lay it on a Difh ready, and fet on a Stewpan with a large Quantity of Hog's Lard; when this is very hot cut out the Pafte which has been done over the Stove.

The proper Method is to cut it out in Pieces of the Length of a Finger, and the fame Thicknefs, and then cut it acrofs at each End; the Confequence of this will be, that in the frying it will open at each End, forming a Kind of double Top; thefe Tops the fancyful People who invented this Difh have fancied refembled the Hollow of a Bilboquet, and thence the Fritters have been named.

There muft be a great deal of Care in the frying of thefe Fritters, for they rife very much, they muft therefore be put in carefully one after another.

As

As they are frying put fome Sugar in the Bottom of a warm Difh; when they are done take them out one by one, lay them in the Difh, and put over them fome fine Sugar powdered: Serve them up hot. They are an excellent Kind.

5. *Point du Jour Fritters.*

Mix together a Glafs of Sack and a Houfe Spoonful of Brandy, or if the Wine be bought at a London Tavern there need be no Brandy added, they never fell it without.

Mix up two Handfuls of Flour into a Pafte with luke-warm Milk, and with this Brandy and Wine among it, beat up the Whites of four Eggs to a Froth, and add them to the Batter.

Add alfo an Ounce of candied Citron Peel fhred fine, half an Ounce of frefh Lemon Peel rafped, and as much Salt and Sugar as will feafon and fweeten it to the Palate.

Let all this be perfectly well worked and blended together into a good Body, but fo foft as to run.

Set on a fmall deep Stewpan with a good Quantity of Hog's Lard, and when it is thoroughly hot drop in fome of the Batter, and fry it brown.

This is the whole Compofition of the Point du Jour Fritter; but there is a peculiar Method ufed in fhaping and finifhing it for the Table; the Method is this:

A Tin Funnel muft be made on purpofe, pretty large in the Body, and with three Pipes; when the Lard is hot, and ready for the Batter, the Funnel is to be held over it, and a little of the Batter is to be poured in with a Ladle; it is to be kept moving over the Pan till all is run out, and this throws the Fritters from the three Streams into their intended Shape.

As foon as the Batter is all out of the Funnel turn the Fritters, for they brown prefently, then put one of them upon a Rolling-pin, and it will get the Shape

of

of a rounded Leaf; that is the proper Figure of thefe Fritters, and they are expected to come up fo at every genteel Table.

There is a great deal of Art and Dexterity required to do thefe right, and nothing does a good Cook more Credit than a Difh of thefe Fritters of a due Form, and made every Way handfome.

They muft not be too thick, and this is to be contrived by getting a right Quantity of the Batter to fpread fufficiently.

When the firft is made, that muft be laid as a Pattern for all the reft; if it be too thick, lefs Batter muft be poured into the Funnel for the next; if too thin, a little more; but this laft is rarely the Fault.

The Stewpan fhould not be broader at the Bottom than a Plate, and the Lard muft be very fine and very hot.   Thefe are the principal Cautions that are needful, and with a proper Regard to thefe it will not be eafy to make any Miftakes.   Care muft be taken to keep the Batter of a due Thicknefs, for any Error in that will altogether difturb and fpoil the Operation.

The common Way of ferving up thefe Fritters is as the others, in a hot Difh, with fome Caftor Sugar at the Bottom, and fome more over them; and this Way they are very elegant, and very much efteemed; but the Italians have hit upon an Improvement in this Article; they cover them with melted Sugar, and before that can harden ftrew over them a Quantity of the little Nonpariel Sugar-plumbs, green, red, and yellow, and fend them up juft as the Sugar is hardened.   This is the Method efteemed there, but it makes them a Holiday Difh for Children, rather than Part of a good Entertainment.

6.   *Elder Flower Fritters.*

Gather four Bunches of Elder Flowers juft as they are beginning to open, for that is the Time of their Perfection, they have juft then a very fine Smell and
a fpirited

a fpirited Tafte, but afterwards they grow dead and faint. We complain of thefe Flowers having a fickly Smell, but this is only when they are decaying; when frefh and juft open they have the fame Flavour, but it is fpirited, and juft the Contrary of what it is afterwards.

The Elder Flowers being thus chofen, break each Bunch into four regular Parts, lay thefe carefully in a Soup Difh, break in a Stick of Cinnamon, pour to them a Wine Glafs of Brandy, and when this has ftood a Minute or two add half a Pint of Sack; ftir the Flowers about in the Liquor, cover them up, and let them foak about an Hour, uncovering and ftirring them about at Times, to fee how they are kept moift.

Put a Handful of the fineft Flour into a Stewpan, add the Yolks of four Eggs beaten, and afterwards their Whites beat up quite to a Foam, add fome white Wine and a little Salt, and put in the Whites of the Eggs laft.

Let all this be very perfectly and thoroughly mixed.

When the Batter is thus made fet on a Quantity of Hog's Lard in a Stewpan, when it is very hot fry the Fritters. The Method is this:

The Elder Flowers are to be taken out of their Liquor and put into the Batter, and the Quantity for each Fritter is one of the Bunches of Elder, with as much Batter as agreeably covers it and hangs well about it.

While they are frying heat the Difh they are to be fent up in, rub a Lemon upon it not cut, and lay in the Fritters as they come out of the Pan, ftrew a little of the fineft Orange-Flower Water over them, and ferve them up.

7. *Apricot Fritters.*

Gather a Dozen and a half of Apricots juft beginning to ripen; they muft not be mellow, nor they

muft

muft not be green : This is a very material Circum-
ftance, for this is a nice Kind of Fritter, and cannot
be made in Perfection unlefs the Degree of the Ripenefs be exactly hit.

They are juft as they fhould be when they can with
fome Difficulty be opened, and the Stone feparated.

Having gathered the Apricots in this State frefh
from the Tree, they are to be prepared for the Fritters
in this Manner :

Put into a very clean Stewpan a Quarter of a Pint
of French Brandy, and a Table Spoonful of the fineft
Sugar powdered ; open the Apricots, take out their
Stones, and put the Halves into this Liquor ; fet
them for two Hours over a very gentle Stove, ftirring
them from Time to Time with Care not to break
them.

Make a Batter with a large Handful of the fineft
Flour, and as much Mountain Wine as will bring it
to a proper Confiftence.

Set on another Stewpan with a large Quantity of
Hog's Lard, and when it is thoroughly hot begin
to throw in the Fritters, made in the following
Manner :

Throw half an Apricot into the Batter, take it out
with as much as hangs about it, and drop it at once
into the Lard.

Set a Difh before the Fire to heat, ftrew a little fine
Sugar over the Bottom of it, and put in the Fritters
hot as they come from the Pan.

Let the Fritters be pretty well browned, which they
will be very fpeedily, and when there are a proper
Number in the Difh hold a hot Fire-fhovel over them
for fome Time ; this will glaze them, and then they
are to be ferved up hot ; no Sugar is to be put over
them.

The French Apricot Fritters are better than ours,
but it is owing to the Goodnefs of the Fruit : They
only dip the Half Apricots in Flour, and fry them ;
but this has been tried here, and does not anfwer,
ours being too watery.

8. *Ba-*

8. *Bavarian Fritters.*

Thefe are a Kind of Apple-Fritters, made in a peculiar Manner.

Chufe for this Difh, fome fine, well tafted, and hard Apples; pare them, quarter them, take the Core clean out, and then cut them into round Bits; prepare thefe in the Manner of the Apricots, by putting them for two Hours in a Stewpan, with a little French Brandy, fome Sugar, and a Stick of Cinnamon broken.

No Batter is to be made for thefe Fritters, but we may make them bare as the French do the Apricot Kind.

Set on a Sewpan with Lard; when it is hot enough, drain the Apples, ftrew them over with a good Quantity of the fineft Flour, and put them into the Pan; they will brown up, and make a very fine Kind: Set a Difh to heat by the Fire, put the Fritters into it as they come from the Pan; ftrew a little Sugar over them, and then glofs them with a red hot Fire-fhovel, and ferve them up hot; ftrewing Sugar round the Edge of the Difh.

C H A P. XIII.

Of Creams.

A R T. I. *Fried Creams.*

PUT into a Saucepan a Pint of Cream, half a Pint of Milk, a Stick of Cinnamon broken, and a little Sugar; fet it over a flow Fire in a Stove, and keep it fcimmering a quarter of an Hour.

While this is fcimmering, break eight new-laid Eggs, throw away two of the Whites, and put all the reft into another Saucepan; beat them about with a wooden Stirrer, and then add by Degrees, a quarter of a Pint of Cream, and a Handful of the fineft Flour. Mix all this perfectly well together.

Nº. XXIV.   4 T   Take

Take the Cinnamon out of the Cream that is all this Time fcimmering hot, and pour it into this other Saucepan, to the Eggs and Flour.

Set it on the Fire, put in a little Salt, make it boil pretty brifkly, and ftir it very well about all the Time.

When it has boiled fome time, mince very fine an Ounce and Half of candied Citron Peel; put this in; add a Blade of Mace fhred as fine as poffible, and continue boiling the whole together, till it is of a Thicknefs that it can but juft be ftirred.

Then fet on a Pan with a good Quantity of Hog's Lard; and at the fame Time pour out this thick Cream upon a Marble or on an even Dreffer, floured well over.

Make it run of the Thicknefs of about half an Inch, then flour the Top of it, and with a fharp and thin Knife cut it out into Squares and Lozenges of an Inch big. Throw thefe into the hot Lard, and fry them brown; when they are done enough, lay them on a hot Difh, and ftrew over them a little grated or fcraped Sugar not in too fine Powder, and fend them up very hot.

This is a Difh that very naturally follows the Fritter Kind, for it is little other than a rich and elegant Cream Fritter.

2. Cream Tarts.

Break into a large Bowl a Dozen new-laid Eggs, beat them all up, the Yolks and Whites together.

When they are well beat up, put in half a Pound of Flour: Stir and beat all this again very well together; when thefe are well mixed, break into another Bowl a Dozen more Eggs, and when they have been well beat up, put them to the reft, and work it again very well together.

Set on a Saucepan with two Quarts of Milk; let the Saucepan be big enough to hold all the Ingredients; make the Milk boil, and when it does, pour in the

Flour

Flour and Eggs, ftir all well together, then put in half a Pound of Butter, and ftir it all very well again; then put in fome Pepper and Salt, and then boil it very well, having a great Caution that it do not ftick to the Bottom.

When it has boiled fome little Time, it will be well thickened; then pour it out into another Saucepan, and fet it to cool.

This Quantity will ferve for a very confiderable Number of Tarts; lefs may be made for a fmall Entertainment; or a proper Quantity of this taken, and the reft referved; for it will keep fome Time.

Put as much of this into a Saucepan as will make the Tarts you chufe, if the whole be not made together.

As it warms ftir it with a Slice; and add to it fome melted Butter, the Yolks of three, four, or five Eggs, according to the Quantity ufed; fome candied Citron-peel fhred very fine, and fome Orange-Flower-Water. There is no faying the exact Quantity of thefe on this Occafion, for they muft be proportioned to the Quantity; and in the fame Manner it muft be fugared to the Tafte.

When all thefe additional Ingredients are put in, let the whole be ftirred well together with a Slice; and laft of all, add a good Lump of Beef Marrow.

The Cream is now ready, and the Tart Pan is to be prepared for it: A Puff-pafte Cruft muft be laid in the Bottom, and a Rim round the Edges, then put in the Pan near full of the Cream, and fend it to the Oven. Let it be baked moderately, and when it comes home, hold a red hot Firefhovel over it to glofs it. Send it up hot.

3. *Rice Cream.*

Pour into a fmall Stewpan a Pint of fine Cream, ftir in as much Flour of Rice as will ferve to thicken it; put in a little Sugar, and then ftrain it off.

Then put it into another Stewpan, and add to it a

Stick

Stick of Cinnamon broke, a Piece of freſh Lemon-peel whole, and a Table Spoonful of Orange-Flower-Water.

Keep it over the Fire about eight Minutes; then take out the Cinnamon, and the Lemon-peel, and pour the Cream into Cups.

Heat a Fire-ſhovel quite red, and hold it over the Cups to gloſs the Cream: This done, ſet it by to cool a little, and then ſerve it up; four Cups do very well upon a Plate.

4. *Velvet Cream.*

Clean a couple of Fowls Gizzards perfeɔtly well, ſlaſh them with a Knife, and ſet them in Readineſs.

Set a Pint of Cream over the Fire in a Stewpan with a little Sugar; when it is hot, and the Sugar is melted, ſet it off. Put the Gizzards into a Cup, and pour upon them four or five Spoonfuls of the boiled Cream; when it has ſtood to cool a little, ſet the Cup over warm Embers, and watch the Cream, after a little Time it will take: Then put in all the Cream to another Stewpan, and mix this from the Cup with it; it will make the whole anſwer in the ſame Way, and gives it an excellent pleaſant Softneſs.

When it is all as it ſhould be, ſtrain it, and repeat this three or foɔr Times.

Then ſet a Diſh upon ſome hot Embers, and take Care that it be placed exaɔtly even and ſteady; pour in the Cream, and cover it with another Diſh. Upon this lay ſome hot Coals, not to melt it; and thus keep it for about a quarter of an Hour, in that Time it will be perfeɔtly done. Take away the Coals, and ſet the Diſh to cool.

It will be excellent if ſerved up juſt when it is properly cooled but it may be Iced, and no Cream whatſoever anſwers that Purpoſe better. The Way to do this, is to put it into a Tin Mould made for that Purpoſe, and bury it among a Heap of Ice.

The

The Italians who are very fond of this Velvet Cream, ufe only the inner Skin of the Gizzard, and they chufe that of a Turkey, rather than a common Fowl; but the Difference in that refpeft is not material; and as to the ufing of the Skin alone, it will very well anfwer the Purpofe, but the whole Gizzard gives a Flavour.

5. *Chocolate Cream.*

Set on a Quart of Cream in a Saucepan with a Stick of Cinnamon, a Roll of frefh Lemon-peel, a Lump of Sugar, and a quarter of a Pound of Chocolate fcraped very fine; let the whole boil together, and when the Chocolate is perfeftly diffolved, and mixed, take it off the Fire, and take out the Lemon-peel, and Cinnamon.

Break fix new-laid Eggs, put away the Whites, beat up the Yolks, and mix them with the Chocolate; then ftrain the whole thro' a Sieve into a Difh.

Set on a Stewpan, the Top of which is juft big enough to take in the Bottom of the Difh the Cream is in, and not big enough to let in the Rim; fill this three Parts with Water, fo that when the Difh is fet over it, the Bottom may reach a Straw's breadth into the Water. Set this Stewpan on the Fire, put on the Difh of Cream, cover it with another Difh that will lay clofe over it, and when the Water is hot, let there be fome live Coals laid on the Top-Difh. This with the Heat of the Water below, will perfeftly well do the Cream.

When it has ftood thus about a quarter of an Hour, remove the upper Coals, and take up the Cream; fet it by till it is grown a little cool, and then ferve it in: This is one Way, and another is to have it entirely cold, which is alfo very agreeable.

6. *Tea Cream.*

Set on a Quart of rich Cream in a Silver Saucepan, put in a Lump of very fine Sugar, and a quarter of an Ounce of fixteen Shillings plain green Tea, let it
boil

boil up four or five Times, ſtirring the Tea about in it ; in this Time it will have diſſolved the Sugar, and taken the Taſte of the Tea.

This Cream is to be velveted ; therefore let ſome Gizzards be got, and uſe either the entire Gizzards, or only the inſide Skin. As we gave the Method of uſing the Gizzard entire before, we ſhall here give that of the Skin ; that the Houſekeeper taking her Choice, may on this, or any other Occaſion, uſe the one or the other according to her Choice.

Take two Gizzards of Fowls, waſh and clean them very well, then ſtrip clean off the Skin that covers the Inſide : Waſh this again, and then cut it very fine with a Pair of Sciſſars ; put it into a Cup, pour on it ſome of the Cream, ſet it on hot Embers ; when it has taken, put it to the reſt of the Cream. Then ſet the whole on ſome hot Cinders, and cover it with a Diſh ; put more hot Cinders over it, and then let it ſtand about a quarter of an Hour. In this Time the whole will take, and having been firſt properly ſtrained three or four Times over, as we have directed for the other Creams of this Kind, it will be fit to uſe when it is ſet by to cool.

7. *Coffee Cream.*

Put a Quart of rich Cream into a Stewpan, put to it a Piece of Sugar, and an Ounce of freſh ground Coffee ; let it heat gently, and then boil five or ſix Minutes.

Set it off, and velvet it in the ſame Manner as the others, by ſtripping two or three Gizzards, and waſhing and cutting to Pieces the Skin, and ſtewing it firſt in a little of the Cream, and then in the whole.

When it is compleated as the other, ſet it to cool ; and ſerve it up either cooled in this Way, or Iced by means of a Mould as mentioned before.

8. *Burnt Cream.*

Beat up the Yolks of five new-laid Eggs without any Whites, mix them up in a Stewpan with a Pint

of

of Milk, and a little Duft of Flour. Put in a Stick of Cinnamon broke, and a Roll of thin Peel of a frefh Lemon ; then put in two Ounces of blanched Almonds pounded, and two Spoonfuls of Orange-Flower-Water.

Set it over a brifk Fire in a Stove, and let it be ftirred continually, left it ftick to the Bottom.

Set another Stewpan over a Stove with a very fierce Fire ; put in fome Sugar, and a very little Water ; when it is coloured, pour in the Cream, and then draw together the Sugar with a Knife from the Border of the Cream, and ferve it up immediately hot ; not cold as the other Creams.

9. *Italian Cream.*

Set on a Pint of good New-Milk, put to it a little Salt, a Lump of fine Sugar, and a Stick of Cinnamon ; let it boil up, then ftrain it off, and pafs it three or four Times thro' a fine Sieve, with the Yolks of five Eggs : Set a Difh very even upon fome hot Embers ; pour in the whole, and cover it up with another Difh ; then put fome hot Embers over the Top of the upper Difh, and keep it thus hot about twelve Minutes. The Cream will be very well found by that Time, and is to be ferved up hot.

Cream may be ufed inftead of Milk, and in that Cafe, three Eggs will do inftead of five : It is rich in that Manner, but many prefer the other.

10. *Crackling Cream.*

Beat up five Yolks of Eggs in a moderate Difh, and then pour in by Degrees fome New-Milk, till the Difh is nearly full : Add fome fine Sugar powdered, and fome frefh Lemon-peel rafped, to give it a Flavour ; then fpread fome hot Embers, fet the Difh over them, and let it ftand till the Cream begins to take.

Then make the Fire more moderate, and take out the greateft Quantity of the Cream, laying it on the

Sides

Sides of the Dish, and leaving very little at the Bottom.

It will in this Manner stick every where to the Dish, and the Care must be to keep the Fire so moderate, that it may dry without burning.

When it is near enough, heat a Fire-shovel red hot, hold it over the Cream in every Part to brown it, and then with a Knife that has a very thin Blade, loosen the Cream from the Dish Edge, and put it altogether into the Middle again ; then set it over the Embers again, and it will waste a little, and come to the right crackling Condition in a few Minutes.

11. *Sweet Cream.*

Mix together a Quart of Cream and two Quarts of Milk, put them into a large Saucepan ; set them on to heat, and when it boils, set it off the Fire: Set a Soup Plate ready, take off the Cream with a Spoon and put it into the Soup Plate. Then set the Milk on the Fire again ; when it boils take it off, let it stand a while, and skim it as before ; in this Manner proceed till you have all the Cream, or else as much as is required for the Dish ; then put in some Orange-Flower-Water, and dust over it some Sugar, and send it up.

12. *To make Chocolate.*

We shall give the following Receipts for making Coffee and Chocolate in this Place, though they cannot properly be called Creams.

To a Quart of New Milk add three or four Spoonfuls of fair Water, put it over a clear Fire and let it boil.

In the mean Time shave two Ounces of the best Chocolate ; put this with a Quarter of a Pound of Loaf Sugar into the Milk and Water, and stir it about upon the Fire 'till the Sugar and the Chocolate are both disolved.

Take it off the Fire, beat up the Yolks of two new-laid Eggs very well, put them in, and pour it

back-

backwards and forwards as you would buttered Ale, to prevent it's curdling ; then set it upon the Fire again, and afterwards mill it up 'till it froths, and it will be fit for use.

This is the only true Way of making Chocolate, to be rich and smooth.

13. *To make Coffee.*

To a Quart of boiling Water add an Ounce of Coffee well ground ; set it over the Fire and let it just have a boil up; try that the Spout of your Coffee Pot be clear, that it may pour out. After this let it stand a few Minutes that the Grounds may settle, and it will be fit to drink.

Some sweeten Coffee with Lisbon, and others with Soaf Sugar, but Sugar Candy is better.

And it is now very common for those who like Mustard, to put a Tea Spoonful of the fine Durham Flour among the Coffee as soon as it is ground : This helps the Flavour, and is very wholsome.

S E C T. III.

Pickling and Preserving.

C H A P. XIV.

Of Pickling.

A R T. I. *To Pickle Cucumbers in Slices.*

CHUSE a Dozen of handsome large Cucumbers before they are too ripe; such as are in perfection for eating are fittest for this Use ; and chuse a Couple of sound large Onions.

Cut the Cucumbers into Slices of the thickness of a Crown-Piece, and cut the Onions also in Slices in the same Manner crosswise, having first peeled them.

Lay a little fprinkling of Salt at the bottom of a Difh : Then lay in fome of the Slices of Cucumbers, and Slices of Onions ; and having made an even Bed of them, fprinkle fome Salt over them, and then lay on another Bed of the Cucumbers and Onions.

Go on thus till you have filled the Difh, and always if you do more than this Quantity, allowing the fome Proportion of two Onions to the Dozen of Cucumbers.

When the Difh is full, place another over it ; and fet it by for a Day and a Night.

At the End of that Time, wipe a Cullander very dry and clean, and gently pour in the whole from the Difh : Let them ftand there fome Time to drain.

When they are well drained, put them into a Jarr ; and pour in as much of the beft white Wine Vinegar as will perfectly cover them : Thus let them ftand four Hours.

Then have a clean large earthen Pipkin ready, and pour into it the Vinegar from the Cucumbers : Put in a little Salt, make it boil, and then pour it on the Cucumbers.

While the Vinegar is heating, put into the Jarr with the Cucumbers, an Ounce of whole Pepper, four Blades of Mace, and a quarter of an Ounce of Ginger fliced thin.

Then pour the Vinegar in boiling hot, and fet by the Jarr to cool.

When it is perfectly cold, tie it over with a Bladder, Leather, and Paper, and fet it by four Days ; in that Time the Cucumbers will be fit to eat, and they will continue good all the Year.

The Cucumbers thus done, will not be fo Green as they are in the Windows of our Oilmen ; and the Reafon is very plain, becaufe there is no Verdigreafe among them.

The French have fo much Care of their Health, that they will not fuffer a green Cucumber of any

Kind

Kind pickled, to come to their Tables. They are perfectly right in this, and they have made green Pickles unfashionable; we think it is the great Art of Pickling, and therefore try at it.

Thofe who have written Receipts for this Pickle, order the Vinegar to be boiled up in a Copper Saucepan, and that gives it enough of the Verdigreafe to colour them : Many who make Pickles for Sale, put in Halfpence to help. We have before defcribed of how dangerous a Nature Verdigreafe is, it is nothing but the Ruft of Copper extracted by Vinegar; and they entail Difeafes upon Thoufands who ufe this pernicious Method of preferving their Pickles.

2. *To Pickle Radifh Pods.*

This is a very fingular and very agreeable Pickle, and nothing is eafier than to do it.

Let a Parcel of the Spring Radifhes ftand for Podding, or purchafe the Pods at Market; but when there is a Convenience of a Garden it is much beft to raife them, becaufe their Frefhnefs is a great Article.

They are light, fpungy, and hollow, and the Way to do them in Perfection is to throw them from the Plant to the Brine.

Put fome Spring Water into a large earthen Pan, and put in fo much Bay Salt that it will bear an Egg. This done, and the Salt melted in the Water, gather a Quantity of Pods from the Radifh Plants before they are too large, and put them into this Brine : Let them ftand in it ten Days, laying all the Time a Board over them to prefs them down, and keep them under the Water.

When they have lain thus long, pour the whole into a Sieve; let the Brine run thru', and let the Pods ftand to drain.

Then fet on as much Vinegar in a large earthen Pipkin as will be fufficient to cover the Pods; let it be made boiling hot, and while it is heating, let the Pods be taken out of the Sieve, and put upon a Napkin to dry.

When

When they are all dried, put them into a Jarr, and put with them a few Blades of Mace, fome Pepper, Ginger, All-fpice, and a few Cloves.

Pour in the Vinegar when it boils, and tie over it a coarfe Cloth four double.

Set by the Jarr for four Days; then pour off the Vinegar into the Pipkin: Boil it again and pour it upon them.

Repeat this four Times, and then let it ftand to be cold, and as foon as it is fo, put in a large Quantity of Muftard Seed whole, and fome Horfe-radifh fliced. Tie it over and fet it by for Ufe.

3. *Pickled Cauliflowers.*

Chufe four very handfome Cauliflowers that are white and very hard, yet are fufficiently ripe.

Set on a Stewpan or Preferving-pan with a good Quantity of Water, and fet by you a Pan of cold Spring or Pump Water juft frefh drawn.

Break the Cauliflowers at the Stalk, and then pull them into fmall Pieces as they naturally feparate; cut off the Ends of the Stalks, and pick away the little Leaves that grow among them, fo that nothing be ufed but the pure white flowery Part.

As the Cauliflowers are pulled to Pieces throw them into the cold Spring Water; when all are in ftir them about, pour away the Water, and let them ftand in a Sieve. By this Time the Water in the Pan will boil.

Then throw in a Handful of Salt, ftir it about, and when it is melted, and the Water boils, throw in the Cauliflowers, brifk up the Fire, and let them boil a Minute very quick.

Have a Cloth ready fpread upon the Dreffer or a Table. When the Cauliflowers have boiled a fingle Minute they are enough, take them out with a Slice, throw them into cold Water, and then lay them fingly upon the Cloth, fpread another over them, and

in

in that Manner let them ftand till they be thoroughly cold.

Prepare fome wide-mouthed Bottles very clean and perfectly dry.

When the Cauliflowers are cold put them Piece by Piece regularly into thefe Bottles, and put among them fome Blades of Mace and fome fcraped Nutmeg; then pour in as much diftilled Vinegar as will fill the Bottles; then melt fome Mutton Fat, pour in this, and let it cool in the Neck of the Bottles, covering the whole; this done tie them over with a wet Bladder, and let them ftand a Month or two before they are opened.

4. *To pickle Nafturtians.*

The Part of the Nafturtian that is pickled is the Bud of the Flower; People ufually call it the Seed of the Nafturtian, which they alfo call the *Stertion*, but this is all erroneous.

Gather a Parcel of the largeft and faireft Buds of the Nafturtian that can be found, juft before their opening into Flower, throw them into a Pan of cold Water, ftir them well about, then pour off the Water, and put on frefh; ftir them about again, and pour it off as before, and then lay them on a Sieve to dry; fet the Sieve, fupported, by a Couple of Bricks, or otherwife, in an airy Place, and now and then turn the Buds: They will fade a little, and they will foon be as dry as when juft gathered; and being thus faded they will take the Vinegar better than if they had been quite frefh.

The Buds being ready prepare fome wide-mouthed Bottles, fcrape down two or three Nutmegs, and break a few Blades of Mace; fet by you alfo fome Pepper whole, and a few Cloves.

Put a little of each of thefe Spices into the Bottom of each Bottle, and then fill the Bottle a third Part full of the Buds.

Put in fome more of the Spices of all the Kinds, and then more of the Buds, and thus proceed till the whole Quantity is in.

Then pour into each Bottle as much fine white Wine Vinegar as will fill it up, and tie them over; let them ftand fix Weeks before they are opened, and in that Time the Vinegar will have penetrated them thoroughly, and the Tafte of the Spices will be got into their very Subftance, fo that they will be one of the fineft Pickles in the World.

CHAP. II.

Of Preferving.

A R T. I.   *To candy Clove Julyflowers.*

GATHER a Quantity of Clove Julyflowers when they are full open, but before they begin to fade, pull them out of the Cups fingly, one whole Flower at a Time, and cut off the white Ends with a Pair of Sciffars.

As they are cut put them into an earthen Pan, and fee that no white Part be left, only the pure Purple is to be ufed.

Cover the Pan with a Pewter Plate, and they will keep frefh till you are ready for them.

Break fome treble-refined Sugar into fmall Lumps, dip them one by one into clear Water, and throw them wet into a Silver Saucepan: The Water they thus take up will be enough to melt the Sugar, and it muft be kept on the Fire till it is thick, and will draw in Hairs.

When the Sugar is in this Condition put in the Julyflowers, and ftir them round that they may be well mixed, then pour the whole into Cups and Glaffes; when it is of a hard Candy break it in Lumps, and lay it high, then dry it in a Stove, and
it

it will look like the fineft Sugar-candy, with the Flowers in the Pieces.

Any other Flowers may be candied in the fame Manner, but none does fo well.

2. *To preferve Goofberries whole.*

Gather a Quantity of large well-grown Goofberries before they are ripe, pull off the Eye, but let the Stalk remain on; put them into a Saucepan of Spring Water, fet them over the Fire, and let them ftand to fcald, but take Care no one of them breaks; if any do, fuch muft be taken out.

When they are enough throw them into cold Water, and let them ftand there.

The Goofberries muft be weighed before they are put to fcald, and for every Pound of them muft be allowed a Pound and half of Sugar of the fineft Kind; melt and clarify this, ufing a Pint of Water to every Pound of Sugar.

When this thin Syrup is perfectly clear put it into a Preferving-pan, and drop the Goofberries fingly into it; let the Fire be gentle, and the Syrup by Degrees heat till it boils; let the Goofberries boil in it a little while, but this muft be very gently, other-wife they will break.

Obferve them carefully, and after a few Minutes boiling you will fee that the Sugar has penetrated them; then take them off, fet them by till the next Day, covering them with white Paper.

Take the Goofberries out of the Syrup, and fet it on the Fire alone; boil it till it begins to be thick and roapy; fkim it carefully, and when it is thus thick, and very clear, put it to the Goofberries again.

Set the Pan with the Goofberries and Syrup over a very gentle Heat, and fo keep it till the Syrup is very thick; then take the Pan off the Fire, and fet it by till it is cold, and cover it up with Paper.

Boil fome frefh Goofberries in fair Water, and make the Water very ftrong of them; then ftrain it off,

off, and when it is perfectly clear put to every Pint of it a Pound of treble-refined Sugar ; melt this over a gentle Fire, and juft let it boil up ; ftrain it through a Flannel Bag, and it will be a thin and perfectly clear Syrup. This is what the Confectioners call a Jelly.

Set this by to cool, as alfo the Goofberries, and the next Day put the Goofberries into Glaffes, and fill them up with this Syrup; cover them with Paper, and put them in fome dry Place. They will be very beautiful, and keep good the whole Year.

S E C T.   IV.

Of the beft Methods of preferving Provifions at Sea.

A R T. I. *A Calf.*

WHEN a Calf is to be killed for this Purpofe, fee that it be a very fine one.

Cut it up into Quarters; then firft take off the Shoulder from one of the Quarters, and cut off the Knuckle; then lard the Shoulder with very fine Bacon, feafon it with Pepper and Salt, and ftrew on fome Leaves of fweet Herbs, with grated Nutmeg, Mace fhred, and a little fine Sugar powdered mixed among them.

When the Shoulder is thus prepared cut off the Loins, and blanch them over a Charcoal Fire ; hang them up to be cold, and then lard them alfo with Bacon.

Then take out the Fat, and take off the Kidneys, fplit each of them in four, without quite feparating the Parts, and ftrew thefe over with Pepper and Salt.

Take

Take the Fillets next; take out the principal Bones, then lard them, and feafon them with Pepper and Salt, and with the fame Spices and Sweet Herbs laſt mentioned.

When the whole Calf is thus dreffed let it be put Piece over Piece in a great earthen Pan, and lay over it fome large Slices of Bacon ; then fpread over the whole a good deal of Butter, tie the Pan over, and fend it to an Oven to be done very well, but with a flack Heat, not to be burnt.

This done prepare a Caſk juſt big enough to hold the whole Quantity ; let it be well fcalded, feafoned, and dried.

Cover the Bottom of the Caſk with Bay Leaves, Cloves, Pepper, and Salt, and then lay in a good Quantity of Veal.

When this is preffed down put in more of the fame Seafoning, and thus continue till the Caſk is full.

Then melt a large Quantity of Butter, and when it is juſt luke-warm pour it over the Meat fo as entirely to cover it three Inches thick. This need not be grudged, for it will not be wafted.

As the Butter is poured in let the Caſk be fhook, and the Butter let in among the Pieces, then let it lie over the whole the Thickneſs we have directed. Let it cool, and fet it by in a cool Place till it is taken on board.

This is an excellent Method. The Uſes of the feveral Pieces, and the beſt Way of dreffing them, we fhall particularly fhew hereafter, firſt laying down the Methods here of preferving what it is needful to carry for the Purpofe.

2. *To preferve Tripe and Neats Feet.*

Chufe a Quantity of Tripe and Neats Feet ready boiled, as they are ufually fold, and the beſt that can be got.

Prepare a Cafk of proper Size, and fcald and feafon it well.

Then lay at the Bottom fome Bay Leaves, put over thefe fome Corns of Pepper, whole Cloves, and Bay Salt.

Lay in a Covering of Tripe and Feet, throw in a good Quantity of the fame Salt and Seafoning, and fo put more Tripe and Feet over them; continue this Method, throwing in a large Quantity of the Salt and Spices every Time any of the Feet and Tripe are put in, till the whole is full; thus the Feet and Tripe will lie between Beds of Salt and Spices, and at the fame Time will have a great deal of both get in among them.

When the Cafk is thus filled with the Provifion, pour in foftly as much Vinegar as it will hold, fhaking it often, and giving Time for the fettling of the Vinegar, that as much may be got in as the Cafk can poffibly contain.

Then clofe it up well, faftening in the Cover with Pitch, and let the Cafk be fet by, and kept cool, till the Time of taking it on board the Ship.

3. *Sea Saufages.*

Cut a Quantity of fine Pork, Fat and Lean together, and let it be cut fmall, but not like fine minced Meat.

Seafon it well with Pepper and Salt, Leaves of Thyme and Winter Savoury, and fome Nutmeg; then clean a Quantity of middling Hog's Guts, or of fmall Beef Guts, and ftuff thefe with the Saufage Meat.

Before you proceed too far drefs one of thefe Saufages, and tafte how it is for Seafoning; if not right, make the reft of the minced Meat right before you fill any more.

When they are well mixed and feafoned fill all the Guts, and tie them up carefully with Packthread; then prepare a Cafk, by feafoning it well, lay at the

Bot-

Bottom fome Bay Leaves, and then put in fome Sau-fages, then lay more Bay Leaves, and upon them more Saufages; thus proceeding till the Cafk is full.

Then pour in a great Quantity of Hog's Lard juft melted, and let it fill up all the Spaces among the Saufages, and come over the Top of them feveral Inches; then cover up the Cafk, clofe it well, and fend it on board.

4. *To preferve Geefe a la Daube.*

Chufe eight or ten Geefe for a fmall Cafk, or more, according to the expected Length of the Voyage, let them be picked and drawn, then let them be finged.

Then open the Legs and take out the great Bones, and do the fame to the Breaft, but let the Wings be hanging to the Body.

Having cut the Breaft open lengthwife, and taken out the Bones, cut the Rump, and take out any Blood that may be on the Infide; then take off the Fat, and fet it on the Fire to melt in a Pan.

The Geefe being thus prepared ftrew fome Salt over their Legs, and leave them fo fix Hours.

Then having ftrained the Fat melt with it a good Quantity of Lard, and throw them in to be half done in it, and then take them out, and fet them to drain and cool.

When they are cold prepare the Cafk for them, and put at the Bottom fome Bay Leaves, Cloves, and Pepper Corns, all whole; this done lay them in re-gularly, with more of the Bay Leaves, Cloves, and Pepper Corns among them.

When the Cafk is thus filled with them pour in the melted Hog's Lard and Goofe Fat, fhaking it at Times that the Fat may get in, and let it cover the whole two or three Inches; then clofe up the Cafk, and fend it on board.

5. *To*

5. *To preserve Soals for Sea.*

Scale, gut, and wash the Soals, then drain them, and when they are moderately dried strew some Salt over them, and let them lie so six Hours.

Then wipe them, strew some Flour over them, and split them all along down the Back.

Set on a Stewpan with a good Quantity of Oil,. throw in the Soals, and let them fry till they be pretty brown; then drain them on a Fish-plate.

Prepare a Cask for them, put at the Bottom some Bay Leaves, Cloves, and Pepper Corns; then lay in some of the Soals, upon these put more Bay Leaves, Pepper Corns, and Cloves, and more Soals over them till the Cask is full.

Then pour in some very good Oil till the Cask is quite full, and close it up, and send it on board.

6. *To preserve Greens.*

Chuse some fine well-grown Cabbages, clean them, cut away the Stalks, split them in four, and throw them into boiling Water; let them lie a few Minutes in it, then throw them into a Vessel of cold Pump Water, and when they are thoroughly cold drain them well.

Prepare a Cask, and that being ready make a strong Brine; it must not be quite strong enough to make an Egg swim, but very little weaker: It is best made by boiling up common Salt in Water, and skimming it if any Thing rises.

When this is cold, and the Cask ready, lay in the Cabbages very evenly and carefully, pressing them down gently, but not squeezing them too much; when a Parcel of them are in put in some of the Brine.

Then lay in more of the Cabbages, and pour in more Brine; in this Manner proceed till the Cask is filled, and the Brine swims to some Depth over the

Top

Top of the Cabbages; then put on the Lid of the Caſk, and cloſe it well down.

French Beans, and almoſt every Kind of Greens, are to be preſerved in the ſame Manner.

When they are to be dreſſed they muſt be firſt ſweetened, by putting them into freſh Water for a few Hours, and they will eat very well.

7. *To preſerve Roots dry.*

Cut ſome Carrots into Slices, cut ſome Parſnips alſo in the ſame Manner, and peel ſome Onions, and cut them alſo in the ſame Manner.

All theſe are to be prepared in the ſame Manner for preſerving, and therefore the ſame Rules will ſerve.

When the Roots are ſliced ſet on a Stewpan with a good deal of freſh Butter, put in ſome of any one of the Roots, for they muſt be done ſeparate; and preſerved ſeparate, and when they are fried to a good brown take them out, and put in more.

As they are taken out, Parcel after Parcel, place them on Hair Sieves to dry, and the next Day ſend them to be baked in a very ſlack Oven.

This will thoroughly dry them; they muſt then be put up in Boxes, and kept dry.

They will thus keep longer, and be fitter for Uſe than if carried on board in their natural Condition: They are ready for all Soups, Raggoos, and the like.

8. *To dry Muſhrooms.*

Clean a Parcel of large Muſhrooms, cut out the Stalks, peel them, and ſcrape out the Gills.

Set them over the Fire in a Saucepan with a little Salt, and let them ſtew a while in their own Liquor, then throw them into a Sieve to drain: When they are tolerably dry ſend them to a ſlack Oven upon Tin Plates, and let them be thoroughly dried; then pack them up in ſhallow Boxes, and keep them in a dry Place.

9. *Muſhrooms*

9. *Mushroom Powder.*

Clean a Quantity of large Mushrooms, then set them over the Fire with a Handful of Salt, a good deal of Pepper, some Blades of Mace, and an Onion stuck with Cloves; let them stew a little, then throw in a Stick of Cinnamon broken.

A great deal of Liquor will come from them, and they must stand over the Fire 'till that is entirely wasted; then they must be taken out, laid on a Sieve to dry a little, and after that, laid on Tin Plates and sent to be dried in an Oven, and then beat to Powder: This Powder must be put up in Jarrs, and is ready for various Uses: It must be kept well rammed down.

10. *Anchovy Sauce to keep for a Voyage.*

Chop to Pieces two Dozen of fine Anchovies Bones and all; shred very fine a Dozen Shallots, and scrape a good Handful of Horse-Radish: Shred a quarter of an Ounce of Mace, cut a Lemon in Slices, and put all these into a Saucepan; add a Dram of Cloves, and a quarter of an Ounce of whole Pepper, then pour in half a Pint of rich Anchovy Liquor, a Pint of Water, and a Quart of white Wine, and a Pint of Red.

Boil all these together for half an Hour, then strain off the Liquor, and bottle it up.

C H A P. II.

Of dressing Sea Provisions.

A R T. I. *To roast a Loin of Veal preserved as before shewn.*

TAKE a Loin of Veal out of the Cask, and spit it carefully; rub a Couple of Sheets of Paper with a good Quantity of the Butter that comes out with the Veal; wrap it up in these Papers, and roast it in the usual Manner.

Serve

Serve it up with a Sauce made of Portable Soup and Mushroom Powder.

2. *To stew a Fillet of Ship Veal.*

Take out one of the Fillets of Veal from the Cask ; take out some of the Butter with it, put this Butter in a Stewpan, set it on with a little Flour, and make it brown.

Then put in a little Gravy made of a small Piece of Portable Soup thrown into Water, and put in the Fillet of Veal : Let it stew some Time, then turn it ; pour in more of the same Gravy, and cover it up to stew 'till well done.

Then put in some Capers chopped small, some dried Mushrooms, and a Piece of Butter rolled in Flour ; thicken it, give it a good Relish, and then send it up, pouring the Gravy round the Veal.

3. *To dress Ship Tripe and Onions.*

Set on a Stewpan with some Butter, when it is melted, throw in some dried Onions according to the foregoing Receipt.

When these have had a Tofs up together, take out some Tripe from the Vinegar in their Cask ; cut them into thin Slices, and put them into the Stewpan.

Strew on them a little Flour, and moiften the whole with a little warm Water.

Let these stew a while, then cut in a small Clove of Garlick.

Let it stew some Minutes longer ; then break four Eggs and beat them up, get in a little of the Liquor of the Stewpan, and then mix this with the rest. This will thicken up the Liquor very agreeably, and the whole will be a very agreeable Dish.

4. *To dress preserved Soals.*

Take half a Dozen of the Soals out of their Oil, and lay them on a Sieve to drain.

Melt some Butter very thick ; then when the Soals are drained lay them in a Dish, pour this Butter

over

over them, and turn them in it, that they may be perfectly melted with it.

Duft them over with fine Crumbs of Bread, and then broil them. Serve them up with a Sauce of Shallots and Gravy.

4. *A Harrico of French Beans.*

We have directed the Method of preferving French Beans in the ufual Way, but befides thefe, there fhould be carried out a Quantity of the Seed Beans dry in the manner of Peafe; thefe are to be ufed for this Harrico, and they may be employed alfo on many other Occafions.

Take a Pint of thefe dry Seed Beans, pick them over that there be no Dirt among them, and put them into a Saucepan with two Quarts of Water; let them boil two Hours.

If the Water waftes too faft, it muft be fupplied by putting in fome hot out of another Veffel.

While the Beans are doing, peel a good Quantity of Onions, and flice them very thin, let there be the Quantity of two double Handfuls.

Set on a Stewpan with fome frefh Butter; let it melt, and when it makes no more Noife, throw in the Onions, and fry them to a fine brown.

Stir them about from Time to Time, that they may be all of a Colour.

When this is done, pour off the Water from the Beans into a Bafon, and put the Beans into the Stewpan, with the Onions and Butter. Add to the whole two Tea Spoonfuls of beaten Pepper and fome Salt, and let it ftew fome time: Pour in fome of the Water the Beans were boiled in, and make it of what Thicknefs you chufe.

Break a Couple of Eggs, beat up the Yolks with a little Vinegar, and mix the whole into the Stewpan; then when all has been once well heated and ftirred together, pour it off into a warm Difh.

A great Caution in this and all other Made Difhes at Sea is, that they be not made too falt.

C H A P.

C H A P. III.

Diſhes for Sea Service.

A R T. I. *Bouride.*

THIS is a particular kind of Soup very much eſteemed on board of Ships, a Baſon of it being taken in a Morning. It is to be made thus.

Put two Quarts of Water into a Saucepan, and put into it a Couple of large Onions cut very ſmall, and a Lump of Butter. Stir it about; when it boils break in four Biſcuits, and then ſeaſon it with Pepper and Salt; then let it boil 'till half is conſumed, and add to it ſome Gravy, and a little white Wine: Let it boil up once when theſe laſt are in, and then ſerve it up in Baſons hot.

2. *Gravy Soup.*

This for Sea Service is delivered in a ſhort Direction; we have in a preceding Number given the Method of making Portable Soup; a Quantity of this ſhould always be taken to Sea, and then the Gravy Soup is made with little Trouble: Boil a Quantity of ſoft Water, as much as is required for the Diſh, and put in ſome of the Portable Soup, ſtir it about, and ſalt it a little; taſte it, and if it be not ſtrong enough, put in ſome more of the Soup: Bake ſome Sippets, lay them round the Sides of the Diſh, and pour in the Soup. If any freſh Meat be boiled, put about a Pound in the Middle.

3. *Peaſe Soup.*

Set on a Quart of Peaſe in eight Quarts of Water, and boil them 'till they are tender.

Let a Piece of Salt Pork be laid in Water the Night before, and when the Peaſe are tender, put it into the Pot.

Put with it two large Onions peeled, ſome Celeri if there be any, and a Bundle of Sweet Herbs; and put

N°. XXV.   4 Y   in

in at the fame Time half a Table Spoonful of whole Pepper.

Let the whole boil 'till the Meat is enough, and probably the Soup will alfo be enough by that Time; but if it be not, the Meat muft be taken out, and the Soup boiled longer.

When it is enough, ftrain it thro' a Sieve, fet it on again, and rub in a good deal of dry Mint. Keep the Meat all this Time hot, and when the Soup is enough, put it in again; let it boil three Minutes that all may be hot together; then put in a Piece of Portable Soup, and let it boil up for that to diffolve; ftir all well together, and ferve it in hot.

This may be made with Beef as well as Pork, and without the Portable Soup; but this is the Way that makes it beft of all, and there is no great Expence in the Addition.

4. *Beef Pudding.*

Lay a Piece of the Sea Beef in Soak for four and twenty Hours; then prepare a Cruft with Flour, Water, and a good Quantity of Mutton Suet fhred fine, or if there be none of that, fome Beef Dripping will do. Let the Cruft be thick and firm; put in the Beef, and ftrew over it a little Pepper; roll it up in the Cruft, tie it in a Cloth, and boil it four Hours. Then ferve it up hot.

5. *Rice Pudding.*

Tie up fome Rice loofe in a Cloth, and boil it in foft Water an Hour.

Then take it up, untie the Cloth, pour the Rice into a Difh, and put to it a good Piece of Butter; ftir this well in, and then grate in half a Nutmeg.

Then put it into a Cloth again, and boil it an Hour more. When it is done melt fome Butter, with a little white Wine and Sugar, by Way of Sauce; and take up the Pudding, untie the Cloth in a Difh, and turn the Pudding out whole; then pour over it the Sauce.

6. *Plumb*

6. *Plumb Pudding.*

Shred a Pound of Suet very fine, and mix it up with a Pound of Flour; add two Tea Spoonfuls of beaten Ginger, and a large Spoonful of Tincture of Saffron.

Stir up thefe together, then put in a Pound of Currants wafhed and picked, and half a Pound of Raifins ftoned. Put in as much fweet Water as will make it up pretty ftiff; mix it all well together, and then either boil or bake it.

7. *Sheep's Liver Pudding.*

So long as live Provifions laft, every Part of them is to be made the moft of, and this is one Inftance of a very good Difh made out of an ordinary Part.

When a Sheep is killed let the Liver be cleaned, and fhred very fine, weigh it, and weigh half the Quantity of Suet; fhred this very fine, and mix it with the Liver. Then grate as much Bifcuit as there is Suet, and mix this with the reft. Shred an Anchovy, and mix with it: Then grate in fome Nutmeg, and add fome Sweet Herbs picked from the Stalks, and chopped very fine, and a little Pepper and Salt.

When all is well mixed together, add a Piece of Butter, and a little Anchovy Liquor, and then make a Cruft as we have before directed; put in the whole and roll it up clofe, then tie it up in a Bag and boil it. It will require three Hours.

8. *An Oat Pudding.*

Get a Pint of Oats once cut after the Shelling; fhred a Pound of Suet, and add to thefe a Pound of Currants wafhed and picked, and half a Pound of Raifins ftoned. Mix all together, and add a little Salt; tie it in a Cloth, and leave Room for fwelling; boil it three Hours, and fend it up with a Slice of Butter upon a Saucer, for thofe who chufe to put it upon a Slice of the Pudding.

9. *Rice*

9. *A Rice Pudding for baking.*

Pick a Pound of Rice very clean, and boil it in Water 'till it is juſt tender ; then pour it into a Cloth, put over the Top of a Pan, and let all the Water run gently from it without ſqueezing.

While it is hot, and when it is pretty well drained, ſtir in a good Piece of Butter ; then add ſome fine Sugar, and a little Salt ; grate in ſome Nutmeg, and ſeaſon it in all theſe Reſpeĉts to the Palate, taſting at Times, and adding where the Quantity is not ſufficient of any Kind.

Waſh and pick half a Pound of Currants, and when all the reſt is well mixed, put theſe in ; ſtir all very well together, and then prepare a Pan to hold it. Butter the Inſide of it very well, pour in the Ingredients, and ſet it into the Oven ; let it be well baked : It will come out of a fine Brown, mellow, and very pleaſant.

10. *Peaſe Puddings.*

Tie up a Quantity of Peaſe in a Cloth, and boil them a conſiderable Time ; when they have boiled long enough to be tender, take them up ; untie the Cloth, pour the Peaſe into an earthen Diſh and beat them well : Add a good Piece of Butter, and work it well in ; then add ſome Salt and Pepper, and beat it up once more thoroughly.

When this is done, tie it up again, and boil it an Hour longer ; then take it up ; take it out of the Bag, lay it handſomely in the Diſh, and cut a round Hole at the Top ; pour ſome melted Butter into this, and duſt over it a little Pepper ; ſo ſend it up.

11. *White Bread Dumplings.*

When there is white Bread to be had at Sea, a very agreeable Variety is made upon the Table by this Dumpling.

Shred very fine a quarter of a Pound of Beef Suet ; grate all the Crumb of a Two-penny Loaf, or of a

like

like Quantity of white Bread of any Kind ; mix thefe together, and grate to them half a Nutmeg ; add a little Salt, and half an Ounce of powdered fine Sugar.

Mix all thefe well together, then break two Eggs, beat them up with half a Glafs of Mountain, and mix this with the Ingredients : Work all well together into a ftiff Pafte, and roll it up in Dumplings of the Big-nefs of one's Fift.

While the Dumplings are making let the Water be fet on to boil them ; when it boils put them in, and let them boil half an Hour.

When they are taken up lay them in a fmall Difh, and melt a Bafon of Butter with fome Mountain ; pour this over the Dumplings, and then ftrew over them, and over the Sides of the Difh fome fine powdered Sugar.

Thefe, and many other of the Sea Difhes, may be fent up any where, and to Sea People they are very pleafing, and to others becaufe of their Novelty, and the Variety they make in the Entertainment.

12. *To bake Fifh.*

There are often Opportunities of taking Fifh at Sea, and they never are eaten in fuch Perfection as when they are put out of the Sea to the Fire. Bak-ing is an eafy Way of managing many Kinds, and when it is properly done anfwers extremely well.

We need not particularize the Fifh, for it will do for almoft any, and whatever comes to the Net on this Occafion is Fifh, in the true Senfe of the Proverb.

Prepare a Pan according to the Size or Quantity of the Fifh ; if they be fmall a great many may be done together, but this Method of drefling does beft for larger, and when very big they may be cut, or only a Piece ufed at a Time.

Butter the Infide of the Pan, then lay in the Fifh, duft fome Flour over it, then fprinkle on a little Salt,

and

and put in a little Water, and an equal Quantity of Wine.

Cut an Onion into fix Pieces, and put it in; then put in a Bunch of fweet Herbs; and after all thefe are placed ftick fome Pieces of Butter all over the Fifh, and fo fend it to the Oven. Let it be baked to a fine brown.

Then heat a Difh, take the Pan out of the Oven, take up the Fifh, and lay it upon the Difh.

Skim off all the Fat in the Pan, and then ftrain the Liquor, add to it fome Gravy, or a Bit of Portable Soup, and a little Catchup; thicken it up with a Piece of Butter rolled in Flour, and fend it up in a Bafon: The Fifh will be of a fine delicate Brown, and this Sauce excellent.

13. *A baked Oatmeal Pudding.*

Set on a Saucepan with a Quart of Water and a little Salt; when it boils ftir in fome Oatmeal, a little at a Time, till the whole is fo thick that a Spoon can hardly be ftirred in it; then take it off the Fire, and add a good Glafs of Mountain, and a Spoonful of Sugar, and grate over it a little Nutmeg; then ftir in Half a Pound of Currants wafhed and picked.

When all is ready butter the Infide of a Pan, and pour in the whole; fend it to the Oven, and let it be well done.

14. *A Sea Chicken Pie.*

Make a proper Quantity of good rich Cruft, roll it out, and cover a Difh with it; cut fome Bacon into thin Slices, and lay them over the Bottom, covering it entirely; prefs them down flat and even, ftrew over the Bacon a very little Pepper, and a few Leaves of fweet Herbs dried.

Pick and draw a Fowl, or well-grown Chicken, put fome Pepper and Salt into the Belly, a Lump of Butter, and a Piece of Bacon rolled in dry Leaves of fweet Herb; finge it, and then lay it handfomely in the

the Pie, preffing it a little down; cut fome more Slices of Bacon, and pepper them, and duft over them a few Leaves of fweet Herbs; then cover the Fowl carefully with thefe, and put in a very little Water, and then put on the Lid.

Let this Pie be put into the Oven, and baked two Hours.

When the Time of its baking is near expired, fet on Half a Pint of Water in a Saucepan, when it boils put in a Piece of portable Soup, and let it diffolve; this will make a rich Gravy.

When the Pie comes out of the Oven take off the Lid, take away the Bacon that has covered the Fowl, and fkim off the Fat that is upon the Liquor, then pour in the hot Gravy out of the Saucepan, put on the Lid again, and fend it up hot.

Pork may be ufed inftead of Bacon, but as the Sea Pork is ufually very falt, it will be beft to fet it to foak four and twenty Hours before it is ufed, and then to cut it out into thin Slices to cover the Bottom of the Pie, and afterwards to lay over the Fowl.

15. *A Sea Pork Pie.*

Cut fome boiled Pork into thin Slices, and flice a Quantity of fine Potatoes, firft carefully peeled; and let there be at leaft as much Potatoes as Pork.

Make a good Cruft, cover a Difh with it, and then lay in a Quantity of the Pork.

Strew a good deal of Pepper over this, and then lay in fome Potatoes; pepper thefe a little.

Then lay in more Pork to cover the Potatoes, and after feafoning it, more Potatoes upon it, and fo on, one Layer over another, till the Pie is full.

Put a good Quantity of Butter in feparate Pieces at the Top, then pour in Water till the Difh is nearly half full; put on the Lid, and fend it to the Oven; let it be well baked. The Potatoes will take off the Saltnefs of the Pork, and all will eat very well together.

The

The only Caution is, that the Pie be not put into an Oven that is too hot, for it muſt ſoak.

16. *Sea Veniſon.*

When a Sheep is killed on board let the Blood be carefully ſaved, and let a Perſon ſtir it continually from the Time it comes from the Sheep till is is cold; this will prevent it from congealing.

Then cut up the Sheep, and cut the Leg of one Side like a Haunch of Veniſon.

Then cut off the Shoulder and the Loin, and the Neck and Breaſt in two.

Put firſt the Leg into a deep Pan, and pour ſome of the Blood to it; then put in the other Pieces, and pour more of the Blood as they are put in, and laſt of all pour the whole over them.

Thus let them ſtand ſoaking as long as they will keep good.

Then when the Blood begins to turn bad, for that will taint a great while before the Meat, take out the ſeveral Pieces, and hang them up out of the Sun; keep them thus as long as they will keep freſh, then roaſt the Haunch of the Mutton in all Reſpects as if it were Veniſon; make ſome Gravy Sauce of the porta-ble Soup, and ſerve it up.

The other Joints might be dreſſed in the ſame Way at the ſame Time, but as ſo much Veniſon is not wanted to be dreſſed at once, the beſt Way of treating them is this: Lay them in a large Pan, with the fat Side downwards, and when they are preſſed flat with the Hands, pour gently over them a Bottle of red Wine; then when they are well ſoaked with this pour in a Quart of Vinegar, and thus let them lie all Night.

After this take the Neck, Breaſt, and Loin out of the Pickle, but leave the Shoulder in to ſtay a Week longer; rub it with a Handful of common Salt, and a large Spoonful of coarſe Sugar, mixed with

Half

Half an Ounce of Salt Petre, and the fame Quantity of Bay Salt.

The Breaft and Loin fhould be made into a Pafty, and the beft Way of doing this is firft to bone and feafon them, then make a good Cruft, and make the Pafty in the ufual Way, as we have directed in its Place.

While the Pafty is baking let the Bones be boiled to make Gravy, with fome Pepper, Salt, and dry Leaves of fweet Herbs, and a Blade of Mace broken.

When the Pafty comes home take off the Lid, and pour in this hot Gravy, then fend it up.

The Shoulder will eat extremely well boiled, with a Peafe Pudding, in the Manner of Pork.

SECT. V.

Of Brewery and Liquors.

CHAP. I.

Of Wines.

A R T. I. *Goofeberry Wine.*

GATHER a good Quantity of Goofeberries when they are well grown, but not ripe, bruife them in a Tub with the Peftle of a large Marble Mortar; put them into a Horfe-hair Bag, and prefs them heartily, but not by fo violent a Method as to break the Seeds.

Meafure out the Juice, and to every Gallon of it put three Pounds and a half of the fineft Powder Sugar.

Chufe a Veffel that will juft hold the Quantity, and pouring in the Liquor fill it quite up.

N°. XXV. 4 Z Let

Let this ſtand a Month in a cool quiet Place, and then draw it from the Lees.

Waſh out the Veſſel, and then pour it in again.

Let it ſtand as before, three, four, or five Months, according to the Quantity, then bottle it off. It will be a ſtrong and pleaſant Wine.

2. *Currant Wine.*

Chuſe a dry Day for gathering the Fruit, gather it full ripe, ſtrip the Berries clean from the Stalks, and put them into a large earthen Pan.

Bruiſe them with the Peſtle of a Marble Mortar till they be all thoroughly broken.

Let them ſtand four-and-twenty Hours in the Pan: In this Time they will ferment, and the Juice which was thick will by that Means grow thin; then pour the whole into a Hair Sieve ſet over a Pan large enough to hold the Juice; it will run freely through, and it is not to be ſqueezed or forced at all.

The Juice being thus obtained, to every Gallon of it put three Pounds and a half of Liſbon Sugar, ſtir it well together, and put it into the Veſſel.

If you have ſix Gallons of it put in a Quart of Brandy, and the ſame Proportion to any greater or ſmaller Quantity.

The Veſſel ſhould be full, and it ſhould ſtand ſix Weeks.

Then let it be examined, and if it be fine bottle it off.

If it be not fine enough for bottling let it be drawn from the Lees into another Caſk, and from that bottled after it has ſtood a Fortnight, for in that Time it will generally grow thoroughly fine and clear.

3. *Raſberry Wine.*

This is to be made much in the ſame Manner of the Currant Wine, and indeed ſo are all of them; they are to be fermented with a due Quantity of Sugar,

and

and ftrengthned as they may require, and then fet to be fine for bottling.

This is the general Rule, and we have explained the Nature of the whole in a preceding Part; fo that it will be familiar from a fhort Account on thefe particular Articles.

Let a Quantity of fine red Rafberries be gathered when they are perfectly ripe, and in the Middle of a dry Day.

Let them be put into a Marble Mortar, and bruifed gently, but not beaten with the Peftle; then let them be ftrained through a Flannel Bag that the clear Juice may run through freely.

To a Gallon of the Juice put four Pounds of double-refined Sugar, ftir the Juice and Sugar well together, and let them ftand three Days; then pour the clear Liquor from the Settlement at the Bottom.

This may be made into a Wine in the ufual Way, by putting it up into a Cafk; but the beft and moft elegant Method is, to add double the Quantity of good white Wine to the Juice thus got clear, and it is to be immediately bottled off. It will this Way be fit to drink in a Week, and it will be a very rich and pleafant Wine.

If Brandy, or very pure Melaffes Spirit be put to the Juice and Sugar inftead of the Wine, it makes the beft Kind of Rafberry Brandy.

4. *Englifh Frontiniack.*

This is a Wine made of Sugar and Raifins, and flavoured highly with Elder Flowers, which give it a rich and elegant Tafte, extremely refembling that of the foreign Frontiniack Wine. The true Way of making it is this:

Chop very fmall fix Pounds of the fineft Raifins of the Sun; beat to a coarfe Powder twelve Pounds of Lump Sugar, and put both thefe into fix Gallons of Water: Set this on the Fire, and boil it an Hour.

Gather

Gather a Quantity of Elder Flowers that are perfectly ripe, and let them be gathered an Hour or two after Sun-rife, but not late in the Day : Being thoroughly ripe the Flowers will eafily rub off the Bunches, and there are to be the Quantity of half a Peck of the pure Flowers thus collected.

Put thefe into the Liquor, and fet it by.

The next Day fqueeze into it three good Lemons, and add four Spoonfuls of Ale Yeaft.

Let this ftand together two Days, then ftrain it off, and put it into a Veffel.

To every Gallon of this Liquor put a Quart of Rhenifh Wine, and then put a Bung lightly into the Veffel; let it remain thus a Fortnight, and then ftop it down clofe.

Let it ftand in this Manner fix Months, then try if it be clear, and if it is draw it off into Bottles; if not, draw it from the Lees, and let it ftand till it is fine, and then bottle it.

This will be a found rich Wine, and will have a moft true Tafte of Frontiniack.

C H A P. II.

Of Brewing.

A R T. I. *Of Malt in general.*

IN order to have Beer in Perfection, the firft Thing fhould be the Care of the Malt. There are fo many People who do amifs in this Article, that we fhall advife the Farmer, when he has Convenience, to make his Malt himfelf; and when he cannot do this, yet at leaft to go as far in it as he can : And that he may not be at a Lofs for Inftructions on this Head, we fhall give him the beft fhort Rules. The Gentleman will find Advantage alfo in obferving of them ; for whether a Thing is practifed or not, the better it

is

is underftood the more likely the Perfon will be to efcape Fraud who is concerned in the Article.

Barley to make good Malt fhould be itfelf very good in its Kind, of a full Body, mown when ripe, and well cured; and in the making the Malt the Nature of the Fuel fhould be greatly regarded: Some make it with Wood, and others with Straw; in fome Places it is made with Fern, but that is worft of all: The beft Fuel is Coke, and the next is Welch Coal. The Reafon of all this is very plain, for the Smoke of the Fuel muft come at the Malt as it is drying, and will give it a Flavour; therefore the beft is that which has no Smoke at all, and the next beft that which has the Smoke fweeteft.

Coke is Cinders of fine Coal burnt till the Sulphur is gone, fo that they will afterwards make neither Smoke nor Smell, and yet will give a brifk, fteady Heat; this is therefore beft of all, for the plaineft Reafons in the World.

Welch Coal is not to be had in all Places, but when it can be got is excellent, for it makes a clear, clean Fire, and has no Smell.

The very worft is Fern, whofe Smoke is four and fuffocating: None ufe it but Country People who have no Choice of their Materials, and not much Niceity in their Palates.

There are fome Counties in England where all the Malt Liquor is fpoiled by this Flavour from Fern Smoke: Cuftom inures them to it, but others cannot tafte it.

Wood has fome Sournefs, but not nearly fo much as Fern; and as to Straw, nothing is fweeter; though there be a great deal of Smoke it is little hurtful.

From thefe Hints the Perfon who is about to purchafe Malt for Brewing will know what are the Defects, and to what they are owing; fo that he can be guarded againft them, and he who fhall be in the

W'ay

Way of making it himſelf will be able to do it with
moſt Advantage.

C H A P. III.

Of the Choice of Water for Brewing.

NEXT to the Choice of the Malt is that of the
Water. There are particular Places where all
the Beer is ſpoiled by the Badneſs of the Water, as
there are others where it is by the Malt.

Thus the mineral Taſte of the Waters in Rutland
give all the Malt Liquor brewed with them a Taſte of
Allum; and in the ſame Manner elſewhere much
Hurt is done when it is leſs perceived what is the
Reaſon.

Theſe however are Particulars which it is only
needful to name, that in ſuch Caſes they may be
underſtood, that People may guard againſt them.
One general Rule will hold : If the Beer in any Place
be univerſally bad, and the Malt nothing particular,
and the more if Beer brewed with Malt from other
Places ſtill have the ſame bad Quality, then it is the
Buſineſs of the Brewer to examine the Water ; if his
Taſte diſcover nothing, let him deſire ſome Chemiſt
to try it by Experiments. A little of ſuch bad Ingredients will ſpoil it for Brewing, and the Art of thoſe
People, ſuch of them as underſtand their Buſineſs,
will diſcover the ſmalleſt Quantity.

If it be found that all the Water is bad, and there
is no large River near, for that cannot well be all
ſpoiled, the Remedy is to ſave Rain Water.

March and October are good Months for Brewing,
and there is Rain enough about that Time : Let this
be ſaved, and the Beer probably will be good that is
brewed with it, though all elſe in the Neighbourhood
be bad.

There is more in this than many can think. The
Thames Water makes London Porter ; the high dry-

ing

ing of the Malt helps, but there cannot be this Liquor made well and properly with any other Water.

In all Places the Brewer has his Choice of two or three Kinds of Water, ufually of more, and it is proper he know the Difference; Liquor he calls it, for it is a Forfeit in a Brewhoufe to fay Beer is made of Water.

The feveral Kinds are, Well Water, River Water, Pond Water, and Rain Water.

Of thefe, Well Water is the hardeft, and Rain Water is the fofteft of all.

River Water is fofter than Well, and Pond Water than River. The general Rule is, that the brown Malts fhould be brewed with foft Water, and the pale with hard.

This is what is fit to fay in general, and we fhall in a fucceeding Chapter come to the Particulars; but as we have here delivered the Nature of Waters of various Sorts, we fhall return to the Malt, and explain in a few Words what is the Change and Difference in that, according to the drying.

C H A P. IV.

Of the feveral Kinds of Malt.

THE Maltfters diftinguifh their Goods under three Names; the pale Malt, the Amber Malt, and the brown Malt.

The fame Corn will make one as well as the other, the Difference is only in the drying.

The pale Malt is the richeft of all the Kinds; it takes more Time in the making, becaufe it muft be dried flowly and leifurely, but then it fells for fome-what more, fo that as much is advanced in the Price as is taken up in the Time of drying; and then it goes farther in the Brewing, fo that the additional Price is no real Charge upon the Purchafer; thus on

all

all Accounts the pale is the beft Malt; it is fulleft of Flower, and moft perfect; it is the moft near the real Nature of the Barley Corn from which it was made, and the richeft and moft wholfome.

The beft Method of Brewing with this is to ufe Well Water; for as it is the loofeft and lighteft of all Malts, the hardeft Waters will take its Strength, and they will amend its Quality.

The Malt that comes properly next after this is what we call Amber Malt; it is of a middle Nature between the pale and the brown, having been dried with a middle Degree of Heat and Time.

Many prefer this to any other; it obtained its Name from the Colour of the Beer that is brewed of it; for when this is well performed the Colour is juft the clear Yellow of a fine Polifh Piece of Amber.

The beft Method of Brewing this is with half River and half Well Water.

Thofe who are very nice about it ufe two Parts Well and one Part River Water.

I have known excellent Beer brewed from this Malt with Well Water alone; but the beft I ever tafted of the common Kind was at Mr. Child's, and upon enquiring into the Way of managing it, that Gentleman very obligingly told me his Secret, which was, he brewed it with all Well Water, but he let that Water ftand two Days expofed to the Sun before he ufed it.

Amber Malt may be brewed either with all Well or all foft Water. In the common Way of Brewing with all Well Water frefh drawn, the Beer looks like the pale Kind, but it has not the fine Flavour, nor does it go fo far: In the other Way of Brewing it with all River Water, it makes the moft Beer, but it is not fo pale as it fhould be.

I have feen in Suffex Amber Malt brewed with all Pond Water, and one could not tell what Kind of Malt the Beer was made of.

Brown

Brown Malt is high dried, it is finished in a little Time, and with a confiderable Heat, and by that Means it becomes burnt up.

There are Ufes for which this Malt ferves beft of all, but there are great Errors about it.

In the firft Place the Maltfter, becaufe he fees his Cuftomers like it for being hard and brown, burns it fometimes to a Coal, till it is too hard to be bitten by the Teeth, and till the greateft Part of the Subftance of the Flour is gone.

In the next Place the Confumer makes the fame Kind of Miftake, and both have very difagreeable Confequences; becaufe brown Malt will colour a great deal of Water, he fuppofes it will make a great deal of Beer; but that is a Miftake, for none makes fo little; he fhould confider that Colour is one Thing and Strength is another: In general, the darker and more burnt the Malt, the lefs Flour and Subftance it has, and this is what gives the real Strength to the Beer.

Let the Perfon who defigns to brew with brown Malt chufe fuch as is not over dry and hard, but what has a good deal of the Strength and Body remaining in it; and when he has thus fuited himfelf with a proper Kind, let him remember that he is to allow a fomewhat larger Quantity than he does of the pale Kinds.

Then the Confideration will be what Water to ufe, and in this his Reafon muft guide him: As brown is the Oppofite of pale Malt, the oppofite Kind of Water is to be ufed in brewing it. The hardeft is beft for that, as we have fhewn, and therefore the fofteft is fitteft for this.

There are many Reafons for this Choice, but the plaineft is this: As the brown Malt has leaft Strength, it fhould be brewed with that Water which takes the Strength out of it beft; this is always the fofteft: More Beer by a confiderable Quantity may be made from any Malt with foft than can with hard Water.

N°. XXV. 5 A Befide,

Befide, the Fault of the brown Malts is, that the Beer made from them is apt to four more than any other, and Experience fhews that Beer with the fofteft Water keeps longeft.

Having thus given the confiderate Reader an Infight into the Nature of Malt and Water in their various Kinds, we fhall clofe the Account with one Caution regarding the Grinding, which, though little regarded, is of great Confequence.

Moft People, out of an over Care, run into the Fault of grinding their Malt too fine; this makes it run thick in the Wort, and troubles and difgraces the Brewing.

The Malt fhould be only juft broke in the Mill; and all the Care needful in this Refpect, is to fee that it be in Reality all broke: And when it is brown Malt the beft Method is to have it ground ten Days before it is ufed, and let it be kept that Time in a dry Place; this mellows it, and gives it a true fine Flavour.

It is a good Method to keep all Malt fome Time after it is ground before it is ufed in brewing, but the browner it is the longer it fhould be kept, for the fiery Particles go off this Way.

C H A P. V.

Of Brewing in a private Family.

IT has been fuppofed impoffible to brew either with Advantage or any great Succefs in a private Family, for Want of the Conveniency of a great deal of Room and a great many Veffels; but we fhall fhew that to be an Error, and at the fame Time advife and invite all private Families to brew, by fhewing them the plain Method, directing the Quantities, and calculating the Profit and Advantage.

The

The Mafter of a Family knows from what has been faid already, how to chufe his Malt for his Purpofe, and to fuit his Water to the Kind of it ; we are now to tell him the Quantities, and fet down the Method of the Work, which is fo eafy that the meaneft Servant may be enabled to perform it, either by reading the Inftrudtions here, or receiving them from the Mafter.

Doubtlefs there are Advantages in great Veffels, and the working of great Quantities together, but thefe are principally in the making a fomewhat larger Quantity of Drink from the fame Malt. This is not to difcourage the private or Family-Brewing, becaufe we fhall fhew that, notwithftanding this Difadvantage attending the working fmall Quantities, the Balance of Price is greatly in Favour of the private Brewer ; and as to almoft all other Particulars the Advantage is on the private Side.

The common or publick Brewer cannot have his Malt ground fo long before, nor kept with fuch Care, as the Mafter of a Family who brews only for himfelf; and Cleanlinefs, which is a very great Article, is altogether in Favour of Family-brewing.

The Veffels for this Purpofe are free, and can be eafily cleaned, fweetened, and aired, and there is Time for the doing it between one Brewing and another; but this is not the Cafe with the publick Brewer, his Backs and Coolers are all fixed, and cannot fo well be cleaned, and the Brewing is repeated fo quick that there is not Time for airing them or fweetening as in the other Manner.

Then the Family Brewer can fkim off his Top Yeaft, and leave his Bottom Lees behind, which the publick Brewer cannot fo well do.

Thefe, and a Number of other Particulars, make it very apparent, that any Man may brew better Beer at Home than he can buy of any Brewer, and that it will come much cheaper; neither is there any

vaft

vaſt Charge in the Purchaſe of ſuch Veſſels as will be required for it.

Suppoſe there is a Copper, which, when brim full, holds a Barrel, that is, twelve Pails of Water; this is no great Size, indeed it is what few Families in the Country are without, or can be, for various Occaſions; with this Copper, and a few Tubs, the Owner may brew five Buſhels of Malt very well, and this is entirely ſufficient for the Demands of a moderate Family.

Let ſuch a Perſon chuſe his Malt carefully according to the Kind of Beer he prefers, and ſuit the Water to it as we have directed.

Let him have the Malt ground ten Days, or thereabout, before he brews, and for Fear of Cheats in the grinding, which we can aſſure him in this Caſe are very common, let him put a Quarter of a Peck of Oats among it; this will keep the Grinder honeſt, and it will not do the leaſt Hurt whatſoever to the Beer.

When the Malt has ſtood its Time let him fill his Copper with Water, and make his Fire ſound and good under it.

When the Water is moderately hot let him throw on Half a Peck of common Bran, this will make the Water boil much ſooner, and it always helps the Beer by keeping in the Spirit of it.

When it boils let the Bran be ſkim'd off, and it will ſerve for Hogs, ſo there is no Waſte by it; let the Water then be let off into the Maſh-Fat, and let it ſtand there a Quarter of an Hour.

Then ſave about Half a Buſhel of the Malt, and pour all the reſt in.

Put it in by a little at a Time, and let a ſtout Perſon ſtand over the Vat all the Time, ſtirring it well that the Malt do not gather in Lumps.

When the whole is in let it reſt.

This

This is not the common Way of brewing, but I have found by Experience that it anſwers much better,

If a good deal of Ale and a ſmaller Quantity of ſmall Beer be intended, the hot boiling Water muſt be ladled in ſo ſlow that one Bowl may juſt come off before another is put on; and in this Way the brewing of five Buſhels will take up about ſixteen Hours; and in this Caſe the beſt Way is to let it run out of the Tap as ſmall as a Straw, and perfectly clear, for Ale thus made will very ſoon be fit for the Table.

If leſs or weaker Ale be intended, and better ſmall Beer, then the ſecond Copper of boiling Water is to be put in expeditiouſly, and drawn off with a quick Stream.

When the firſt ſtirring of the Malt is done, the Half Buſhel that was reſerved muſt be put in; this will ſoon ſpread itſelf all over the Surface of the reſt, and then it will be very proper to ſpread ſome coarſe, thick Cloths over to keep in the Steam and Spirit of the Malt.

Thus it is to ſtand three Hours, and then more Water is to be put in from the boiling Copper; this is to be poured in a Bowl at a Time, at ſmall Diſtances, till as much is in as will make the Quantity running off nearly enough to fill the Copper.

This is the Time for the Hops; Half a Pound of ſuch as are fine, freſh, and fragrant, is the right Quantity to be uſed now; theſe are to be tied looſe in a Canvas Bag, and they are to boil half an Hour, and then to be taken out, and ſuch a Quantity of freſh Hops muſt be put in as will be enough for the whole Brewing if it be for Ale, but if it be for Beer a freſh Quantity muſt be put in every half Hour, and boil briſkly.

While the firſt Copper is thus boiling off, the Malt in the Maſh-Tub ſhould have freſh hot Water Bowl by Bowl thrown on it, and run off in ſuch a Manner that

that there may be the Quantity of a fecond Copper ready by that Time the firft is boiled off.

This is to be boiled in the fame Manner as the firft.

Thefe make the ftrong Beer, and after this a Quantity of fmall Beer may be made by boiling up the next Wafhings of the Malt, with the old Hops boiled over again that before ferved for the Ale.

By this Management, out of five Bufhels of Malt may be made a Hogfhead of Ale with the two firft Coppers of Wort, and a Hogfhead of fmall Beer with the other two.

It is a middling Ale that is brewed with this Proportion ; thofe who chufe it ftronger or weaker have nothing to do but vary the Proportions, allowing more Malt as they would have it ftronger.

Now with Refpeft to the Tafte, Flavour, and wholfome Quality of this Drink, there is no Comparifon with that of the common Brewers, for if it have been made according to thefe Directions it will be in every Refpeft vaftly preferable to that from the beft Brew-houfes.

As to the Advantage in Price, that comes next to be named ; and to do it in the moft fair Manner, we will fuppofe the Owner have chofe his Beer a little ftronger than according to this Rule, and that he has put fix Bufhels of Malt to the fame Quantity of Ale and fmall Beer, ftill we fhall find the Profit altogether on his Side againft the buying, though we take in every Article.

The fix Bufhels of Malt, allowing the Market Price to be two Shillings and eight Pence, will be fixteen Shillings ; we will call the Pound of Hops one Shilling and fix Pence, then allowing half a Crown for a Man's Wages the Day, and a Shilling for Fire, which is the moft, here is the Price of a Hogfhead of Ale and a Hogfhead of fmall Beer, which in the whole amounts juft to a Guinea : Whereas the Hog-

fhead

fhead of Ale bought of a Brewer in London would be four and twenty Shillings, and the Hogfhead of fmall Beer nine Shillings, in the whole one Pound thirteen.

Twelve Shillings therefore will be faved, all Expence being fet at the higheft, and the Beer will be pleafanter, ftronger, and wholfomer than if bought at the beft Brewer's.

S E C T. V.

Of GARDENING.

C H A P. I.

Of the Flower Garden.

THIS is a Month in which the Eye will have a great Variety of pleafing Objects in the Flower Beds, and that fhould encourage the Poffeffor to take all due Care for a Succeffion. What he fees this Year, is in great Part the Product of the laft, for the Gardiner is a Kind of Creator with refpect to thefe Things. Therefore he is now to lay in the Sources of his fucceeding Stores.

Many of the Annuals that now make a Shew in the Garden, will not ripen their Seeds, and this from the plain Reafon that they were fown late in Spring; fuch are feveral of the Lupines, the Annual Stock, the Sweet Scabious, and the like: Therefore the End of this Month is a good Time to fow them for a better Chance next Year.

Many of thefe Kind of Flowers being fown late in Summer, will ftand the Winter in a low State, and then will be ftrong and early the next Spring; they will flower very finely, and have Time to ripen their Seeds well.

The

The common Practice of Gardiners is very wrong on this Head, and the sowing in this Manner would be a great Improvement.

This is a very good Seafon for propagating feveral Flowers by cutting ; all the Lychnis Kind will anfwer thus very well, and will get a great deal of Strength againft the next Year.

The beft Method is to take the Cuttings from the main Stalk ; they fhould be fix Inches long or more, and a Couple of Joints fhould be put into the Ground and one left above: This muft be done in a fhady Place and in good Ground, and the Cuttings muft be watered ; there will then be no great Hazard as to their Succefs.

Let the Eye be now carefully carried over the Borders, and fee where luxuriant Nature has loaded her-felf too much, as is very frequent. The Top of a flowering Plant will at this Seafon be too heavy for the Stalk ; the Wind will have too much Power over it, and will either break it off at the Surface, or if it ftand that, will loofen the Root in the Ground. This is to be prevented by tying them up to Sticks, and there is more Good done by this Practice than moft are aware ; for nothing hurts a flowering Plant fo much as to be fhaken at the Root : The fame Plant will throw out twice the Number of Flowers, and every one twice as big, that fhall be well fupported, which would have ripened only a few, and thefe poorly loofe.

While this Care is taking of the rifing Generation, the Ground fhould be cleared of the paft ; dead Stalks croud up Borders in a very unpleafing Manner : Nothing looks fo well as clean Earth about a flowering Plant, and nothing makes it flower fo vigoroufly ; therefore both to pleafe the Eye, and to advance the Perfection of the other, let all decayed Plants be cut away.

It is a Rule that no Seed fhould be fuffered to ripen upon a Plant, unlefs it be intended for Ufe, be-

caufe

caufe it exaufts the Root; at the fame Time that the Plants paft Flowering are cut down, the Weeds will alfo be taken away; and if thefe be removed once in Fortnight, as there will be Occafion at thefe Seafons, the Garden will always look frefh and flourifhing.

Let the Tufts of Sweet Williams be examined, and there will be found a great Number of Shoots ftragling on every Side : Let thefe be laid, and they will get Root, and furnifh an Encreafe for the next Seafon.

Pinks will be found in the fame Condition, and the fame Care fhould be taken of them. A little Trouble at this Time is a Source of Plenty for the fucceeding Summer.

Whatever Bulbs were left in the Ground the preceding Months, fhould be now taken out; and fuch as do not bear to be kept out of the Ground any Time fhould be now tranfplanted; for this is the Seafon that their Flowering being over, they are in a State of Reft. The Fritillary is to be removed at this Time, and the whole Family of the Narciffuffes are in this Condition.

We have directed the Gardiner in our Spring Months to fow feveral of thofe Flowers which do not Flower 'till the fecond Year; and a particular Management required for thofe Plants, one Part of which regards the prefent Seafon. They will now be of fome Height, and as they fhould be twice tranfplanted, this is the Time of the firft removing them. The Hollyhocks and French Honeyfuckles, and the Lychnis Kinds, with the Campanulas, and many other Flowers come under this Denomination. They fhould at this Time be removed into fome good Border, and be well nourifhed during the Remainder of the Summer, by having a due Space of Ground for their Roots to roam in. In the Seed Buds they ftood too clofe, and it is not a Time yet for putting them where they are to ftand all the Winter.

N°. XXV. 5 B They

They fhould be tranfplanted in a dripping Seafon; and having ftood about two Months in their new Places, they will be fit to be removed again, and fet where they are to Flower next Year.

Such of the Plants that have Flowered the laft Month, and have been marked for Seed, fhould now be watched for its Ripening: Thefe are the only ones that are to ftand fo long, but thefe deferve their Place very well by their Ufe; it is not by their Beauty. When their Seeds are ripe they muft be gathered with a great deal of Care, Hufks and all, and laid on a Shelf or in a Cupboard feparate, to dry leifurely: They fhould not be fhook out of the Pods 'till the Time of fowing them.

The Flowers in Blow at this Time muft alfo be examined for the fame Purpofe, and fuch as are fineft marked for Seed by placing a Stick at them: This will fave them when the reft are cut down after Flowering; and then their Seeds are to be gathered in the Manner we have juft named for thefe.

We are to recommend to the Curious in a particular Manner at this Time, the propagating his flowering Shrubs by inoculating; this is the fineft Month of the whole Year for that Purpofe.

There is no Way like this for the propagating the choice Rofes, and the like, and when it is performed in a judicous Manner at this appropriated Seafon, it fcarce ever fails.

Carnations will be now coming into Bloom, and this is a Time at which they require a great deal of Care, when the Hufk, which ignorant Gardiners call the Pod, burfts on one Side, it fhould be flit open on the other, that the Flower be fpread equally; and then they are to be guarded from Infects, which are more dangerous to them than to all other Flowers.

We have advifed the making Layers of Sweet Williams and other Flowers this Month; but the Reader will remember we directed him to do the fame in the two preceding. Thefe he is to watch

and

and water; and such as have taken Root, he is to take up: The best Method is to plant them in a Border by themselves for the present, and toward Autumn to remove them again into the Places where they are to remain: In each of these Removes they must be carefully watered and shaded, or they will not well take Root.

Seedlings of the choice Flower of the Auricula and other Kinds, should about this Time be transplanted, and the only Direction needful to this is, that they be placed in good Mould and have the Advantage of Shade.

C H A P. II.

Of the Kitchen Garden.

THE Products of the Spring Sowing are now many of them in their Perfection, but the Gardiner should remember while he is gathering one Crop to make Preparation for another: There is the Winter to come, in which the Products of the Kitchen Garden are always very desireable, and there is also a Consideration to be had for the succeeding Spring, for there is no Time better than this for sowing many of the useful Crops that are to come in very early.

Winter Spinage is to be sown this Month, and Onions for the Spring. Carrots sowed at this Time and kept clear of Weeds, will also come in very well in Spring, before those sown later: And Colworts and Turnips may be sown now with great Advantage.

The late Cauliflowers should now be planted out; and all of the Cabbage Kind intended for Use early in Spring.

Many Seeds will be now ripening, and they must be watched and gathered in due Time: Spinage naturally ripens now, and the Seeds of many of the Spring Salletings. They must be gathered in a dry

Day,

Day, and dried on a Floor in an airy fhady Place, after which they muft be got out of the Heads and Pods, and put up for Ufe. The Seeds of Flowers we have directed to be preferved in their Pods; for they are but a fmall Quantity, and they are of a more tender Nature: Thofe of Kitchen Products are hardier, and will bear being kept naked; and there would not eafily be found Conveniencies for keeping them in the Hufks.

Several of the early Crops will be gathered off by this Time, and the Stalks fhould in this Cafe be carefully cleared away. There can be no Good in fuffering the dead Stems of Plants that are paft Ufe to remain upon the Ground; they are offenfive to the Eye, and they are a Harbour and Shelter for Vermin.

The Cucumber Plants will now be in full Bearing, and they muft be taken Care of; Water is what they principally want, and they muft have it or their Produce will come to little; they are a large Plant, and the Fruit large, and the whole is full of a watery Juice, which muft be fupplied at this Time, or they will not bear half their natural Product.

Endive is an Herb fo very ufeful by its Continuance when others are gone, that there always fhould be frefh Sowings of it fo long as the Seafon calls for it. This Month will be a very proper Time; we have advifed it to be fown in the preceding Months, and what is raifed by thefe Sowings will laft the Summer; but what is fown at this Time, will ftand thro' the Winter.

The little Kind that is called Silver Endive, is very proper for this Sowing; it requires no bleaching, and will come into Ufe foon, and a great deal of it will ftand 'till the next Spring.

This is a very good Seafon alfo for fowing Brocoli for Spring; it is a Time few Gardiners mind for this Purpofe, but he that fhall do it, will have Brocoli at a Time when they have none, or when they have it very poor.

He

He will have ripe Heads when they have nothing but fide Shoots remaining. Thofe who chufe Spring Salleting in too advanced a Time of Summer may have it, for the Seeds will grow at no Time more regularly or fpeedily; they fhould be fown in a North Border at this Seafon, for when they have more Sun, they will foon be too rank for Ufe.

There is as much Advantage in very late Crops, as in very early ones, tho' there be not fo much Profit in them : At this Time it will be proper to fow French Beans, and fuch as are fown now will bear 'till the very coming on of Winter : It fhould be confidered that they will be expofed to Frofts in this Time; and they fhould for that Reafon be planted in a defended Place.

Celeri and Endive are now to be planted out for bleaching, and let it be a conftant Care at this Time to water thofe Things that have been tranfplanted, for otherwife in thefe dry Times they will come to little.

Onions will fhew they now begin to be fit for pulling by the Leaves fading. The fame will be feen in the Shallots and other Plants of that Kind ; and the Notice muft be obferved by the Gardiner. They are now in Perfection for taking up, and they muft be laid in an airy Room fpread at a Diftance upon the Floor, and upon Shelves, that they may be thoroughly dried on the Outfide, and may have a fufficient Quantity of their Juices gone from within, to prepare them for keeping.

The Endive and Celeri planted out in the preceding Months, will be now fit for blanching. The Celeri is to be blanched by earthing up, and the Endive by tying it. The great Care in drawing the Earth up to the Celeri, muft be not to bury the Head ; and a proper Time fhould be taken for tying up the Endive ; the Middle of a dry Day is the proper Time ; for if it be in wet Weather, or even when

there

there is but a large Quantity of Dew upon the Plants, they will rot inftead of blanching.

The Melons will now ripen in large Numbers, and Care muft be taken of them that they ripen properly, and are gathered in due Time.

The Gardiner muft not carry on one of our Inftruٵions to another Species; for what is proper for one Kind is wrong for another, often when they feem nearly related in Nature to each other: In the prefent Cafe there is a ftrong Inftance of this. The Cucumber and Melon may naturally feem related, and an unfkilful Perfon might thence fuppofe, that whatever was ordered for one, muft be proper for the other; but this is not the Cafe, the Cucumbers we have direٵted fhould be largely watered, but the Melons muft at this Seafon have very little.

The Value of this Fruit is its delicate Flavour, much watering will make the Melons large, but it will entirely take away their delicate Tafte.

If Afparagus Beds have been made in the Spring or young Artichokes planted, this is the Time for preparing and finifhing them up. The Afparagus Beds muft be carefully looked over, and where any have failed, the Lofs muft be fupplied by new ones; and as to the Artichokes, great Care muft be taken that they be cleared from Weeds, and the Ground muft be well dug about them.

The Letuces fown laft Month will be fit for planting out, and they muft be watered for three or four Evenings after; for thefe and for the repairing the Afparagus Beds, there muft be chofen a dripping Day, and it is better to defer it a Fortnight, than to do it in improper Weather; we may affift the Deficiencies of Nature by artificial Waterings: They do not anfwer like the real and proper Drops from Heaven: *Set Wet* is an everlafting good Rule.

C H A P.

CHAP. III.

Of the Orchard.

THE preceding Month was a very favourable Time for the *budding* of Fruit-Trees, but this will not be amifs, therefore let fuch as have omitted it entirely begin now; and let the Gardiner who has been more careful to begin in Time, recollect whether he has omitted any Thing; it may very well be done this Month, and will fucceed beft in a cloudy Day; otherwife the Evening is the beft Time.

After every Shower it will be proper to walk the Rounds among the Fruit-Trees, to look after Snails; they will now be feen crawling Abroad; and much good Fruit may be faved by deftroying them.

The Trees that have been budded or grafted the preceding Seafon, are now to be carefully looked over. If there be any Shoots from the Stalk, the Buds or Grafts will be poorly nourifhed: Such muft therefore be rubbed off, and the whole Store of Nourifhment obtained from the Root muft be directed that Way.

In the fame Manner all fore-right Shoots fhould at this Seafon be rubbed off from Wall-Trees, and Efpaliers, that the Nourifhment may not be drawn by them which are ufelefs, from thofe which fhould be encouraged.

This is a good Seafon for cutting off Suckers from the Roots of young Trees; they are like the fore-right Branches of the others, only worfe; they are of no Ufe, and they draw a great deal of Nourifhment. Thefe being cut off, the Weeds fhould be cleared away, and the Ground dug about the Trees: This will give them the greateft Strength and Vigour.

Snails are not the only Devourers of fine Fruit, Wafps will eat into it, and even fo contemptible an

Infect

Infect as the Ant will be vaftly mifchievous; the Way to guard againft thefe, is to tempt them from the Fruit with fomething they like better; for this Purpofe let little Gallipots of coarfe Sugar and Water be ftuck in the Forks of the Trees, and wide mouthed Bottles of the fame Syrup tied to the Branches, they will be decoyed into thefe, and the Fruit will efcape.

One Caution however is needful in this Refpect, which is, that the Danger be feen before the Remedy be ufed; let there be none of thefe Pots and Bottles fet 'till the Wafps come, for they may bring them.

From Lady *Montague's* Book.

The moft proper Time for gathering Herbs or Roots.

ALL Kinds of Herbs and Leaves are fulleft of Virtue from *Spring* to *Midfummer*; the Stalks from *Midfummer* to *Michaelmas*; and the Roots during the *Winter Seafon:* For it is an unerring Rule, that Roots of all Kinds are fulleft of Strength and Virtue when the Plant is without Leaf.

In the drying of Herbs it is moft proper to let them be expofed to the Air, in fome Room or Place that is fhaded from the Sun; for by this Precaution they will better retain their Virtue.

PUBLISHER'S NOTE

This edition is ongoing, but should be complete by the end of 1998. Those who have bought it in parts may apply to the publisher for a box to house the full set.

If you would like to be notified of the appearance of subsequent volumes, please write to the publisher at the address below. If you would like to **subscribe** to them at a reduced price, write also.

PROSPECT BOOKS, ALLALEIGH HOUSE, BLACKAWTON, TOTNES, DEVON TQ9 7DL. Telephone 01803 712269. Fax 01803 712311.
E-mail: kal69@dial.pipex.com